PC Power!

Stephen J. Dougherty

PC Power!

Boosting Your PC's Performance

- Applies to all 286, 386, and 486 PCs
- Covers Windows 3.1
- Loaded with performance tips and techniques

Stephen J. Dougherty

M&T Books

M&T Books
A Division of M&T Publishing, Inc.
411 Borel Avenue, Suite 100
San Mateo, CA 94402

Printed in the United States of America

Library of Congress Cataloging-in-Publication Data

Dougherty, Stephen J., 1951-
PC Power!: Boosting your PC's Performance/Stephen J. Dougherty
p. cm.
Includes index.
ISBN 1-55851-250-0
1. Microcomputers—Maintenance and repair. 2. Microcomputers—Upgrading I. Title
TK7887.5.D66 1992 92-30908
621.39'16--dc20 CIP

95 94 93 92 4 3 2 1

Project Editor: Laura Moorhead
Cover Design: Lauren Smith Design
Layout Design: Margaret Horoszko
Production Supervisor: Cindy Williams

This book is dedicated to my wife, Suzanne, who has lived with nearly every technique mentioned in this book being installed and uninstalled on her computers.

Contents

Acknowledgments

Thanks to the engineers who make computers possible. In particular, thanks to those who have taught me so much: Joe Kua, Kam Chow, Joe Kierouz, and Paul Tien. And thanks to the nonengineers who have shared my passion for making PCs faster: Andrew Choi, Steve Manuel, Bob Brose, and Geary Rowe.

Special thanks to Richard Power. Without his time and effort this book would never have made it. And thanks to Kevin Strehlo and the staff of M&T Books for their assistance.

Why This Book Is For You

This book is for you if you are a 286, 386, or 486-based PC user who wants to increase the speed and efficiency of your machine.

Written in an easy-to-understand style, *PC Power!* teaches you how to analyze, diagnose, and troubleshoot your system for maximum results. It includes complete coverage of cache, memory, I/O tuning, clock speed, MIPS, and CPU design. You'll also find dozens of performance techniques and tips for fine-tuning Windows and other popular applications.

While the main focus of this book is on ways to improve performance at a minimum cost, it also covers some of the more exotic and sophisticated techniques that can be used to unlock your system's true potential.

Improving your computer's performance can be easier than you might imagine. And with the tips and techniques presented in this book you will quickly be on your way to faster, more efficient computing.

CHAPTER ONE

Understanding the Data Funnel

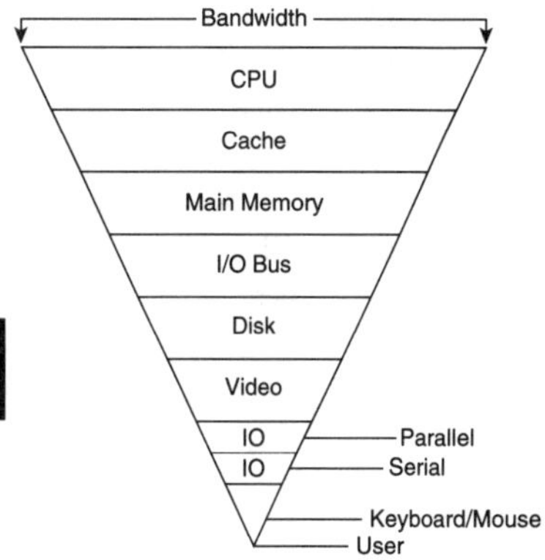

Data Funnel

Improving computer performance can be much easier, and less costly, than you might imagine.

In fact, the goal of this book is to demystify the concepts that go into enhancing computer performance so that you can deduce for yourself how to make personal computers run faster without spending a lot of money. Rather than simply telling you how to make a PC run faster in a particular situation, this book teaches you the principles of solving performance problems. It's like teaching people how to farm instead of just giving them food—over the long run they'll be better off for it.

The primary principle for achieving performance improvement in any system, whether it's a computer or another kind of system, is avoiding, reducing, or eliminating bottlenecks.

In the traditional block diagram of a computer system, as shown in Figure 1-1, it's difficult to get a sense of where the bottlenecks in the system occur. It's easy to see what is connected to what, but that doesn't tell us much about which components are faster and which are slower.

Probably the most important first step toward making your computer run faster is to understand why it is slow (or at least slower than you would like it to be). To this end, this book asks you to look at computers differently than you have probably ever looked at them before.

This book uses a concept called the *data funnel* as a tool to diagnose performance bottlenecks and prescribe effective, economical cures. The data funnel is an artificial construction that helps you visualize where system bottlenecks occur, which in turn helps you conceive methods to eliminate them. Of

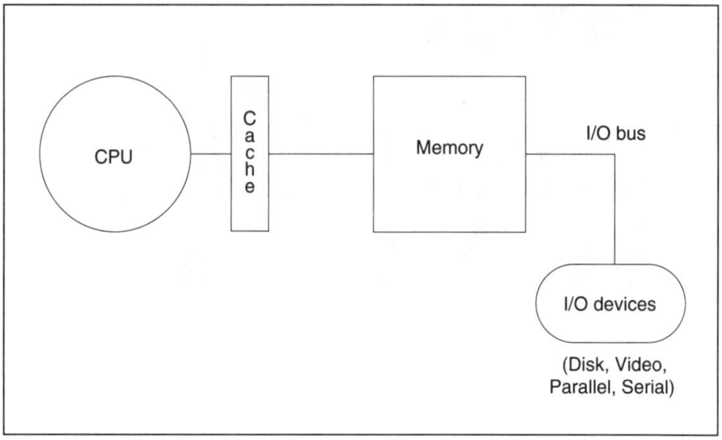

Figure 1-1. The traditional depiction of a PC system doesn't tell us much about where bottlenecks might occur.

course, the concept of the data funnel is a gross oversimplification of a very complex device, the computer.

Use the data funnel to visualize your entire computer system. The different levels of the funnel represent the various subsystems and components that make up the computer (see Figure 1-2), which includes the central processing unit (CPU), memory, a bus to get data and instructions in and out of memory, various storage devices and input/output devices, video, printers, modems, and keyboards. The data funnel puts these components together so that you can quickly see potential bottlenecks. (If any of these terms are unfamiliar, please see the Glossary at the end of the book.)

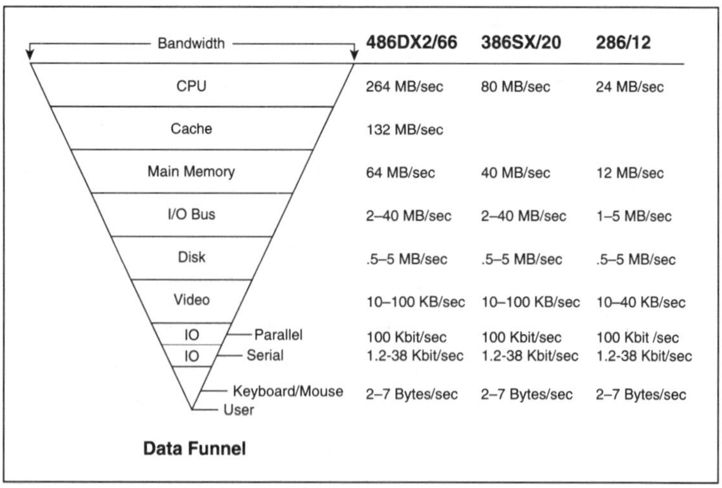

Figure 1-2. The data funnel, showing performance levels (bandwidths) of various systems and subsystems

Bottlenecks occur at the narrowest part of the funnel through which a particular computer operation must pass. You can see this by imagining that a program is a liquid that you pour into the funnel. If you chop off the lower narrow sections, the liquid only has to pour through the wide section, and it will go very quickly. On the other hand, if the liquid must flow through the entire funnel, including the very narrow part, the speed at which the program flows slows.

The data funnel's width at any given point, therefore, matches the bandwidth of one of your computer's subsystems or components; the bandwidth is the potential amount of data that can move through a component or subsystem during a given period of time.

Since computers operate at millions of cycles per second and because people commonly refer to bytes of information, a convenient measure of bandwidth is *megabytes per second (MBps)*.

Although the most common measure of computer performance is *millions of instructions per second (MIPS)*, this only applies to CPU processing speed. CPU power can also be considered in terms of the speed with which data flows through it. For example, the 386 and 486 can transfer 4 bytes (32 bits) of data every clock cycle; at 25 MHz, that is the equivalent of 100 MB per second. If you view it this way, the CPU fits well into the data funnel, which consists of subsystems that data move through and areas where data are stored.

Still, it is better to look at the funnel less empirically. Just remember that the width of each section is a rough approximation of how quickly data moves through the subsystem it represents. The wider a particular part of the funnel, the more data can be moved through that subsystem.

Bottlenecks and Logjams

The CPU is at the top of the funnel because it operates on the data faster than the other parts of the system provide data to it. In other words, the CPU processes data only as quickly as preprocessed data can be given to it and processed data taken away.

If the data you need to process already resides in the CPU, it can be processed quickly. In such a situation, speeding up the CPU speeds the overall operation. On the other hand, if the data must be input through the keyboard or read from the hard drive, processing will take much longer. Likewise, if the data must be output through a slow parallel port to an even slower printer, the system slows considerably. In fact, the entire system slows to match the performance of the slowest component through which data must pass.

In the worst case, you'll have the CPU at the top of the funnel, which can move 100 MBps or more, waiting for data to pass through the bottom of the funnel at the rate of a few bytes per second.

It would be nice if you could always keep things at the highest part of the funnel, but some operations can't happen there. Since users aren't able to communicate directly with electronic subsystems, for example, there is a need for the slower, mechanical processes like keyboard entry and printing that occupy the lower levels of the data funnel. The interface between computers and users is still very slow.

Although sometimes it is inevitable that data pass through the narrow (slow) sections of the funnel, the key to performance enhancement is to keep the data in the wide sections of the funnel as often as possible.

The Memory Mix

The data funnel provides a clear view of a key principle of computer design, a concept called *memory hierarchy.* Computers have a memory hierarchy of very fast, very expensive memory or storage, such as cache memory, and storage that is much slower but much cheaper per megabyte, such as disk drives. This corresponds to the narrowing of the data funnel from cache memory to disk drives.

System architects don't have infinite resources when designing a computer. More accurately, they must assume that computer buyers don't have unlimited resources when they're buying. Therefore, they need to make some trade-offs among the different kinds of memory.

The trick is to design the computer so that most operations take place in the fastest memory. Fortunately, since computer programs tend to require relatively small areas of memory at any given moment, designers get away with using small amounts of fast, expensive memory for holding data and program instructions that are accessed frequently, while using larger amounts of slower, less expensive memory for data and program instructions that are accessed less frequently.

Making Trade-offs

Such trade-offs in memory and all other subsystems are based on system architects' need to design computers that deliver optimum performance within a certain price range. In general, the higher a subsystem in the data funnel, the more expensive it is (see Figure 1-3).

Figure 1-3. Subsystem speed and cost comparison

Subsystem	Technology	Typical Size	Average Access Time	Transfer Rate	$/Byte	$/Megabyte
CPU registers	HCMOS	32-208 Bytes	20-60 ns	40-200 MB/sec	0.25-2.00	$250,000-$2,000,000
On chip cache	HCMOS	0-8 KB	20-60 ns	40-200 MB/sec	0.03-0.06	$3,000-$6,000
Cache (SRAM)	CMOS	32-256 KB	40-125 ns	20-100 MB/sec	0.001	$1,000.00
Main memory (DRAM)	CMOS	1-32 MB	100-200 ns	20-80 MB/sec	0.00005	$50.00
I/O Bus	Copper	16 or 32 bits		1-8 MB/sec		
Bus memory	CMOS	4-32 MB	250-500 ns	1-8 MB/sec	0.000075	$75.00
Hard disk	Magnetic	40-1,000 MB	15-30 ms	.5-5 MB/sec	0.0000035	$3.50
Floppy disk	Magnetic	1-2 MB	100 ms	.2 MB/sec	0.000000625	$0.63
DAT	Magnetic	1,000-4,000 MB	25 secs	10 MB/min	0.00000001	$0.01
QIC Tape	Magnetic	60-500 MB	10 min	5 MB/min	0.0000001	$0.10
Optical disk	Optical	128-800 MB	40-100 ms	.2-1 MB/sec	0.0000005	$0.50
Juke box	Mechanical	4K-200K MB	30-60 secs	5 MB/min-1 MB/sec	0.00000001	$0.01

So while computer designers know that they can improve performance by using a faster CPU or more cache memory, they also know that this will add to the cost of the system.

Just as computer designers must make decisions about which mix of components provide the best performance for the best price, so do you. To attain optimum performance from your computer, optimize your component mix for your applications and budget. To do this, make decisions based on the current market price of components and subsystems.

When you choose a computer, you're actually choosing between various manufacturers' ideas of the best price/performance trade-offs. Their ideas of the best trade-offs may not be right for you and your applications, though. Also, over time, component prices change. What may have been an ideal configuration from a price/performance perspective at one point may not be ideal a year later. (The computer wouldn't actually run more slowly a year later, but it could perhaps be configured differently for the same cost and deliver better performance.)

High Performance, Low Cost

The focus of this book is on PC *performance* (how to make your computer run programs faster), not *productivity* (how to use your computer more efficiently). Computer productivity generally deals with which software to use on your computer and how to run it. Performance, on the other hand, deals with how to make whatever you use run faster.

One underlying assumption of this book is that it is better to improve the performance of what you already own than to buy new components, whether that means the computer itself, the CPU, the disk drive, or the video adapter. Whether or not you can afford to buy new equipment, it makes sense to tune what you have for maximum performance.

In keeping with this, the book consistently refers to *optimizing* not *maximizing* your PC's performance. Optimizing your computer is to take what you already have and make it work better. Maximizing your system is to replace everything with faster parts. So to maximize drive performance, buy the fastest drive, and to maximize video performance, buy the fastest video card. Maximum means most, but optimum means best. This book will help you get the best performance from your system without paying for the most.

An important rule for optimization

Always check your assumptions before you commit to a given optimization strategy.

There is no such thing as an optimum configuration that applies to all PCs. Nearly every PC is configured differently and nearly everyone has a different combination of applications which they run. The optimum configuration for your PC will be the configuration that allows your applications to run fastest. After reconfiguring your system to take advantage of an optimization technique run your application(s) and see if it is faster. There may be some additional tweaking involved in order to achieve the absolute best performance. Achieving the best performance possible from a computer is more of an art than a science. But the ideas and suggestions in the following chapters should give you a solid basis to work from.

The bottom line is that keeping your programs executing in the widest sections of the data funnel is the key to optimal system performance, and there are many inexpensive ways to do that.

How to Use this Book

The organization of this book parallels the organization of the data funnel, from the fastest subsystem to the slowest. The more familiar you are with the various parts of your computer and their performance bottlenecks, the less important it will be to read the book in order.

The first several chapters of the book lay a lot of groundwork, explaining how computers work, and focus on the fastest subsystems of computers, which are least likely to be system bottlenecks. So, the number of performance enhancements you'll find in the early chapters is relatively low. As you reach later chapters on the slower subsections, you'll find many more inexpensive tricks and configuration techniques that let you avoid these lower, narrow sections of the funnel.

Not every chapter can possibly cover all the issues surrounding its particular subsystem. But each chapter provides enough of a grounding in how the subsystem works and what affects its speed that you can ascertain whether a bottleneck exists and what might be done about it. You'll certainly know enough to evaluate potential solutions offered by vendors.

Throughout the chapters you will see various icons, calling your attention to particularly interesting or useful information. Here's what you will find:

Warnings tell you what to be careful of, and what to avoid.

Tips are helpful hints and techniques that will save you time and frustration.

Rules of Thumb are general principles to keep in mind when deciding what to do.

Shopping Tips help you decide what to buy and how to get the best deal.

Insider's Views take you behind the scenes, letting you know what's happening now and helping you intelligently guess what will happen tomorrow in the computer industry.

Software Techniques explain how to use software to diagnose and correct performance problems.

Hardware Techniques tell you how to optimize the hardware you have or add a new component.

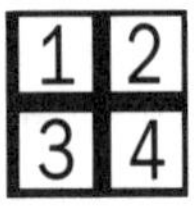

Doing the Numbers explain how to calculate and evaluate the numbers that get tossed around when analyzing computers or computer components.

Highly Technical sections are detailed explanations of how something works.

A Note to 286 and 8088 Users

Although this book often refers specifically to 386- and 486-based PCs, most of what is covered applies to all PCs, regardless of the CPU. The main differences are in areas of memory. If you're running an 8088- or 80286-based system, you don't have 32-bit memory. This book is still for you, just disregard specific references to 32-bit memory and programs like EMM386 or QEMM 386.

If you haven't yet bought your computer, you should strongly consider buying a computer with a 386SX or higher CPU. The 386SX-based PC generally costs only a couple of hundred dollars more than the 286- or 8088-based PC. Unless you're on an extremely tight budget, spend the extra money for the faster computer; it's well worth the extra expense!

CHAPTER TWO

Working with the CPU

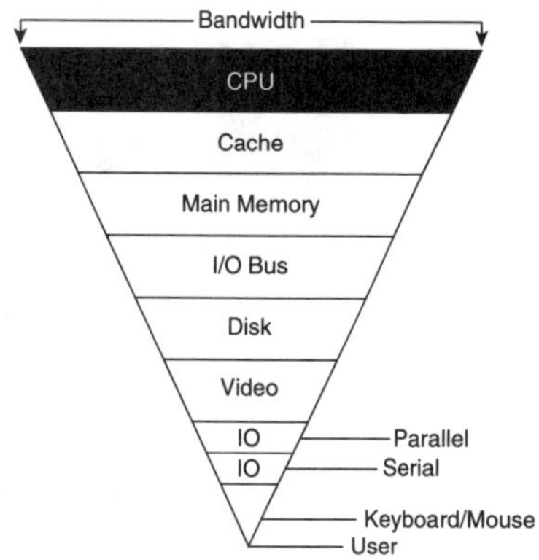

Data Funnel

The *central processing unit* (CPU), or microprocessor, of a computer is the device that adds, subtracts, moves, compares, and performs all the other operations thought of as computing. The rest of the computer exists to get data or instructions into or out of the CPU or to store the information that's not currently needed by the CPU.

The CPU is almost always at the top of the data funnel; it is generally the fastest component of the computer (see the figure above). As such, it determines a computer's maximum *potential* performance level. Most computers, from PCs to supercomputers, cannot deliver their maximum potential because the rest of the system cannot keep up with the CPU. This is both good news and bad news—good because the price of the microprocessors used in PCs is continually dropping and the performance is increasing, bad because it means that you can't have the fastest system by simply installing the fastest microprocessor available.

On the other hand, some computing activities are CPU intensive and, therefore, spend most of the time in the top band of the data funnel. In such a case, you may be able to improve the speed of your computer by upgrading the CPU.

And if your CPU belongs to the 8088 family, it can even be a bottleneck to performance of other system components. In other words, if your microprocessor is slow enough, it may sit below another subsystem in the data funnel and restrict the performance of that faster subsystem.

The key thing to remember is this: If your computer's performance is still not all you desire after implementing the performance tuning tips in Chapters 3 through 12, which deal with subsystems that normally sit below the CPU in

Tests that measure CPU speed

The old standby for testing CPU performance is Norton's SI.EXE, or system information test, which first shipped with the Norton Utilities back in 1983. It was calibrated to award an original IBM PC XT a score of 1.0.

Norton's SI was never a perfect indicator of PC performance. That's obvious, because it only looked at the CPU, ignoring performance in other sections of the data funnel. For example, SI said the original IBM PC AT was 4.4 times as fast as the original XT, when most observers gauged the AT as about 2 to 3 times as fast as the XT, depending on the application.

Also interesting is that Norton Desktop for DOS and Norton Desktop for Windows include a new version, SYSINFO.EXE, that has been recalibrated to eliminate some inaccuracies. Vendors complained when it first shipped because their machines started getting lower scores. For example, my 33 MHz 386 white box scores a 40.4 on SI.EXE but only 35.2 on SYSINFO.EXE. A 33 MHz Compaq is given a 34.7 in the standard SYSINFO performance chart.

Another noteworthy CPU benchmark comes from *PC Magazine*'s lab. *PC Magazine*'s version 6.0 benchmark doesn't give just a single score, however. It breaks things down as follows for my 386 33MHz white box versus an original IBM XT and a Compaq 386/25e:

	IBM XT	Compaq 25e	White Box 386/33MHz
8088 Instruction Mix	45.57	600.00	840.33
80286 Instruction Mix	NA	615.25	876.33
80386 Instruction Mix	NA	663.12	919.43
Do Nothing Loop	48.41	467.38	620.89
Integer Add	12.10	252.00	332.67
Integer Multiply	04.4	121.98	201.39
String Sort	0.09	1.3	1.9
Prime Number Sieve	1.64	29.21	37.81
Floating Point Mix	11.50	272.74	242.04

Notice that the *PC Magazine* benchmark doesn't provide a single number for CPU speed. In fact, it breaks things down even finer than shown here, with figures for the speed of memory and many other factors. If you like this kind of granularity, even though it's not quite clear how to apply these many numbers to the tasks you put your PC to, you can download the *PC Magazine* benchmark from CompuServe, Prodigy, or Ziff-Davis's own ZiffNet. You can find information on how to do that online or by reading any recent copy of *PC Magazine.*

Both the *PC Magazine* and Norton benchmarks don't really try to reflect the kind of performance differential you'll see when you use the machine to do real work. If you want a better indication of the kind of performance you'll get from your machine, you'll have to run the software you use on a daily basis and see what the performance is like. One test of that kind is the BAPCo SysMARK92, which sees how much work a machine can get done in a given amount of time using the most popular business applications.

the data funnel, or if you simply gather from this chapter that your microprocessor isn't up to the tasks you're asking of it, you will need to upgrade your CPU.

Let's take a look at the microprocessors currently used in PCs and what the upgrade options are.

CPU Types

There are four different CPU families available on PCs today: the 8088, 80286, 80386, and 80486.

The 8088

The 8088 is the earliest generation of CPU on which PCs are based. PCs based on the 8088 are generically referred to as XTs. Although the 8088 is a 16-bit processor, it is often referred to as an 8-bit processor since it has an 8-bit data bus. The 8088 was introduced at a clock speed of 4.77 MHz but later became available in speeds of 8, 10, and finally 12 MHz. While the 8088 provides an adequate level of performance for many of the original PC applications, it is inadequate for nearly all of the more recent software.

(Some XT systems use the 8086 instead of the 8088 because the 8086's 16-bit data bus slightly increases speed. The following discussion on 8088-based systems applies equally to 8086-based systems.)

Although many of the performance techniques discussed in this book will apply primarily to PCs based on the 8088, the CPU itself quickly becomes the bottleneck in an 8088-based system. Even the slowest of hard drives can outrun an 8088. If you implement some of the performance tips in Chapter 3 and beyond and still find your system's performance lacking, it's probably best to consider upgrading to a system based on a faster CPU.

While it is possible to replace your current 8088 motherboard with a motherboard based on a faster CPU, that's probably not the best course of action. Most of the peripherals on an 8088-based system are either inadequate or incompatible with 286- or 386-based motherboards. Your current power supply may not be up to the task of supporting higher-powered components, and it is likely that your current disk controller won't work in a 286 or later machine. Most of the keyboards used in early 8088 systems won't work with more advanced systems either. If you have a real need for high performance, consider investing in a more powerful system.

If you can't afford a more powerful system, disk caching will help nearly any system, and disk defragmenting and file organizing are always appropriate (see Chapter 6). Software-related techniques such as batch files and macros can also be useful (see Chapter 10).

While a used 8088 system doesn't have much resale value, it can still be useful. It might make a good beginner's machine, or perhaps it would serve well in a dedicated role for voice mail, as a terminal, or as the basis of a security system.

More memory, of course, will probably also help, but the 8088 can only directly address 1 MB of memory, some of which is used for system housekeeping. That means once an 8088-based machine has 640K of disk operating system (DOS) memory, you cannot add extended memory just by adding chips to the motherboard. Your only option is adding an expanded memory board. (For an explanation of extended and expanded memory, see Chapter 3.)

There are a few CPU enhancement techniques that are available to 8088 systems. NEC America Inc. produces the V20, a CPU that is pin-compatible with the 8088. A V20 runs 10 to 20 percent faster than the 8088 it replaces. (It used to be thought that the V20 was about 60 to 80 percent faster, but that was due to an anomaly in the benchmarks used to measure the performance.) If your machine uses an 8086 instead of an 8088, replace it with a V30 chip for the same 10 to 20 percent performance boost.

The NEC V-series chips cost less than $10 and should be completely compatible with your current 8088 or 8086. You can simply unplug your current 8088 and plug in a new V-20. Make sure you replace your old CPU with a new one rated at the same speed; for example, replace an 8-MHz CPU with an 8-MHz CPU.

Finally, if your 8088-based system is currently running at only 4.77 MHz, you can buy an 8-MHz or a 10-MHz 8088-based motherboard for considerably less than $100. While a 10-MHz 8088 is slow compared to any 386, it's still twice as fast as a 4.77-MHz 8088. All the peripherals from your 4.77-MHz motherboard should work with the faster 10 MHz board.

The 80286

The 80286 CPU was first used in a PC by IBM in 1984. The 80286, like its less powerful brother the 8088, is a 16-bit CPU, but unlike the 8088, the 286 has a 16-bit interface to the rest of the system. The 286 also runs at higher clock speeds (typically 8 to 20 MHz). As shown in Figure 2-1, the result is that the 286 is considerably more powerful than the older 8088.

The 286 runs most of the earlier-generation software on the market, but it is too underpowered to run most of the latest software at an acceptable level of

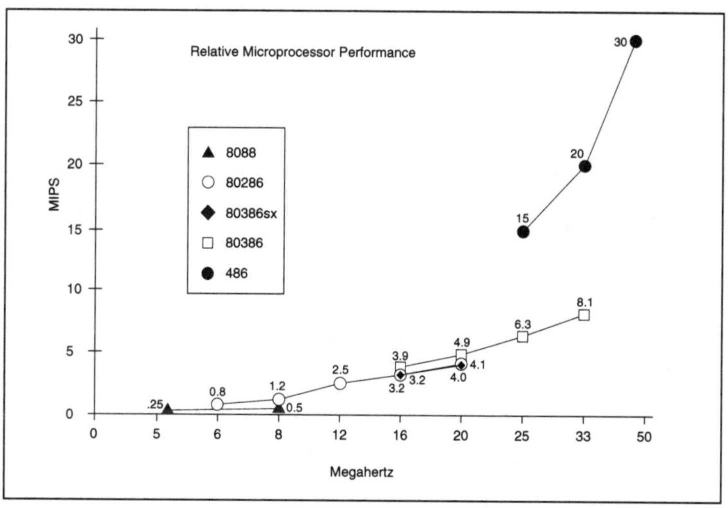

Figure 2-1. Relative CPU performance

performance. Of course, what constitutes an acceptable level of performance is subjective. When the original 286-based 6-MHz machines first appeared, some users questioned the need for such a powerful machine. As users have become accustomed to the quicker response of 386- and 486-based systems, a 286-based system seems relatively slow. In absolute terms, most 286 systems are more powerful than many minicomputers running businesses. If you haven't been spoiled by using a faster PC, a 286 probably won't seem unacceptably slow. So if the idea of upgrading your current 286 system to one based on a faster CPU is not desirable or feasible, don't despair: The tips from Chapter 3 on in this book will still help you get more performance out of your system.

For example, you can add memory, either extended or expanded. If you do, be aware that the memory on the motherboard will be faster than memory on a card in the I/O bus, which is probably running at only 8 MHz. So if you need to add extended memory, add it to the motherboard if possible. Remember also that because 286-based systems use 16-bit memory as opposed to the 32-bit memory of 386- and 486-based systems, techniques that require 32-bit memory will not apply.

Unlike an 8086-based system, which cannot be upgraded with a 386- or 486-based motherboard, a 286 system can be upgraded to a higher-performance motherboard relatively easily. Your current power supply will probably be adequate and most disk controllers that work in a 286-based system will also work in a 386- or 486-based system. So before you write off the motherboard upgrade to be about as feasible as replacing your car's engine, investigate a little further. The cost and effort are probably far less than you think; a 386SX motherboard can cost less than $200 and be installed in about an hour.

The 386 (SX and DX)

The 386 microprocessor first appeared in PCs in 1986. It later became known as the 386DX to distinguish it from 386SX, which was introduced in 1988 as a lower-cost alternative to the original 386. The 386DX is a 32-bit processor, which means that it operates internally 32 bits at a time and has a 32-bit interface to the rest of the system. In addition to 32-bit operations, the 386 includes much more sophisticated memory management capabilities than a 286. The 386 microprocessor also has the ability to directly address as much as 4,000 MB of memory, while the 286 is limited to addressing only 16 MB directly.

The 386SX is functionally identical to the original 386 (again, it is now called the 386DX) except the 386SX has only a 24-bit address bus and 16-bit data bus instead of the 386DX's 32-bit data and address buses. The 386SX does retain the ability to execute 32-bit instructions and operate internally with 32 bits. However, because of its 24-bit address bus, it has a maximum directly addressable memory space of only 16 MB (2^{24} bytes), as opposed to the 386DXs potential of 4 GB (2^{32} bytes). And because of its 16-bit data bus, the 386SX is slightly slower than a 386DX running at the same clock speed.

To put it simply: The 386SX can run all the software that a 386DX runs; it just runs it a little slower. PCs based on the 386SX have become the generally accepted entry-level computer. Given the small price difference between 386SX- and 286-based PCs, you should consider the 386SX a minimum acceptable processor if you haven't yet bought a PC.

The most common reason for upgrading from a 286 to a 386 is to access the 386's better memory management capabilities. The memory management programs available for 386s (including 386SXes) are far superior to those of their 286-based counterparts in terms of both performance and features. For example, the 386 has the ability to keep track of the 1 MB addressable memory spaces of several "virtual" 8088 processors, which allows the 386 to run a number of DOS programs at once without additional hardware. This capability is tapped by such software as Windows 3.x, OS/2 2.0, and DESQView.

There's no question that at higher clock speeds such as 25, 33, and even 40 MHz the 386DX is considerably faster than even the speediest 286. A 33-MHz 386 is approximately six times as fast as an 8-MHz 286, and a 40-MHz 386 is nearly eight times as fast.

But there has been a lot of controversy over whether the 386 CPU is faster than the 286 when both are running at the same clock speed. In fact, a 386SX-based PC delivers roughly the same performance as a 286-based PC running at the same speed: A 16-MHz 286 or 386SX in a well-designed system will both run at slightly over 3 MIPS. On the other hand, a 386DX in a well-designed system is about 25 percent faster than either a 286 or a 386SX running at the same speed. This means that moving from a 286-based system to a 386SX-based system running at the same clock speed will not deliver higher performance. Nevertheless, there are other compelling reasons for moving to a 386SX-based system (such as taking full advantage of software like Windows 3.x).

But again, the bottom line is that if implementing disk caching, faster video, and some of the other techniques found later in this book still doesn't raise the performance of your 286-based system to an acceptable level, you should probably upgrade to a faster CPU.

If you are contemplating a motherboard or CPU card upgrade (discussed later in this chapter), keep in mind that even though your current peripherals will work with a faster CPU, they may be a considerable bottleneck to the new CPU's performance. True, your drive and video subsystems will always be something of a bottleneck to the performance of a 386- or 486-based CPU. However, using the slow drive and video card from an older 286 might bog down your system's performance too much. If you're going to end up replacing your memory, drive, drive controller, video adapter, and monitor, you may be better off getting a completely new system.

The 486DX

The 486 microprocessor, introduced in 1989, includes all the features of the 386 and more. The 486 has its own on-chip 8-KB cache and an on-chip 387 coprocessor as well. (See next section for details on the 486SX, which lacks the math coprocessor.) The 486 delivers about 80 percent higher performance than a 386 operating at the same clock speed. There are many reasons the 486DX is faster than the 386DX, but we'll limit our discussion to the two most important ones: the presence of the on-chip 8-KB cache, which accounts for most of the performance boost, and that some of the instructions that are in microcode in the 386 are hardwired into the 486. (See Figure 2-2.)

Why the big boost from the 486's cache? A quick glance at the data funnel shows that the cache memory on most 386-based PCs is about half as fast as the CPU itself. Thus, the cache memory, fast as it is, is a bottleneck in a 386-based system. In contrast, the 486 is not slowed when it needs to access data or instructions in its on-board cache, which is accessible much more quickly than the separate cache on a 386-based motherboard.

What is microcode, and what does it have to do with the improved performance of the 486? Many of the instructions that a 386 and all other microprocessors perform are actually stored on the chip contained in a special type of software called microcode. *Microcode* is a set of instructions that express a complex operation as a series of simpler hardware instructions. Thus, instead

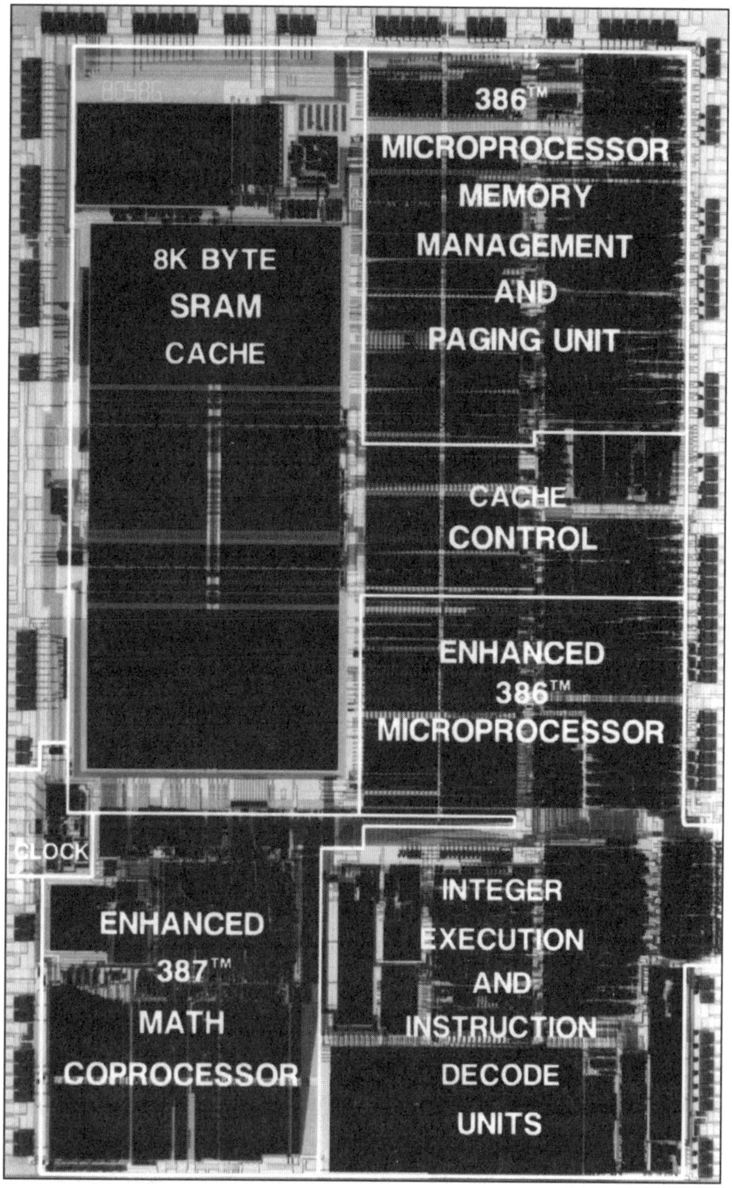

Figure 2-2. The Intel Corp. 486 CPU

of performing an operation in a single hardware instruction when an operation is expressed in microcode, the chip must decode and execute several hardware instructions, which takes more time. The reason instructions are placed in microcode instead of included in hardware is that the more circuits a CPU contains, the more difficult (and expensive) it is to build. The 486 includes many more circuits for hardwired instructions than does the 386; the 486 microprocessor contains circuitry equivalent to 1.2 million transistors, compared to the 386's 275,000.

Since the 486 has its own on-chip cache and has more hardwired instructions than the 386, the 486 can deliver higher performance than the 386, even when both are operating at the same clock speed (see Figure 2-1).

IBM's 486 SLC2

IBM has a very close working relationship with Intel—so close, in fact, that IBM owns rights to the design of both the 386 and 486 chips and has taken the liberty of improving upon both for IBM's proprietary use.

In the case of the 386SX, IBM shipped the 386SLC, which improved upon the performance of the SX by as much as 80 percent or more. Yet the 386SLC, like the 386SX, interfaced to the outside world as a 16-bit chip, which meant it could work with the less expensive external circuitry of systems like IBM's PS/2 Models 56 and 57.

IBM has also shipped a 486SLC2 that is based on the 486SX. In this case, however, Intel's 486SX is a 32-bit chip (the difference between it and the 486DX is 486SX's lack of math coprocessor). Given that, IBM did something extraordinary—it made the 486SLC2 interface to the outside world as a 16-bit chip, which meant it could still be used as an upgrade chip in a system designed to use a 386SX, like the Model 56 or 57.

Upgrading one of these systems from a 386SX to a 486SLC2 does an amazing thing: it doubles the total performance of the system as measured by BAPCo's SysMARK92, from 35.41 to 74.40. The SysMARK92 measures performance by

The 486SX

The 486SX is a lower-cost alternative version of its predecessor, the 486DX. Unlike the 386SX, which is less expensive because it skimps on the data and address buses, the 486SX includes the full 32-bit data and address buses of the standard 486. The only functional differences between the 486SX and DX are that the 486SX is available in a clock speed of 16 MHz and does not include a built-in, 387-compatible coprocessor. (Early 486SX chips actually include the coprocessor circuitry, but that portion of the chip is disabled.)

The important thing about the 486SX is that most systems based on it include a special socket called the performance enhancement socket. This socket is the basis for Intel Corp.'s long-term plan for making all PCs based

running the best-selling business software through a series of typical application scenarios and seeing how long it takes the system to perform the work. That makes the performance doubling measurement particularly impressive; it also shows how important the bandwidth at a single point in the data funnel can be to overall performance.

Unfortunately, these upgrade chips are available only for a few IBM PS/2 models. If IBM were a merchant chip seller and had told all of the system vendors buying its chips that an upgrade would be possible if particular design considerations were followed, we'd all be able to benefit from this impressive engineering. Instead, these upgrades are proprietary IBM features.

In both the 386SLC and the 486SLC2, IBM improved performance chiefly by applying one of the standard tricks advocated in this book: IBM added cache memory. In the case of the 386SLC, IBM added 8K of two-way set associative cache to a chip that had none, and in the case of the 486SLC2, IBM doubled the size of the on-board cache. By letting the processor access data at CPU throughput speeds, rather than at slower main memory speeds, IBM was able to get a huge increase in performance for both chips, as you might guess by glancing at the data funnel. IBM also optimized a few of the more commonly used processor instructions on both chips. And on the 486SLC2, IBM also used clock doubling: the 486SLC2 runs at 40 MHz internally while interfacing to the outside world at 20 MHz.

on the 486 and beyond upgradeable by simply adding a new processor (see "The Ultimate Upgradeable Architecture" later in this chapter).

If you have a 486SX-based PC, you'll be able to plug in an upgrade chip that operates twice as fast as the 486SX installed and this nearly doubles CPU performance. This upgrade chip called OverDrive also includes a very fast 387-compatible coprocessor.

Eventually, users can expect to see this chip level upgradeability available on all 486-based PCs. This feature offers a powerful incentive for users to select a 486SX-based system over a similarly priced 386. On the other hand, if you're deciding which system to purchase and think you'll need a math coprocessor, consider a 486DX. You may still be able to take advantage of the upgrade socket to double the internal clock rate, as we'll discuss further (see "The Ultimate Upgradeable Architecture" later in this chapter).

Non-Intel CPUs

Until 1991, the only source for 386-compatible processors was Intel Corp. (IBM [International Business Machines] produces its own 386-compatible CPUs, sold only in IBM computers.) In 1991, Advanced Micro Devices Inc. (AMD) began shipping a chip that was a clone of the Intel 386. The performance of the AMD chip is identical to that of the Intel chip when both are running at the same speed. AMD decided, however, to ship a chip that could run reliably at 40 MHz, 20 percent faster than 33 MHz, the highest clock speed 386 available from Intel. Taking advantage of this higher clock speed requires a system that supports the higher clock speed processor. Simply plugging a 40-MHz part into a 33-MHz system will not increase performance. (For more information about changing CPU clock speeds, refer to Appendices D and E.)

In 1992, you should start seeing 386-compatible processors from companies other than Intel that deliver higher performance than the original 386, even when running at the same clock speed. Chips and Technologies Inc. has already announced such a chip, as has Cyrix Corp., and other companies are expected to follow. Currently, none of the parts from these other manufacturers are drop-in performance upgrades for the original 386. It remains unclear whether there will be any new CPUs that are "plug compatible" with the original 386, which lets you remove your old 386 chip and replace it with a faster 386. Nevertheless, these new 386-compatible CPUs promise to deliver higher

Figure 2-3. Arche Technologies Inc.'s Master 386/40 system board with AMD 386 CPU and CYRIX 387 coprocessor. This board also includes two special 32-bit slots for additional memory.

performance in systems designed specifically to take advantage of them, at approximately the same cost as a standard 386. (see Figure 2-3.)

The Motherboard

The motherboard is the main circuit board that holds the CPU and its support logic. While replacing it can be a viable option, try implementing the techniques in Chapters 3 through 12 first. If you're still unhappy with your computer's level of performance, replacing your motherboard is worth considering.

Even if you don't intend to replace your motherboard in the near future, it may be something to keep in mind when purchasing a new PC or upgrading your current system. Whenever possible, try to upgrade with components or peripherals that can be used in your next computer or on a new motherboard. For example, suppose you're adding memory and your current PC uses 100-nanosecond (ns) memory. If you can get 80-ns memory for just a few dollars more, it may be wise to purchase the faster memory in case your next PC or motherboard requires it. The same might apply to the computer itself. If you have a choice between a computer that uses standard AT or baby AT components (such as motherboards, power supplies, or video cards) and a system that uses proprietary components, the standard size may prove to be beneficial in the long run. There are literally hundreds of sellers of standard components and peripherals, which makes it easy to change any part of your system.

Indeed, changing a motherboard is surprisingly easy. They tend to be secured to the computer case with four screws. The only other connection to worry about is the line from the power supply. While you'll probably have to take all the other components out of your machine in order to do the swap, there is nothing complicated about making the swap itself. You should guard against discharges of static electricity when handling the motherboard, of course. At the very least, touch an exposed metal piece of the case to discharge static you may be carrying before handling any computer circuitry; that also goes for handling any computer board or chip outside of the static-free bags in which they are ordinarily shipped.

If you have a standard size motherboard, it's also easy to put that motherboard into a new chassis if necessary (if, for example, you decide that you need more room for hard drives). Similarly, if you have a standard size chassis, it's easy to upgrade your power supply or disk drives.

The two extremes of nonstandard and standard components can be represented by a Compaq Computer Corp.'s Deskpro and a no-name clone. The Compaq is very difficult to upgrade with anything other than genuine Compaq replacement parts. If you purchase a Compaq system, forget about replacing the drives with any off-the-shelf drives or replacing the power supply with an off-the-shelf one. On the other hand, if you buy a clone, nearly all the parts should be interchangeable with other clone parts. You can easily replace the motherboard, chassis, power supply, and use off-the-shelf drives.

This is not to suggest that you shouldn't buy a name-brand computer like a Compaq. Name-brand computers offer a lot of warm fuzzies that you won't get with a clone. For example, if you're buying computers for your business, it's reassuring to know that there's a large company standing behind its product. The service provided by a name-brand vendor may be superior since the dealers are often better trained. But if you feel comfortable working under the hood of your PC and don't mind providing most of your own service, consider buying the clone; it can be much less expensive in the long run.

Motherboard prices have become very competitive, and it's now possible to buy a very high-performance motherboard for as little as $150 to $500 more than the price of a CPU itself. That means you can purchase a 20-MHz 386SX motherboard for just over $200 and a 33-MHz 486 for less than $1,000. That's still a lot of money, but it's probably a lot less than you'd pay for a complete system using the same CPUs.

Tips on changing a motherboard

First check your system's setup screen (the boot screen usually tells you how). Write down all relevant data, particularly the disk drive and display information.

Now turn the computer off and unplug it. To make sure you don't discharge static that could wipe out chips on the new motherboard or your other boards, attach a 10-gauge wire to your computer's chassis and run it to a ground like a cold water pipe.

If your system doesn't function properly when you first install the new motherboard, you could lose everything on the disk. So the next step is to back up your hard drive.

Next, remove all components from the computer: the drives, cables, power supply, I/O boards, and finally the motherboard. A simple screwdriver should be the only tool you'll need. To make sure you won't have any trouble reconnecting cables, use masking tape to indicate where each wire ran (from where to where).

Now put the new motherboard into the chassis. It probably attaches with four screws. Make sure that you replace the insulating washers, too. If your system uses plastic standoffs instead of screws, put them into the slots in the cabinet first, and then push the stems through the motherboard's mounting holes.

Once the new motherboard is installed, put the power supply back and reconnect the power supply cables to the motherboard. Plug in the video card, attach your monitor to it, and plug the power cable back into the wall. Now power up your system. If you see the memory check counting up the total memory on the machine, and then the screen displays an error message about no drives being installed, you're in fat city.

Now reinstall the boards, drives, and cables, then power the computer up again. This time you should get all the way to a setup screen. This gives you the opportunity to specify drive type, how much memory you've installed, what display your computer has, and so on. In most cases, the system makes a pretty good guess, but you'll definitely have to fill in your drive type, the time, and the date.

Don't try to buy the cheapest possible motherboard. There can be significant quality differences between the various boards. Unfortunately, price isn't always a reliable factor when determining what constitutes a quality board. And most of the factors that add to the board's reliability are not readily visible, either. Choosing a quality board by simply looking at it is much like kicking the tires of a car before buying it; it won't tell you much about the product, but it might make you feel better. The only way to reassure yourself of a good buy when it comes to a motherboard or any other system component is to buy from someone you trust and expect to stay in business for a while. Ideally, you can consult others who have done business with the firm. With the prices of motherboards as low as they are, don't try to save $20 or $100 by buying a low-quality board.

Upgradeable PCs

An increasing number of PC manufacturers are taking advantage of the fact that most users eventually require a higher-performance CPU. The concept of an upgradeable computer is not new; in fact, it predates the PC itself.

Before the introduction of the first IBM PC in 1981, there were a number of microcomputers based on the 8080 and the Z-80 chip. Many of these machines used a common bus called the S-100 bus. In some of these machines the motherboard was just a card that plugged into the S-100 bus along with the memory, video, and other cards. The circuit board that held the bus connectors had relatively little logic itself, and thus came to be called a *passive backplane*. (The backplane is simply the circuit board into which all the other circuit boards plug. Modern PCs based on motherboards are said to have *active backplanes*.) The arrangement was flexible since it was relatively easy to upgrade any part of the system, including the main CPU board. This was particularly desirable at the time because the microcomputer industry was in a period of rapid change. Manufacturers were coming and going quickly and there was no IBM to lend its stability. By using computers based on this easily upgradeable backplane, microcomputer users had less fear of their computer manufacturers disappearing and leaving their systems orphaned.

IBM, which was not keen on the idea of other manufacturers' CPU cards plugging into its computers, did not use the passive backplane in its first PC and, of course, the industry tended to follow in IBM's footsteps. But the concept was reintroduced in the mid-1980s by several companies, including Kaypro

Corp., Wyse Technology, and Televideo Systems Inc. These companies failed to market it well, however, and the idea of an upgradeable PC didn't catch on.

In 1988, my coworkers and I at a PC manufacturer discussed the idea of developing a line of passive backplane CPUs that would be user-upgradeable. But the idea was dropped since the only companies offering such designs at the time were struggling. (The market leaders, IBM and Compaq, avoided such designs, and it was assumed that they had better market knowledge.) Also, the backplane-type architecture would cost more to build (and would be priced higher), and the manufacturer wouldn't be able to maintain a performance edge. In retrospect, it was a technically sound decision but again probably a marketing mistake.

In 1989, AST Research Inc., with great fanfare and a big advertising campaign, announced the introduction of its CUPID (Completely Universal Processor Input-Output Design) architecture. This architecture is a modification of the passive backplane design, but in the hands of an excellent marketing department it became the birth of the "upgradeable PC." ALR and others soon followed with similar announcements. By the end of 1991 nearly every major PC manufacturer had an upgradeable architecture of some kind.

Do you want or need an upgradeable PC? Or if you already have one, should you upgrade? Certainly the ability to upgrade your CPU to a more powerful one is an interesting concept. But is it practical or cost effective? The answer, of course, depends on your needs and the type of upgradeable PC you're considering. And it's probably going to come down to cost.

Most major manufacturers charge heavily for upgrade boards. In fact, some brand-name upgrade boards alone cost more than you might pay for a whole new system. And don't forget to look into *all* the costs. Can the computer be upgraded with just a CPU card, or does it need new memory as well? If it needs new memory, does it need both DRAM (dynamic RAM) and SRAM (static RAM), or just DRAM? How will the performance of your computer compare to that of other computers using the same processor at the same clock speed? Most motherboards are tuned to perform best with a specific processor running at a specific clock speed. (The term *tuned* means that various bus signals are adjusted to consider the speed of the CPU and the delay it takes to get signals from one point to another.) Simply plugging in a new processor board, even if it is significantly faster than the old one, may not provide the expected performance increases; so be sure to look before you leap. Some of the most widely touted upgradeable machines are also some of the slowest PCs, both before and after the upgrade. Finally, before you decide to upgrade, consider the support issue discussed earlier: Will the rest of your system be able to adequately support the faster CPU, or will the CPU be bottlenecked by slow drives, video, or other system functions?

If you haven't yet bought this kind of upgradeable PC but are considering it, remember that you'll generally pay a premium for an upgradeable PC, since they are more expensive to design and manufacture than a nonupgradeable system. Also, try to find out whether the manufacturer will still be offering an upgrade to your PC when you're ready to upgrade. The PC business moves quickly. Today's technology will be outdated soon, and most manufacturers must limit the number of products they continue to support.

A few companies offer 386SX upgrade modules for PCs that were designed and built as 286s. These modules, however, may not substantially improve system performance. Also, the upgrade module must be designed specifically for a particular model of machine, be sure it will be compatible with your system.

Since there's no standard architecture for upgradeable PCs, you have to be careful. With a larger company that manufactures its own motherboards, you'll have to buy the upgrade from that company. Smaller companies and no-name clone makers might be considered an iffy source of an upgradeable PC, since they are less likely to be around when you decide to buy the upgrade board. But since their PCs tend to be built around boards manufactured by either AMI (American Micronics Inc.) or Mylex Corp., you can probably still obtain a compatible upgrade even if your clone maker goes out of business.

Before you invest in a 386SX upgrade to your 286 PC, do a thorough cost analysis. If you can replace the motherboard with a 386SX or 386DX motherboard for a comparable price to the 386SX upgrade card, that's probably a better way to go.

The Ultimate Upgradeable Architecture

Intel's Performance Upgrade Processor concept eliminates the biggest problem with most upgradeable PCs, which is that upgrades cost too much and may not be available when you need them. Companies that build their 486-

based PCs according to designs provided by Intel will be able to make their PCs upgradeable with the addition of a single chip.

Intel announced performance upgrade processors for all three (16, 20, and 25-MHz) 486SX CPUs and the 25-MHz and 33-MHz 486DXs. These chips, dubbed Intel OverDrive, gain increased performance by running at double the old clock rate internally while maintaining the same external clock rate to preserve compatibility with the rest of the system. While the actual performance gains depend on the application, 60 to 90 percent improvement in CPU performance is feasible. Intel says it does not plan a dual-clock upgrade for the 50-MHz 486 chip, however—100 MHz is apparently too much to ask of the 486 design.

Intel clock doubling processors

In 1992, Intel announced one of the most important PC performance enhancements ever, the Intel i486DX2 and i486 OverDrive processors. These new CPUs are called clock doubled or speed doublers because they run at twice the speed of the rest of the system by virtue of a circuit called a phase-locked loop, which effectively doubles the CPUs' frequencies. For example, the i486DX2/50 runs at 50 MHz while the rest of the system runs at 25 MHz. The net effect of this doubling is a CPU that runs at nearly twice the performance level of a standard CPU plugged into the same computer.

These clock doubling CPUs are the source of a great deal of confusion. The two product lines are just different enough that they are not plug compatible with each other (that is, one can't be plugged into the socket meant for the other). The OverDrive's pinout is designed to fit into the performance enhancement socket found only on 486SXes and a few 486DX-based systems. The 486DX2 chip is functionally identical to the OverDrive chip except that its pinout allows it to be plugged directly into a socket designed for a standard 486DX.

The big benefit of this new technology is that systems designed to support lower clock speed chips can now deliver higher performance. Because of the way Intel designed these CPUs, most computer manufacturers were able to simply put one of the new 486DX2 chips in their existing designs and instantly have a system that has twice the CPU performance. Intel thus ensured that users

The bottom line is that the Performance Upgrade Processor is much faster than the CPU it replaces yet requires no special circuitry. Because it runs at the same clock speed as the original CPUs, it doesn't require faster memory. And because it's designed to be an upgrade chip, it doesn't require any additional circuitry on the original motherboard, giving upgradeable computers that use this approach a big advantage over older upgradeable computers. Manufacturers can simply include a socket for the new CPU on the board so all users have

(continued from page 29)
would have access to systems based on very high performance CPUs at very reasonable prices.

Indeed, at the high-end of these CPUs, 66 MHz, clock doubling is the only practical way to improve performance, since at 66 MHz, DRAM can't keep pace. Even if there were affordable memory available to support such high clock speeds, the necessary circuitry to control such memory would be very difficult to implement. Even the latest generation of IBM's mainframes operate at "only" 66 MHz.

Performance impact

What kind of performance can you expect from a system that uses one of these clock doubled chips?

You should be in a better position to answer this question after reading the rest of this book, because as you will see there is far more to a system's performance than just CPU performance. But for those tasks that are CPU or coprocessor dependent, the performance doubles. For those tasks that are bottlenecked by the rest of the system, the performance gain will be proportionately less.

What does that mean, for example, about the performance of the 486DX2/66 versus the 486DX/50? For many operations, the clock-doubled 66 MHz chip will be faster, but for I/O intensive operations the 486DX/50 should prevail.

Upgrading

Does this new development mean you can upgrade your 486-based systems by simply adding a new chip?

The answer is maybe. If your system was specifically designed with a performance enhancement socket (also called the 487SX socket), you can upgrade to the

to do is insert the new chip. (Because space on a motherboard is at a premium, some manufacturers will use a common socket for both the original CPU and the Performance Upgrade Processor. This will require users to remove the original CPU and replace it with the higher-performance one.)

The OverDrive Processor is a major breakthrough for PCs. You can buy a PC without having to understand all the various trade-offs in upgrade architectures. The upgrade chip shouldn't be too expensive since you won't need to buy

clock doubled OverDrive CPU by simply adding the new chip. If your system does not have the performance enhancement socket, the OverDrive chip won't do because it has a slightly different pinout from your current 486 and cannot be physically inserted into your 486 socket.

There is a 486DX2 CPU that would fit into your 486 socket after you remove your current 486, but there are three possible impediments to this upgrade path. The first is that Intel does not sell the 486DX2 chip to dealers for sale to end users. So while your local (or mail order) electronic parts store will be able to sell you the OverDrive processor, they won't have the nearly identical 486DX2 chip to sell. The DX2 chips are only being sold to computer manufacturers for inclusion in new systems. This will prove to be only a minor inconvenience, however, to those willing to seek out a "gray market" chip dealer willing to sell them a DX2 chip.

The second potential problem is that your system's original BIOS may not be able to handle the higher performance chip without an upgraded BIOS that fixes timing loops or other code in the system's firmware that prevents the faster chip from operating correctly. Computer manufacturers may be reluctant to provide you with this new BIOS.

The third impediment comes into play if you own a 50 MHz 486 and would like to pick up a 100 MHz part. It doesn't appear as though Intel will offer a 486 faster than the 486DX2/66. The next CPU after the 66 will most likely be the P5.

What should you be aware of if you are buying a machine now but plan to upgrade to a clock-doubled machine later?

In general, the systems that have been designed with a larger memory cache will perform better with a clock-doubled CPU than those with a smaller cache size. So it would be advisable to buy a 486 with a large or upgradeable memory cache.

it from a computer manufacturer with the normal steep markup but from an electronic parts store at low, commodity-type pricing.

Most of the 486SX-based PCs on the market already offer support for the OverDrive, since the special socket it requires (called the *performance enhancement socket*) is identical to the 487SX socket. Some manufacturers have started to include the upgrade socket on their 486DX designs as well.

Finally, Intel has said that whenever it announces a new processor, it will also announce the specifications necessary to support a higher-performance processor. This means that if you buy a computer based on Intel's next generation chip (code-named the P5), you will be assured of upgradeability to the next level of that chip as long as the computer manufacturer supports the plan by including the appropriate socket on the motherboard.

Coprocessors

Earlier this chapter stated that the fastest part of any system is the CPU. The possible exception to this is the coprocessor.

A coprocessor is a specialized type of microprocessor that has been optimized for specific functions. A coprocessor cannot function on its own; it can only work with the central processor. There are several types of coprocessors, each of which has been designed for specific job functions.

Why is it necessary to build a special processor to perform these specific functions? Why can't the CPU be designed to perform them? One reason is that although these functions could be built into the main CPU, they would require additional circuits, which would increase the cost of the CPU. CPU manufacturers must make certain trade-offs in order to keep the cost of their products as low as possible. Not every user needs all the functions that the coprocessors perform, and users don't want to pay for additional functionality that they don't need. If only a small group of the users require the functions found in a given coprocessor, that group can buy that coprocessor while everyone else buys a less expensive but slightly less functional standard processor.

Another reason why the coprocessor's functions are not included in the CPU is that by keeping certain functions on a separate chip, the chip manufacturer may be able to get the main CPU to market sooner than if it had to design, manufacture, and test all the coprocessor functions first. For a manufacturer, time to market is a critical consideration in the introduction of a new CPU, and any time saved can mean millions of dollars of revenue. The 80387 coprocessor (to accompany the 80386) did not ship until long after the shipment of the 80386 itself. Intel went against this line of thought in the 486, but problems found in the 387 section of the 486 shortly after it had begun shipping caused Intel to stop shipping them and greatly delayed general availability of the chip.

The most common coprocessors are math, or floating-point, coprocessors. These are chips that have been designed specifically to run certain mathematical operations very quickly, as much as 50 times faster than a standard CPU. Math coprocessors are usually designed to support only a certain family of chips. The 8087 was designed to accompany the 8088, the 80287 was designed to accompany the 80286, and the 387 was designed to accompany the 386.

How much does a coprocessor help?

Vendors sometimes claim a math coprocessor can make your PC calculate up to 100 times faster. That claim is true for the duration of a single floating point instruction. But when solving real problems using real software, you'll see no more than a two- to tenfold improvement by adding a mathematical coprocessor—and that's the best possible case.

Word processors and database managers don't tap floating point at all, and even spreadsheet models won't benefit from a numeric coprocessor if all you're doing is summing up columns in a simple departmental budget. However, if you tackle something that calculates future values, trigonometric values, or exotic statistics (anything involving transcendental functions), a coprocessor will kick in and help in a modest way, although performance improvement as low as 20 percent is not uncommon, simply because so many of the operations in a typical model do not involve floating point.

Math coprocessors really come into their own in scientific applications and particularly in rendering complex three-dimensional images. Such graphics require heavy floating-point calculations. So if you run a CAD program or a heavy-duty scientific or engineering package, a numeric coprocessor is a necessity.

Your computer probably didn't come with a math coprocessor already installed, but there is almost certainly a socket for one on the motherboard. Since computer manufacturers realize the majority of users don't really need to do complex, high-precision math, these chips are almost always offered as options rather than being incorporated into the standard configuration. (The exceptions are PCs based on the Intel 486DX, since the 486DX chip includes a very fast 387-compatible coprocessor.)

Applications that benefit from a math coprocessor

The most common area in which a math coprocessor offers performance benefits is Computer Aided Design (CAD). In fact, most of the high-end CAD applications require a math coprocessor in order to run. CAD software developers realize that without a math coprocessor, their products would simply run too slowly; so they make the assumption that users are willing to pay for the chip.

Selecting a coprocessor

Computers that use an 8088 take an 8087 math coprocessor that can operate at the same speed as the main CPU. For a stock IBM PC or XT, that means 4.77 MHz and a stock 8087. For faster, so-called "turbo" XTs, an 8087-2 runs at speeds up to 8 MHz, and an 8087-1 runs at speeds up to 10 MHz.

In an 80286-based computer, the 287 does not have to operate at the same speed; typically the 287 runs slower, but you'll have to check your system's manual, because sometimes a 286 machine is designed with a faster clock rate for the coprocessor. The only 287 still available from Intel, the 287XL, is rated to operate at speeds up to 12.5 MHz, while 287-compatible coprocessors operate at various speeds: for example, AMD's 80C287-16 runs at 16 MHz.

Some early 386 machines can handle either a 287 or 387. If yours offers the choice, choose the 387 because it delivers as much as five times the performance as the 287. The 387 chips currently available from Intel operate at speeds up to 33MHz and match the speeds of that company's microprocessors. A number of companies have developed clones of the 387, including Cyrix Corp. and Integrated Information Technology.

Most engineering and scientific applications also benefit greatly from a math coprocessor, as do three-dimensional modeling applications. Desktop publishing is an area in which programs have just recently started to tap the resources of the math coprocessor. In fact, some desktop publishing programs and other programs that deal with font manipulation are currently using the chip to gain an edge on performance.

Spreadsheet applications are one area in which the benefits of a math coprocessor are unclear. Although coprocessor manufacturers cite statistics that show how much faster a spreadsheet runs with a math coprocessor, typical spreadsheet use doesn't involve the type of mathematical operations for which the math coprocessor is designed. Unless you are using your spreadsheet to perform some very complex mathematical manipulations involving operations such as transcendental functions, logarithms, or square roots, you are unlikely to see a significant performance increase with the addition of a math coprocessor.

Clearly, programs such as word processors and database packages involve very few mathematical operations and are almost certain to see no performance

Installing a coprocessor

The hardest part of installing a coprocessor is finding the socket into which the chip goes. Sometimes you'll find the coprocessor socket in some unreachable spot under the power supply or drive bays.

In systems that accept 8087 or 287 coprocessors (chips that look like centipedes with two rows of 40 legs each), you may be momentarily confused by two vacant sockets for expansion ROMs, either of which could physically accept the coprocessor. Don't be: ROM sockets come in pairs, while coprocessor sockets are always single.

Systems that accept a 387 have a pin grid array (PGA) socket—a square socket that has 68 holes exposed with which to make connections. Such chips can be pushed directly into their sockets. Just make sure the notch that indicates the pin-one corner of the chip matches the notch in the pin-one corner of the socket.

gain from a math coprocessor. Perhaps surprisingly, the same holds true for accounting applications. These are actually more similar to database applications than to complex spreadsheets, performing far more character manipulation than mathematical manipulation.

If you are unsure as to whether your particular application will benefit from a math coprocessor, consult the application's technical support department. Just because the documentation or packaging to your software claims support for a math coprocessor doesn't necessarily mean that adding one will result in a significant performance benefit.

If you decide that your application would benefit from a math coprocessor, be aware that there are several different coprocessors available. If you are using a 286, there are 287-compatible coprocessors available from Intel, AMD, or Integrated Information Technology Inc. (IIT) that should be functionally equivalent. If using a 386, you also have many choices. The original coprocessor to accompany the 386, as mentioned, is Intel's 387, but Cyrix and IIT offer 387-compatible coprocessors that actually outperform the Intel 387 in many operations and are usually priced lower. The chips plug into the same socket as the 387 and are compatible with the same software as the 387.

In addition to the 387-compatible parts, Weitek Corp. makes a coprocessor called the 3167 (see Figure 2-4). This chip is not compatible with the original 387 but offers better performance on certain operations than the 387 or its compatibles. The 3167 is designed to plug into a special coprocessor socket that is actually a superset of the 387 socket. Called the *Extended Math Coprocessor* (EMC) socket, it includes an additional set of pins that makes it slightly larger than the 387 socket. Most manufacturers of 386-based PCs provide an

Figure 2-4. The Weitek 3167 Floating-Point Coprocessor

EMC socket on their motherboards, allowing users to plug in either a 387 or a 3167 coprocessor. The 3167 requires that software be specifically written for it—if your application requires a 387 and you install a 3167 instead, the software won't work. So before you invest in the Weitek chip, make sure that your application can take advantage of it, and if it can, be sure that the resulting performance gain is worth the expense. Again, if you're unsure, consult your application's technical support people.

Some users find that they need both the 387 and the 3167 coprocessor. Since most motherboards don't provide two coprocessor sockets, it is necessary to purchase a small adapter board that accommodates both chips by allowing them to use the same socket. If you want both chips, make sure that the adapter board is available and can fit in your system. However, if you need both a Weitek 3167 and a 387, you may be better off upgrading to a 486DX-based system. The 486DX, with its built-in coprocessor, is faster than the 386/387 combination but completely compatible with it, and in most cases delivers the same performance as the Weitek. By upgrading to a 486DX, you should also enjoy better overall performance in your other applications since the 486 is faster than the 386 in non-mathematical operations.

If you're using a 486SX-based PC, your motherboard should have a socket for a 487SX. Plugging in the 487SX has the effect of adding a math coprocessor. Actually, the 487SX is a standard 486 (that is, one that has not had its coprocessor section disabled) with a slightly different pin configuration; when it is plugged into a 486SX system it simply takes over for the original 486SX on the motherboard and functions as both the CPU and the coprocessor.

Because the 487SX and the 486DX are actually the same chip with a slightly different pin configuration, some 486 manufacturers allow users to upgrade their 486SX systems to 486DXs. If you have a 486SX, decide whether to upgrade with a 486DX or a 487SX based on price, since both parts provide exactly the same level of performance.

If you're using a 486SX-based PC and you require a math coprocessor you will probably be better off installing an OverDrive processor. The OverDrive processor fits in the 487SX socket but will be twice as fast as a 487SX. It's likely that the OverDrive processor will actually cost less than a 487SX. The OverDrive processor has pretty much made the 487SX obsolete.

If you haven't purchased your 486-based PC yet and anticipate that you will not need a math coprocessor, consider buying a 486DX to take advantage of Intel's Performance Enhancement Socket concept. Most 486DX-based PCs will not initially support the new OverDrive Processor, but most 486SXs will. If you don't need a math coprocessor, get the 486SX with the performance enhancement socket. That way you will be able to easily upgrade your CPU later.

Weitek manufactures a math coprocessor called the 4167 to accompany the 486. Many 486-based systems have a socket to support the 4167. The 4167, like the 3167, is not compatible with the 387; so it requires software written specifically to support it (software written for the 3167 also works with the 4167). Although the 486 has a very fast 387-compatible coprocessor built in, the 4167 can perform some operations faster still. For example, the 4167 coprocessor can speed up three-dimensional rendering programs running on a 486-based computer by as much as 40 percent.

It remains unclear whether or not Weitek will introduce a 50-MHz version of the 4167. If the top speed of the 4167 is 33 MHz, the 50-MHz 4167 would have to deliver a 50 percent performance improvement over the 33-MHz 486 in order to outperform a 50-MHz 486. For users with a 486/33 and a Weitek 4167/33, there would be little coprocessor performance gain in going to a 50-MHz 486 if there is no 50-MHz 4167. For users trying to decide between a 486/33 with the Weitek chip or a 50-MHz 486 without the Weitek, the 486/50 will probably prove to be the better solution (assuming there is not a substantial cost difference between the two) since the 486/50 will run both integer and floating-point operations faster.

Other coprocessors

In addition to math coprocessors, there are coprocessors designed to accelerate graphics and to speed data compression, and there are processors designed for disk or peripheral control. These are very specialized processors, not general-purpose processors like the 286, 386, and 486. An advantage of these specialized processors is that they can work independently of the CPU, freeing it to work on other tasks.

There are also chips that are not processors since they cannot be programmed by the user, but that function as coprocessors. The best example of these types of chips are the ones used in graphics accelerator boards. This book refers to these chips as accelerators, not coprocessors.

To further confuse matters, sometimes general-purpose processors are used as coprocessors. Technically, a coprocessor requires the constant support of a CPU and cannot function on its own, but processors such as the Intel i860 are often used as a high-performance coprocessor—in other words, they are used to perform only certain limited tasks—even though they can also be implemented as a main processor. Another example is the use of the general-purpose 80186 as a coprocessor in certain caching disk controllers and intelligent serial cards.

General-purpose CPUs are used as dedicated processors for two reasons: they can be very cost effective compared to specialized chips since they are produced in relatively high volume, and they are often easier to program since they can use the same instructions as the CPU that they accompany. This is the case with the widely used 80186. The i860 is used because it is one of the most powerful chips on the market.

For users with a 486/33 trying to decide if they should add a Weitek 4167 or move up to a 486/50, they may be able to move up to a 486/66 with a simple chip replacement. For more on this, see the "Intel clock-doubling processors" sidebar.

To summarize, there are several types of coprocessors. The job of these chips is to assist the CPU. They are faster than the CPU at certain tasks or are able to do some tasks while the CPU performs other tasks.

Once again, refer back to Figure 2-1 to examine the huge performance variation between different CPUs running at various clock speeds. This book helps you get the optimum performance out of your current CPU, but if you really want the ultimate in PC performance you'll need a fast CPU. As Figure 2-1 shows, a 486 running at 33 MHz is over 50 times as fast as the original 8088 running at 4.77 MHz, and all the performance tricks in the book won't get that XT up to 486 level performance. But if you don't optimize your system correctly, you won't get nearly the performance that you paid for, either.

Summary

The CPU is what determines the ultimate potential performance of your system. How you configure and use the rest of that system determines how much of that performance you'll see. The rest of this book focuses primarily on eliminating bottlenecks that occur in the data funnel (your PC) below the CPU. If you eliminate or reduce the bottlenecks that slow the flow of data and instructions to and from the CPU, you free up the system to deliver its maximum potential. If the elimination of system bottlenecks does not deliver the level of computer performance desired, maximize your PC performance by replacing the CPU. You can replace the CPU with an upgrade card or with a new motherboard. In the case of Intel's performance upgrade CPU, you will be able to replace the CPU with another CPU.

CHAPTER THREE

The Importance of Memory

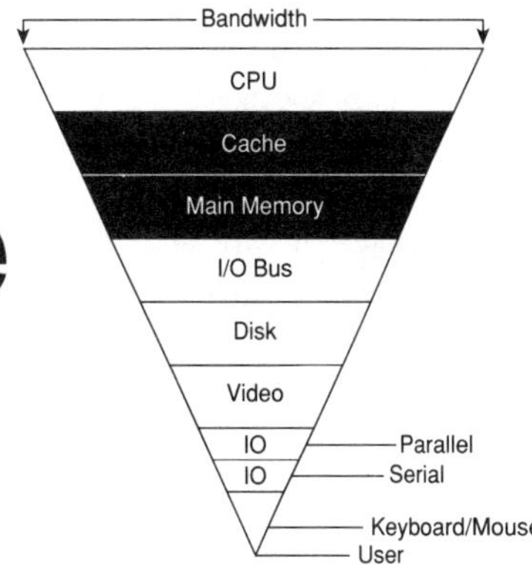

Data Funnel

In Chapter 2, we looked at how faster CPUs and higher clock speeds improve system performance but require the support of faster system components. The most important of these components is memory.

Look again at the data funnel and you'll see that the width of the cache-and-memory section is second only to the CPU itself. In other words, memory is the second fastest component in the computer. Several of the optimizing techniques discussed in this book involve using this speed to close the performance gap between the CPU and the other, relatively slower system components (represented by the narrower sections of the data funnel) as much and as often as possible. How much memory your PC has, how it's configured, and what it's used for have a profound impact on your system's overall performance.

SRAM and DRAM

To sustain the very high levels of performance at which a modern CPU can operate, you must get data into and out of the CPU quickly. In early PCs, *dynamic RAM* (the most common type of memory in computers) could keep pace with the CPU; over time, however, CPUs began to outperform DRAM (see Figure 3-1).

A 386 CPU running at 33 MHz can send and receive 32 bits of data every two clock cycles. That means if you give the CPU less than 64 MB of data per second, you're creating a potential bottleneck. The only way you can provide data at this rate is to use memory rated at better than 30 ns (memory which can be accessed in 30 billionths of a second). Since the fastest widely available DRAM

Figure 3-1. CPU speed and DRAM speed. Notice how CPU performance increases have far outpaced DRAM improvements.

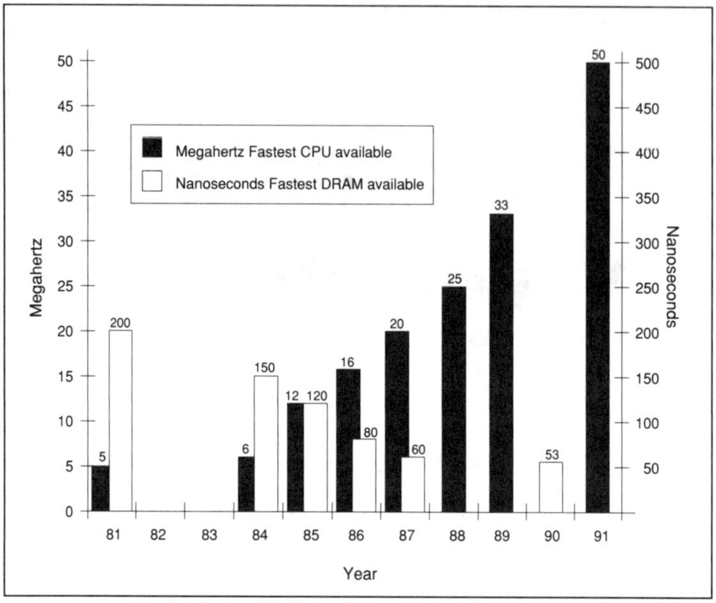

is about 50 ns, you're forced to use *static RAM* (SRAM), which reaches speeds of 15 ns or better.

Why don't system designers simply build in a lot of this very fast memory? The answer is cost: A megabyte of SRAM can run as much as $1,000. If manufacturers added SRAM to their systems, they would drive up the list price of their products in a very competitive and price-conscious marketplace.

Take a look at Figure 3-2, which compares the relative bandwidths, access times, and costs of various system components. Notice that DRAM and especially SRAM have very high bandwidths and offer very fast access times compared to components lower in the data funnel. Only the CPU provides broader bandwidth and faster access times. However, you'll also notice that both SRAM and DRAM are very expensive compared to the slower components, and SRAM is considerably more expensive per megabyte than DRAM is.

Another issue for system designers is available board space. SRAM can take up a great deal of room on the motherboard, a drawback in a field where smaller is perceived as better.

If it weren't for the prohibitive cost and limited board space, system designers might build in massive amounts of fast SRAM memory. However, they have to balance users' demands for fast memory with the need to keep cost

Figure 3-2. Subsystem speed and cost comparison

Subsystem	Technology	Typical Size	Average Access Time	Transfer Rate	$/Byte	$/Megabyte
CPU registers	HCMOS	32-208 Bytes	20-60 ns	40-200 MB/sec	0.25-2.00	$250,000-$2,000,000
On chip cache	HCMOS	0-8 KB	20-60 ns	40-200 MB/sec	0.03-0.06	$3,000-$6,000
Cache (SRAM)	CMOS	32-256 KB	40-125 ns	20-100 MB/sec	0.001	$1,000.00
Main memory (DRAM)	CMOS	1-32 MB	100-200 ns	20-80 MB/sec	0.00005	$50.00
I/O Bus	Copper	16 or 32 bits		1-8 MB/sec		
Bus memory	CMOS	4-32 MB	250-500 ns	1-8 MB/sec	0.000075	$75.00
Hard disk	Magnetic	40-1,000 MB	15-30 ms	.5-5 MB/sec	0.0000035	$3.50
Floppy disk	Magnetic	1-2 MB	100 ms	.2 MB/sec	0.000000625	$0.63
DAT	Magnetic	1,000-4,000 MB	25 secs	10 MB/min	0.00000001	$0.01
QIC Tape	Magnetic	60-500 MB	10 min	5 MB/min	0.0000001	$0.10
Optical disk	Optical	128-800 MB	40-100 ms	.2-1 MB/sec	0.0000005	$0.50
Juke box	Mechanical	4 KB-200 KB	30-60 secs	5 MB/min-1 MB/sec	0.00000001	$0.01

within the range dictated by the market. The technique they came up with is called *caching*.

The Memory Cache

Caching is the single most important concept in this book (see Appendix B). While it can take many forms, the principle is simple: The cache grabs the most recently used data and holds it for future reference. This is possible because most of what a computer does is very predictable. It operates on a certain small number of memory locations at any given time; so for a given period the CPU uses a relatively small amount of memory.

To take advantage of this situation, system designers have developed sophisticated ways to place data the computer needs at any given time in a small amount of very high-speed memory, the memory cache, while the rest of the data is kept in a larger amount of less expensive memory. If a computer normally used only 10 percent of a program, it would need to keep just that 10 percent in very fast memory. Because the computer would eventually need to work with a different section of the program, it must be able to move the unnecessary data out of fast memory and into slower memory and replace it with the new data. In a well-designed system, the necessary data can be in

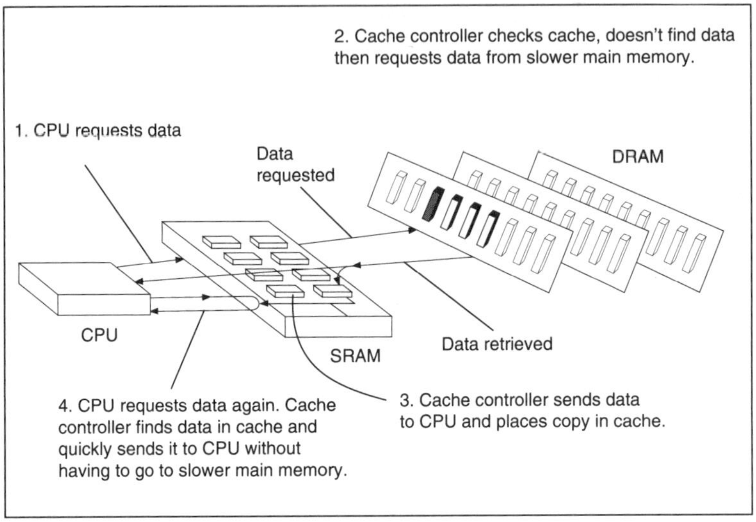

Figure 3-3. How the CPU cache works

the cache more than 90 percent of the time, even if the cache size is only a small fraction of the total memory. (See Figure 3-3.)

Caching strikes a balance between the cost of a small amount of fast SRAM and a large amount of slower (but far less expensive) DRAM. The result is near-SRAM performance at near-DRAM prices.

Adding Main Memory

Just as computer designers have been forced to limit the amount of SRAM they use in a system, they must limit the amount of DRAM or main memory (RAM). They realize that a computer with 16 MB of main memory could be much faster than a computer with only 1 MB, but it will also be much more expensive. That's why manufacturers typically ship computers with a relatively small amount of memory installed.

Fortunately, most computers are designed to accommodate far more main memory than they're configured with. The system boards have extra memory sockets so that memory can be added for only the cost of the additional memory. That way, dealers and users can add to their systems' memory if their particular markets or applications demand more memory (and they usually will).

Manufacturers expect you to need more memory than they ship with the computer. But they assume you'll shop around and get the best price for it rather than having them buy it and sell it to a distributor, who sells it to a dealer, who sells it to you. You're almost certain of getting a better deal if you buy memory and install it yourself. If you're uncomfortable working under the hood of your computer, have your dealer install the extra memory.

A word of caution: Don't try to save money by buying cheap memory. Buy quality memory from a reputable seller. When purchasing single in-line memory modules (SIMMs), avoid third-party memory (name-brand memory chips soldered onto low-cost, no-name SIMMs). If the going rate for memory is $50 per megabyte, you won't save anything in the long run if you pay a questionable source $38 per megabyte.

Adding memory is the single most important action you can take to improve performance (provided you follow some of the suggestions in this book on how to take advantage of that memory). You'll see extraordinary performance boosts if you use it to break up bottlenecks throughout the system. Most of the techniques discussed involve bypassing bottlenecks in the slower subsystems (below the memory area in the data funnel) by moving as much activity as possible into memory. That means you need to have large amounts of memory installed. If you're a typical user and have less than 4 MB of memory installed, you should probably upgrade to at least 4 MB. If you're a power user (that is, you already have 4 MB of memory installed but still wish your computer would run faster), you should have at least 8 MB.

PC Memory Usage

To evaluate your PC's current configuration and decide the best way to add system memory, you need to understand the three ways memory is used in most 386 and 486 computers: conventional, expanded, and extended.

Conventional memory

Base or *conventional memory* normally consists of the first 640 KB. This is the memory DOS can recognize and access directly and is where most applications operate.

In the early 1980s, when the IBM PC was designed, 640 KB seemed like more than enough memory. The most popular microcomputer operating system prior to DOS, CP/M, was limited to only 64 KB, making 640 KB seem like overkill. Indeed, the first IBM PCs were shipped with only 32 KB of memory.

Today, only a decade later, with standard configurations of between 2 and 8 MB and fully configured systems with as much as 64 MB, it's difficult to conceive of motherboards that only accommodated 640 KB. Nevertheless, the PCs designers didn't foresee the need to address more than 640 KB of memory, so they established a purely arbitrary boundary of 640 KB.

At most, the IBM PC could address no more than the hardware limitation of the Intel 8088 microprocessor, which could only address 1024 KB (1 MB) of memory. Of that, IBM decided to reserve the upper 384 KB for system uses (like the system BIOS), limiting DOS to the bottom 640 KB. Today's 32-bit members of the Intel chip family address up to 4 GB of memory, but DOS still only addresses 640 KB. You can only change that limitation by changing DOS, but that would make the DOS application base obsolete.

Because DOS is the problem, one obvious solution is to migrate to a more powerful operating system, such as UNIX or OS/2. Windows also alle-

Tips on adding main memory

First, you must decide what kind of memory you need to add. If you have an older system or an older memory board, you may have to add regular memory chips, called DIPs—the ones with 16 to 20 pins arranged in two rows like the legs of a centipede. Most PCs now use single in-line memory modules (SIMMs) and single in-line pin packages (SIPPs), which are small circuit boards that hold several memory chips. SIMMs use an edge connector; SIPPs, on the other hand, use a single row of long pins.

If you have an older system that takes DIPs be aware that installing them can be tricky. With most PCs using DIPs, the eight bits in each byte plus a parity-checking bit are divided among nine chips (one bit per chip) in a "bank" of memory. Make sure that you align the chips with the semicircular depressions in their plastic cases located near pin 1 on the sockets. When you install the chips, make sure all of the "legs" are straight and parallel. Align one row of legs first, resting them in the socket. Then gently line up the other row of legs with the other side of the socket before pressing the chip into the socket until it's all the way in. It's very easy to bend one or more legs, so be care-

viates some of the problem for Windows-specific applications, without requiring abandonment of the huge DOS application base. But clever hardware and software designers also found ways around the 640-KB limitation for DOS programs.

Expanded memory

At first, applications for the PC were migrated from the 64-KB confines of CP/M, and even 256 KB seemed limitless. As time went on, software developers explored ways to use the PC for increasingly powerful applications. Those programs soon began using the entire 640 KB available to them. Software packages grew larger and larger, as did the data files they generated. Eventually, the programs and their data files ran out of memory.

One way software designers get around this limitation is to overlay the program, meaning that application code and data unable to fit in memory is kept

---

ful—even one incorrectly installed RAM chip can prevent your computer from operating.

For SIMMs, align the plastic pin in the socket with the hole at one end of the SIMM (SIMMs fit only one way). Then push the metal contacts at the bottom of the SIMM into the socket, and press the SIMM back until the plastic tabs at either end snap into position.

If your manual doesn't indicate what type of memory chips to use, examine the chips that are already installed. The chip's size is indicated by digits preceding a dash (256 for 256-kilobit chips, and 1,000 for 1-megabit chips), while digits after the dash represent the access time in nanoseconds. Chips on a SIMM might be marked "P1C1000A-70," which tells you that they're 1-megabit chips with a 70-ns access time.

It's OK to put in faster memory—a 70-ns SIMM on a machine that needs an 80-ns SIMM—but don't use slower chips. Since your PC may not run at all or may stop occasionally and display a message called "parity error."

Using memory rated faster than your current memory will not allow your system to run faster though. Most PCs are designed for a certain speed of memory and must have at least that speed in order to operate but cannot take advantage of memory with a faster access time, that is, memory with a lower number, say 60ns instead of 80ns.

on disk and simply swapped into memory when needed, displacing other program code and data. Of course, a look at the data funnel makes clear that the much slower speed of disk access as opposed to memory access causes a considerable hit to performance.

Some clever computer designers realized that the computer could accommodate and address more than 1 MB of memory even if the applications could only see the first megabyte. To get around the 1-MB barrier, they developed *page swapping* (or *paged memory*) and called it expanded memory.

Expanded memory is a way of tricking applications into thinking more memory is available to them than actually is. A memory manager switches memory from outside the 640 KB (that is, from above the 1-MB area) into an area the applications recognize and access. To be specific, the expanded memory manager reserves an unused 64-KB "window" in the memory address space reserved for system use (the area between 640 KB and 1 MB). Although much of this

Extended and expanded memory

The data throughput associated with each kind of memory depends a great deal on the way the memory is implemented. For example, a software emulation of expanded memory will be far slower than an expanded board that implements page frame swapping in hardware, and both will differ from expanded memory implemented using a program like EMM386.EXE, which uses the memory mapping capabilities of the 386 chip to swap page frames.

The most acute problem, however is measuring the speed of extended memory. Extended memory accessed from DOS's real mode is far slower than extended memory accessed from protected mode—far slower.

Thus, if you were to depend on the throughput of extended memory as represented by a suite like *PC Magazine*'s 6.0 benchmark, you might get the wrong idea about the usefulness of extended memory.

The data throughput numbers of my 33-MHz white box 386 come out like this on the *PC Magazine* benchmark 6.0:

address space was already reserved for use by the system BIOS, video cards, and so on, several 64-KB stretches were still available.

Applications that know how to use expanded memory simply look at data in this 64-KB area, into which the expanded memory manager maps a 64KB data page that lies above the 1-MB limit. The application asks the expanded memory manager to swap these memory pages as needed.

This expanded memory isn't the ideal solution to the memory barrier, however, since the additional memory management wastes CPU cycles.

Extended memory

As time passed, software developers noticed all the additional memory that was potentially available. Why should they have to play the expanded-memory game? Why not address all available memory directly? Fortunately, by the time the 386 started shipping, they were already taking advantage of the CPU's abil-

Memory read .... 4608 Kbytes second
Memory write .... 4535 Kbytes second
Expanded memory read .... 1488 Kbytes second
Expanded memory write .... 1570 Kbytes second
Extended memory read .... 480 Kbytes second
Extended memory write .... 496 Kbytes second

In fact, access to extended memory is not inefficient when a 286 or 386 machine is in protected mode, but only when a PC must switch between real mode and protected mode to access it as the PC hubs benchmark does.

Do not be mislead by outdated benchmark programs; in most PCs extended memory is just as fast as conventional memory. And in most PCs extended memory is faster than expanded memory.

So although we don't include them in the data funnel, the key point to retain is this: expanded memory is about one-third the speed of ordinary RAM. And although you can't see it from these numbers, extended memory accessed from protected mode in an operating environment like Windows is quite efficient. That's why it's usually better to configure memory above 1 MB as extended memory rather than expanded.

ity to address far more than 1 MB of memory; it was the operating system DOS that was memory-bound.

The enabling technology for this advance was a group of products called *DOS extenders.* These extenders allowed software developers to address and use memory that DOS alone could not. The developers rewrote their programs to take advantage of all that memory beyond 1 MB. This additional memory, which could be recognized and accessed without being swapped into conventional memory, is known as *extended memory.* This term applies to all linearly addressable memory in the system beyond the first megabyte.

Some DOS programs, such as the Oracle Corp.'s Professional database, require the presence of extended memory in order to run. Other programs, such as FoxPro and Paradox, simply use extended memory if it's there, either to buffer data or to keep program code in memory that would otherwise have to be brought in as needed from disk.

Still, extended memory can only be used by the relatively small number of DOS applications that are written to be aware of and take advantage of it. Fortunately, the number of such applications is increasing. UNIX and its applications access extended memory directly, as do Novell Inc.'s NetWare, Banyan Systems Inc.'s VINES, and other network operating systems. Windows 3.x can also take advantage of extended memory.

Questions and Answers About Memory Configuration

The following are some of the questions that may arise when adding memory to your system. This book assumes you already have plenty of conventional memory; most of you probably have at least 640KB. If you don't have at least 640KB, you'll want to take care of that deficiency immediately.

Should I install extended or expanded memory?

If you have a 386- or 486-based machine, most likely you'll want to install extended memory. Even if you want expanded memory because that's all your older DOS programs can take advantage of, it's better to install it as extended and then use a memory manager like Quarterdeck Office Systems' QEMM to utilize the memory mapping capabilities of the 386 to convert extended memory to expanded.

On 8088 and 286 machines, which lack the 386 and 486's ability to map memory, a special board with memory management hardware is required for efficient access to expanded memory. You can install extended memory on the motherboard of a 286-based machine, but it won't be usable as expanded memory. For an 8088-based machine, extended memory is not an option because of the 1 MB address space limit, and an expanded memory board is your only option for access to more memory.

In general, extended memory is more useful for obtaining improved performance from your computer. It typically has the advantage of being supported directly on the motherboard—you just add chips without the need for an additional memory card. And unlike expanded memory, it doesn't require a memory manager.

Although your current applications might only take advantage of expanded memory, future versions of those programs will probably use extended memory to achieve better performance. Even programs that support expanded memory generally can't *run* in expanded memory; they only use it to store data files. Extended memory is also typically faster than expanded memory.

On the other hand, in some 286- and 386-based PCs, this is not the case. That's because of the way the original IBM PC-AT accessed extended memory and that many computers followed suit to maintain compatibility with the AT standard.

To access memory above 1 MB, the AT switched from real mode, which addresses the same 1 MB of address space as the original 8088, to protected mode, which lets the chip use the additional memory addressable by the 286 and later chips in the Intel family. This switching between modes required that the system perform a *system reset.* On the AT, the system reset was activated through the keyboard controller. Even on the original AT this was a slow process, but as machines got faster it seemed slower still. No matter how fast machines became, the keyboard controller still operated at 5 or 8 MHz. Using an 8-MHz keyboard controller to perform the reset on an 8-MHz PC wasn't so bad, but as PCs sped up to 16 MHz, 20 MHz, and faster, using the keyboard controller for the reset function became a serious bottleneck. This wasn't a problem when using expanded memory because no system reset is required. As a result, PCs that followed the AT method of accessing extended memory are slower when addressing extended memory than when addressing expanded memory.

This problem is corrected in most PCs by implementing circuitry called fast Gate A20 (A20 being the first address line for memory over 1 MB). The fast Gate A20 circuitry allows the computer to address extended memory without going through the slow system reset process.

On the other hand, extended memory accessed through fast Gate A20 circuitry does not solve all memory problems. Many DOS applications still do not recognize extended memory. Extended-memory programs also sometimes conflict with each other (expanded-memory programs are generally better behaved). For more information, refer to Chapter 11 and Chapter 12.

If your applications can't take advantage of extended memory, use memory managers to turn the extended memory in your system into expanded memory that many more programs work with. The latest versions of MS-DOS include memory managers (EMM386.SYS or EMM386.EXE), but you may want to buy

Slow Gate A20 and a way to avoid it

Some 386-based computers that tried to maintain 100 percent compatibility with the IBM PC/AT are very slow when switching from protected mode to real mode. This problem will manifest itself in the PC Labs extended memory benchmark. With this test, a computer that has fast scores for conventional memory and expanded memory has very slow scores for the extended memory benchmark as well. This problem normally will not manifest in actual applications; it usually just shows up in this particular benchmark. If you are concerned about a slow score in this benchmark or you seem to be accessing extended or expanded memory much slower than you would expect, slow switching from protected to real mode may be the problem. The solution is to use a memory manager such as QEMM or 386-to-the-Max. These programs normally hold the A20 line and prevent it from slowing memory accesses.

If you see a line in the computer's data sheet that says something like "Fast Gate A20 support," it is referring to this issue. Presumably the designers of that system have taken care of the problem for you. But as I said, normally the A20 problem is a non issue, except for the PC Labs benchmark.

one of the third-party expanded memory managers. Two excellent products are Quarterdeck's QEMM and Qualitas Inc.'s 386-to-the-Max.

Where does additional memory get installed and what speed should it be?

Most PCs ship with standard configurations from 1 to 4 MB of memory but have additional sockets for increasing memory on the motherboard. If you have such a computer, this is generally where you want to place any additional memory. If your system is a 386DX or 486, memory added to the system board should be 32 bits wide and run at the same speed as the CPU. If you have a 286 or 386SX, system board memory should be 16 bits and run at the same speed as the CPU. Such memory is added in the form of DIP chips (although these are becoming less common) or SIMMs (see Figure 3-4). In order to install 16-bit-wide memory with chips, 18 DIP or 2 SIMM chips must be added at a time. A 32-bit system requires 36 DIP chips or 4 SIMMs to be added at one time.

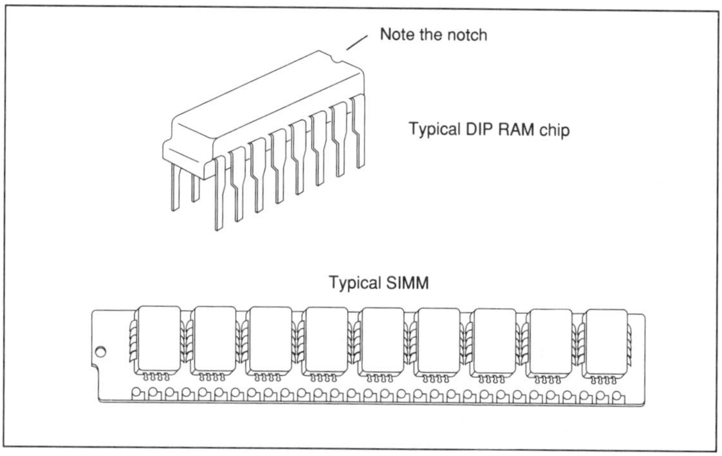

Figure 3-4
SIMM and DIP-style RAM chip

What if no sockets are available on the motherboard?

Some 386DX and 486 systems are designed with a built-in 32-bit memory expansion slot. Of course, this requires buying a 32-bit memory card to plug into the slot. The advantage of using such cards is that you install 32-bit memory and it runs at the same performance level as the memory on the motherboard.

Any 32-bit memory added with an expansion card in a proprietary 32-bit memory slot should run as fast as the memory on the motherboard, but verify this with your computer's manufacturer or your computer dealer before proceeding. Sometimes what appears to be a 32-bit memory card is actually something else, and in some cases, 32-bit cards run slower than the memory installed directly on the board.

What if I'm out of room on my 386 or 486 motherboard or its 32-bit memory board, or there is no 32-bit memory slot?

All is not lost; you can still buy a memory card that plugs into the I/O bus. At the time of publication, no memory boards available are designed specifically for the EISA (Extended Industry Standard Architecture) bus; however, you can use standard AT-bus memory cards in the EISA slots.

What if I have a 286 or 386SX and I've filled the available memory sockets on the system board?

The solution given for users with 386s and 486s also applies to those with 286 and 386SX systems. If you've filled the memory sockets on your system board, install a 16-bit memory card (see Figure 3-5).

If I'm installing an I/O-bus memory card in a 386DX or 486, should I expect a drop in performance?

Although these bus-based memory cards are now very common and fairly inexpensive, they aren't the most desirable way to upgrade a PC's memory. This should be your third choice (after adding more memory directly to the motherboard and installing a 32-bit memory card, if that option is available to you). That's because a PC's I/O bus typically runs at either 8 MHz (ISA and EISA) or 10 MHz (Micro Channel), while memory on the motherboard should run at 25, 33, or 50 MHz (or at least closer to the speed of the CPU itself). Therefore, the CPU accesses memory on a card plugged into a slow I/O bus much more slowly than if the additional memory were installed on the motherboard or in a 32-bit memory slot.

Look again at the data funnel and notice how the I/O bus area is much narrower than the memory areas above it. Memory installed on the I/O bus can't be accessed any faster than the bus itself. However, that doesn't mean you shouldn't install a memory expansion card if you really need to add memory and the only place to add it is on the I/O bus. As you'll see in later chapters, you

Figure 3-5.
The Acculogic Ram Plus AT is a 16-bit AT bus memory expansion card.

can use that extra memory to handle operations that normally happen way down in the data funnel, so that I/O bus speed is a marked performance improvement. I/O bus-based memory, whether it's on the ISA bus or the Micro Channel bus, can be useful for disk caching, creating RAM disks, and other techniques mentioned in this book.

If you're using 16-bit I/O bus memory to move applications out of the lower sections of the data funnel into, say, a disk cache, I/O-bus memory is acceptable (though 32-bit motherboard memory is preferable). On the other hand, if your application ends up executing in a portion of that I/O-bus memory, you may unknowingly be slowing that application's performance significantly. It's very important to keep your applications executing in the faster 32-bit memory and only use I/O-bus memory for those operations that would normally be further down in the data funnel.

Fortunately, applications can run in the lower parts of memory; in fact, most run in the first 640 KB. Therefore, the extended memory you add will probably only be used for operations such as disk caches and RAM drives.

However, let's say you have an 8-MB system and want to add 2 MB on an I/O bus card to be used as a disk cache (reserving the 8 MB for the operating system and applications). Unfortunately, when you put the additional memory on the I/O bus, it's entirely possible that the program will put itself into the top 2 MB of the total system memory (the memory on the I/O bus). If that happens, you may find that the disk cache has access to the very fast 32-bit memory on the motherboard and your applications are running at a much slower speed on the 16-bit I/O bus. Thus, instead of improving performance, you suffer a net loss in overall throughput.

Although this generally doesn't happen, it's important to be aware that it can, especially with those programs that use the Phar Lap DOS extender. I/O-bus memory is great if you' re using it for disk cache; if you're adding it to give applications more memory, though, just be aware that it may slow them down considerably. I'll go into detail on ways to take advantage of additional memory in the following chapters.

Summary

Memory is one of the most important components of computer performance. Not only is it important to have enough memory, but it is important to have the memory configured in such a way that your CPU and applications take maximum advantage of available memory. Although the people that built your computer realize the importance of memory, they probably did not sell it to you with as much memory as you require for optimum performance. Fortunately, memory has gotten to be relatively inexpensive; so adding memory is one of the least expensive ways to improve computer performance. Considering the low cost of memory relative to the cost of hardware and software you are likely to install on your system, it is probably well worth the cost to add the necessary memory to obtain maximum performance.

CHAPTER FOUR

The Input/ Output Bus

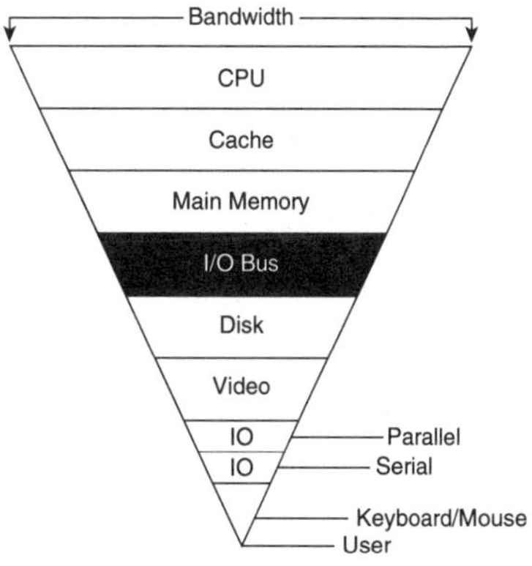

Data Funnel

The *input/output (I/O) bus* is a hardware path inside a computer that connects the CPU, coprocessor, and memory banks to the controllers for each peripheral device, including your hard drive, printer, video monitor, and others. (Sometimes, as in the case of memory or cache cards, the boards themselves are the devices.)

The bus is divided into two channels, the address bus and the data bus. During a data transfer to or from one of the peripheral devices, the address bus designates the destination of the data, while the data bus actually carries the data moved between the two locations.

There are three principal PC bus interface standards: ISA (Industry Standard Architecture), EISA (Extended Industry Standard Architecture), and MCA (Micro Channel Architecture). They differ in terms of speed, number of lines available for addressing, and form factor, as explained in more detail later in this chapter.

In general, however, the operation of the various buses is the same. When you insert a network interface card, a tape drive controller, or other expansion board into one of your system's open *slots*, you are actually connecting it to the bus controller, which resides on the motherboard (see Figure 4-1.) Literally, the bus controller contains the circuits that connect the slots to the motherboard and, in turn, allow the cards in the expansion slots to control data transfers to and from peripherals across the I/O bus.

Figure 4-1. Expansion slots for different bus standards

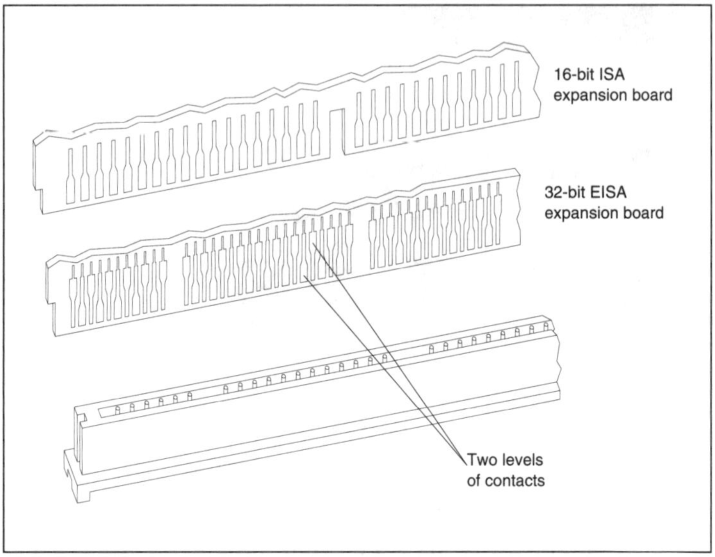

The I/O Bus Relative to the Rest of the Data Funnel

Unfortunately, the I/O bus is slow relative to the main memory of the computer and to the CPU. You can see this by looking at how narrow the data funnel is at the I/O bus section in relation to the sections above it.

Since much data (including everything read from and written to disk) has to go through the I/O bus, the bus can be a major bottleneck in overall system performance. The severity of this problem depends on how much time the CPU and motherboard RAM wait idle while information flows to and from peripherals through the I/O bus.

Rival Bus Interface Standards: ISA, EISA, and MCA

Let's look at each of the interface standards in terms of impact on overall system performance.

The ISA bus

Most PCs in use follow the ISA. The ISA bus was originally used on the IBM XT and was expanded for the AT. It can have an 8- or a 16-bit data path. In AT machines, it typically runs at about 8 MHz. Although data theoretically travels at a maximum of 4 MB per second on an ISA bus, it rarely reaches this speed. Rather, data usually travels over the AT bus at 1 MB per second or less. Thus, the bandwidth of an ISA bus is only a fraction of the bandwidth of main memory, which ranges from 20 MB per second to 64 MB per second, or of CPU bandwidth, which ranges from 80 MB per second to 200 MB per second.

EISA and MCA

Computer designers have tried to alleviate the I/O bottleneck by expanding the bus even further—from 16 bits to 32 bits. Such an expanded data path means that more data can travel over the path, or bus. EISA and MCA are the best known enhanced PC buses (see Figure 4-2).

EISA extends the ISA bus specification for faster data throughput. In contrast to the 16-bit ISA bus, the EISA bus has a 32-bit data path. EISA is compatible with the ISA standard: ISA expansion cards function when plugged directly into EISA bus slots. However, you won't benefit from EISA's 32-bit transfer rate unless you use EISA expansion cards, which cost more.

Like EISA, MCA can be implemented as a 32-bit bus. But unlike EISA, the MCA bus, introduced by IBM in its PS/2 line, is not compatible with the ISA standard. IBM argued that developing a more efficient bus meant abandoning

Figure 4-2. Mylex MAE486, a typical 33-MHz EISA system board

the AT-bus standard. Others said that IBM developed the proprietary standard to differentiate its machines from those made by PC clone vendors.

The Bus Wars: Hype or High-Performance?

While it is difficult to give a precise throughput rate, both EISA and MCA have theoretical maximum throughput rates of more than 30 MB per second. However, data rarely moves across either of these buses at speeds greater than 5 MB per second. In fact, most machines rarely sustain a rate of 5 MB per second. Therefore, even though EISA and MCA are high-performance buses, they are still slow when compared with the 200-MB per second bandwidth of a 50-MHz 486 CPU or the 100-MB per second bandwidth of a 25-MHz 386 CPU. If a system's processor can move data at a rate of 100 MB per second, but the I/O bus is only running at 1 MB per second, 2 MB per second, or even 5 MB per second, obviously there is a significant bottleneck in the data funnel. The width of the data funnel in the I/O bus section then is actually much narrower than it appears in the data funnel drawings.

Thus, any I/O bus—whether ISA, EISA, or MCA—even when performing at its highest throughput rates, provides a fraction of what the system needs for maximum performance. And as yet there is no practical (cheap or easy) way to upgrade your system's I/O bus because the I/O bus is intimately connected with the PC's motherboard. If you replace the I/O bus, the motherboard must be replaced also.

While replacing the entire motherboard may be an option, it probably will not be worth the trouble. You are unlikely to buy yourself much of a performance boost by upgrading from an ISA bus with a 2-MB per second bandwidth to an EISA or MCA bus with a 5-MB per second bandwidth unless you use very fast peripherals extensively. If your applications frequently go back and forth over the I/O bus to access peripherals, then reduce the amount of time they spend doing so by switching to a faster bus. If you are interested in replacing the motherboard and bus, please refer to Chapter 2.

However, your biggest performance gains are going to be achieved by avoiding the I/O bus as much as possible. For example, if you have a choice, install motherboard RAM rather than RAM on an expansion board. But in general, there aren't many cases where the bus itself is a significant bottleneck since the I/O devices accessed through the bus are often far slower than the bus itself.

In short, switching buses isn't a sound solution for eliminating the I/O bottleneck, and users should be wary of vendor claims for EISA and MCA; real-world performance rarely matches theoretical maximums.

Bus Mastering

Bus mastering is another feature that distinguishes the EISA and MCA buses from the ISA.

A *bus master* is a card that functions with its own chip so that it has enough intelligence to operate independently of the CPU. Thus, the bus master performs its tasks while the CPU attends to other tasks. The most common example of a bus-mastering device is a bus-mastering disk controller. Such a controller should be able to read and write data to and from the hard disk while the CPU performs other tasks.

The ISA or AT bus can accommodate only one bus master, and even that device is often difficult to install correctly. On the other hand, EISA and MCA support multiple bus masters with fewer headaches. However, there are a couple of "gotchas." Bus masters will probably not significantly improve system performance in a single-tasking environment, such as DOS. Also, bus masters cost considerably more than standard cards. Thus, only consider bus masters for particularly high-throughput applications, such as the use of a PC as a file server. For example, when several bus-mastered network interface cards independently process network traffic in parallel, leaving the main CPU free for other work, you are likely to increase network throughput greatly. But installing a single EISA network interface card (NIC) on a single node on a network will most likely not show a performance gain over a similarly configured PC with an ISA bus and ISA NIC.

In demanding applications, whether you're installing bus masters on the EISA or MCA bus or not, use cards that take advantage of EISA and MCA bandwidths. While standard EISA and MCA cards are not as expensive as EISA and MCA bus masters, they are still priced higher than ISA cards.

Local Bus

A PC's I/O bus can be a major bottleneck when it comes to PC performance. Most computer designers realize the potential performance bottleneck introduced by a slow I/O bus based on the over 10-year-old standards (the PC's I/O bus dates back to 1981, the year IBM introduced PCs). The problem computer designers face is that for a PC to be successful (that is sell in profitable quantities), it must conform to standards.

If a computer manufacturer came out with a new model that offered a much faster I/O bus but there were no peripheral cards to take advantage of this special bus, there would be little demand for the bus. During the 1980s, several computer manufacturers did exactly this. The most notable attempt to create a fast I/O bus that was not based on the previous standards was AST's SmartSlot Architecture. The SmartSlot was a special bus in some AST computers that was designed to run at close to CPU speeds rather than the standard 8 MHz of the AT bus. Unfortunately, the manufacturers of peripheral cards didn't feel as though there would be enough of a demand for a peripheral that would work in only one company's computers, so they didn't build cards for this slot and the SmartSlot quietly disappeared.

The need for a faster I/O bus has not gone away, though, simply because it requires a departure from the AT bus standard. In fact, as other components of the system on either side of the I/O bus increase in performance (CPUs are now about 100 times faster than the original PC I/O bus and disk drive throughput has increased about 10 times) the need has become even more apparent. Recently, a number of PC manufacturers have decided to implement a faster I/O bus on some of their systems, even if it means departing from the standard bus. Systems with these new I/O buses, often called a *local bus*, are now being touted as having performance of up to 20 times faster than similar systems that use a standard 8 MHz bus. While it is obvious that claims are limited to only a few operations, not the overall performance of the system, these systems with faster buses are, in fact, able to deliver higher performance in at least some areas. Most of the performance increases being touted by these new local bus systems are in the area of video.

While improved video performance is an admirable achievement there is an important downside to these video bus implementations.

The problem with most of the local bus implementations that are starting to appear is that they are all proprietary (that is, they belong to the company that developed them and thus by definition are not industry standard). This means that if you want any peripherals to take advantage of these high performance buses, you will have to buy the peripherals from the same company that made the computer.

The most obvious problem with this arrangement is that the peripherals for these new buses are going to cost more (the laws of supply and demand dictate that if the supply is limited then the price will be higher). But there is an even bigger problem with these proprietary buses. The companies that are building computers with these new buses have most of their expertise in the areas of designing and building computers, not in designing and building peripherals. Most of these companies will not be able to design peripheral products that are as advanced or as up-to-date as similar products from companies whose entire focus is on designing and building peripherals. There are companies that are very good at building graphics adapters and there are others that are good at building disk controllers but there are very few companies capable of building advanced PCs and high performance PC peripherals. And unless the companies that are building these PCs with proprietary local buses also deliver the high performance peripherals and drivers required to take advantage of the bus, there will be little point in buying computers that include these proprietary buses.

There is some relief from this problem in sight. A number of companies have banded together in an association to try and develop advanced peripherals for PCs. The Video Electronics Standards Association (VESA) has created a specification for a high performance I/O bus, called the VL-bus, with the hopes that it will become the high performance I/O bus for PCs. Because VESA is an industry-wide group it should gain support for the VL-bus by both the PC manufacturers and the peripheral manufactures. If that happens, there will be some relief from the I/O bus bottleneck.

To put this development into perspective though, the VL-bus will only be available on computers that were designed with it. If your motherboard doesn't include support for the VL-bus (and at the time this was written none did) you won't be able to take advantage of the bus or its peripherals. But before you succumb to the inevitable hype and performance claims that will surround this new standard, keep in mind that unless the high performance peripherals are available to claim potentially high throughput, a faster bus won't make a computer any faster than the reliable old AT bus.

Summary

Although you can sometimes optimize I/O bus performance by simply avoiding heavy throughput on the I/O bus, in general the I/O bus bandwidth can be improved only by buying a new motherboard. Even so, the impact of the I/O bus on performance in single-user systems is minimal. Thus, in the remainder of this book, the term *bus* may come up in discussion in the context of avoiding I/O on the bus, but distinctions between ISA, EISA, or MCA are unimportant.

CHAPTER FIVE

Understanding Disk Performance

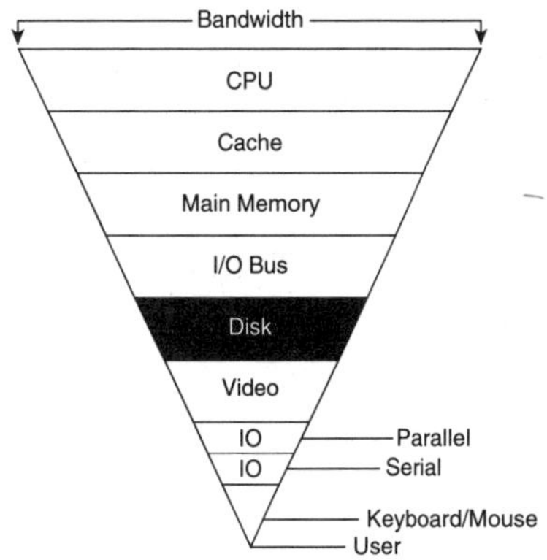

Data Funnel

With the exception of the CPU, the disk drive probably has more impact on performance than any other single component or subsystem of a computer. Fortunately, disk drive performance is one of the easiest aspects of overall system performance to improve. You do so through a variety of changes to hardware and software configuration that we'll discuss in Chapter 6. Such changes are inexpensive and do not require replacing your disk drive.

The Disk Drive and the Data Funnel

When considering performance in terms of the amount of data a system component can process per second, the hard disk drive is shown to be very slow relative to the CPU, the main memory, and the I/O bus of your computer. The reason for this deficiency is easily explained—disk drives are mechanical devices. Those system components higher in the data funnel, which are those capable of greater throughput or bandwidth, are all electronic devices. A mechanical device moves at a much slower pace than a semiconductor device, where the only moving parts are very fast electrons.

The fact that disk drives have moving parts introduces a new element to data throughput. The maximum amount of data transferred per second is lower for disk drives than for memory or CPUs, and there is also delay introduced in a disk drive while the mechanical parts move into position to read or write the desired piece of data (see Figure 5-1.)

Performance is measured in terms of millionths or billionths of a second for a semiconductor device like a CPU or a memory module. The clock rate of a CPU is measured in megahertz (millions of cycles per second), and access

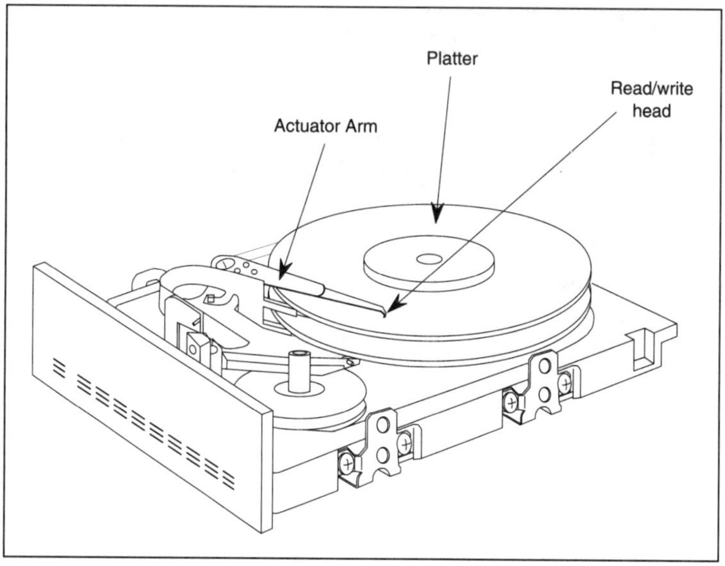

Figure 5-1. Components of a hard disk drive

time of memory chips is measured in nanoseconds (billionths of a second). But when you drop to the disk drive section of the data funnel, performance is measured in thousandths of a second. For example, the average seek time of fast drives only recently approached 10 milliseconds (10 one-thousandths of a second, or one hundredth of a second).

In other mechanical mass storage media, performance slows even further to fractions of a second for CD-ROMs (roughly the speed of hard drives from the original IBM PC XT, which had average seek times longer than one tenth of a second). In the case of tape drives, performance slows to seconds or even minutes.

Elements of Disk Drive Performance

Before discussing the ways in which you can improve the performance of a system's hard disk drive, let's take some time to understand how disk drive performance is evaluated and why the disk drive is slow relative to other major components. If you don't care why disk drives are slow or you aren't interested in the arcane details of measuring drive performance, just skip to Chapter 6.

There are two aspects of disk drive performance to evaluate: *latency* (delay) and *throughput* (speed). In other words, the impact of a disk drive on performance is affected by *access time* (the amount of time needed for a drive to begin transferring data) and the *data transfer rate* (how fast the drive transfers the data once the transfer begins). The amount of delay before the drive starts transferring data can be considerably different than the amount of time necessary to transfer the data. While these factors can be severe bottlenecks to overall system performance, their relative importance depends on the operation you're performing.

For example, if you're transferring a single bit of data, the latency period before the transfer starts will be very important. If, on the other hand, you're transferring a large chunk of data situated on disk such that the disk drive head can read or write that data continuously, the average access time will be unimportant compared to the data transfer rate.

Average Access Time

The average access time is comprised of two elements: average seek time and rotational latency.

In practical terms, average access time tells you how long it's going to take to find any single piece of information on the disk drive. It does not tell you how fast data moves once a transfer begins if the data you're accessing is located contiguously on the disk, which we'll discuss later in the chapter.

Average seek time

Seek time is the amount of time needed for the read/write head on the disk drive to move and position itself over a particular track on the disk. The *average seek time* is the average amount of time required for the read/write head to position itself over a track (see Figure 5-2).

The principal factors in determining what that average seek time will be are how long it takes the read/write head to move over the surface of the drive and how many cylinders the drive has. (That is, how fast can the drive's actuator arm move the heads and how far do they have to travel? Since you have one head per cylinder, a disk with many cylinders is faster than a disk of the same storage capacity with fewer cylinders. See Figure 5-3.) Average seek times are normally given in milliseconds (ms), thousandths of a second. Seek times have improved considerably over the years, going from over a tenth of a second in 1982 to close to a hundredth of a second on today's fastest drives. Unfortunately, the access time is not determined solely by the seek time.

Figure 5-2.
Tracks and sectors. Each track consists of a series of sectors.

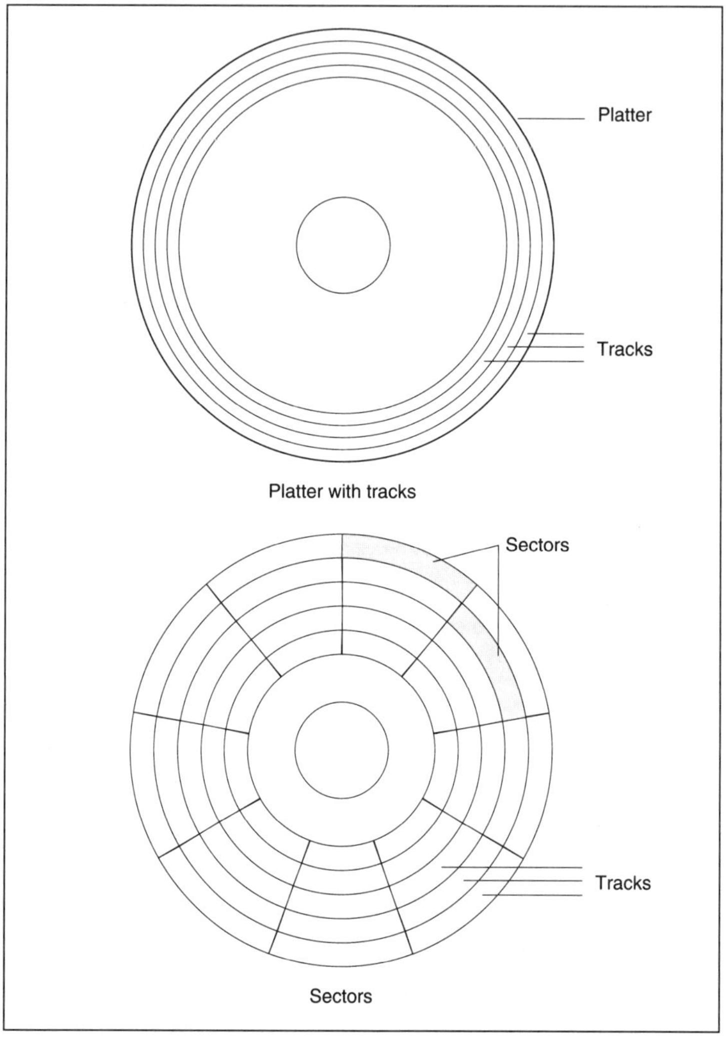

Figure 5-3.
A drive cylinder

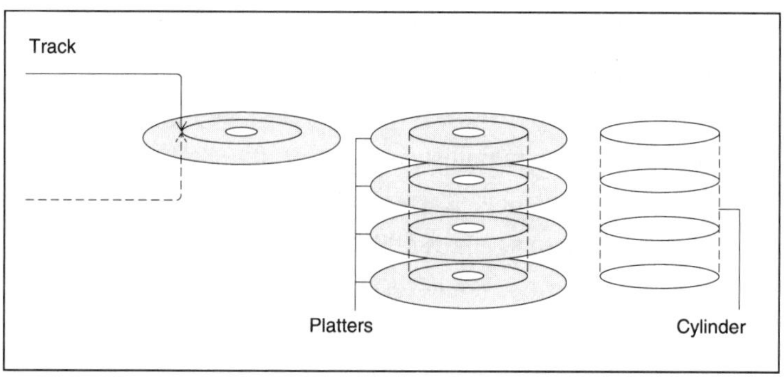

Rotational latency

Even though some disk drive manufacturers try to convince customers that average access time equals seek time, it's not true. The seek time is only a measure of how long it takes to move the head over the correct track. Once the actuator arm has moved the read/write head over the track it has been seeking, there may still be a delay while the platter rotates the correct sector into position. Often when the actuator arm moves the read/write head over the track it seeks, the head ends up over a different sector than the one it requires. In this case, there is a delay while the drive platter rotates until the correct sector is under the read/write head. Only when the platter has rotated this sector into position can the read/write head commence its reading of the sector(s) it needs to access. This delay is called the *rotational latency.*

The rotational latency is the average delay experienced while the disk drive platter rotates so that the required sector comes under the read/write head. Unfortunately, while seek times have improved considerably, the rotational latency of disk drives is a factor that really hasn't improved very much since the introduction of the PC/XT. A typical disk drive in 1982 rotated at about 3,600 rpm; that's the same speed at which a typical disk drive rotates today. Starting with a rotational speed of 3,600 rpm, the computation of rotational latency is straightforward (3,600 rpm/60 = 60 rps, or one rotation every 1/60 of a second). On average, the head reaches the data in half a rotation, or 1/120 of a second. (1/120 of a second is .00833 seconds or 8.33 milliseconds, which is the rotational latency.) Thus, the average time needed for the platter to rotate under a head before it can start reading information from the sector it's been waiting for is about 8 milliseconds (or 8 thousandths of a second).

The importance of access time

It's easy to see why computer vendors want to call the seek time the access time. As seek times improved by roughly a factor of 10 over the last decade, rotational latency stayed the same for the vast majority of disk drives, and thus became a larger and larger component of access times (seek time plus rotational latency).

In 1982, with the arrival of the XT, hard drives had an average access time of just a little over a tenth of a second (100 milliseconds). At that point, average seek time and average access time were close to each other, because rotational latency didn't add very much to the total of the average access time. It took 100 milliseconds for the arm to position the read/write head over the proper track, and only 8 ms more for the platter to rotate so that the head was over the right sector. In other words, in those days, rotational latency accounted for less than 10 percent of the average access time.

In today's marketplace, a very fast drive is expected to put the head over the right track in about 15 thousandths of a second (15 milliseconds). So in the ten-year span since the inception of the PC, average seek times for hard disk drives have improved a factor of about six. However, since our rotational latency has remained relatively unchanged, the overall average access time is still more than 20 milliseconds on all but the fastest drives (see Figure 5-4).

A few state-of-the-art disk drives operate at significantly increased rpm. Some are actually spinning platters at 5,400 rpm rather than the older standard of 3,600 rpm. The rise in rpm from 3,600 to 5,400 results in an increase of 50 percent in terms of rotational speed. This increase translates into a rotational latency time of about 5 milliseconds versus 8 milliseconds for most drives.

Figure 5-4. The growing impact of rotational latency

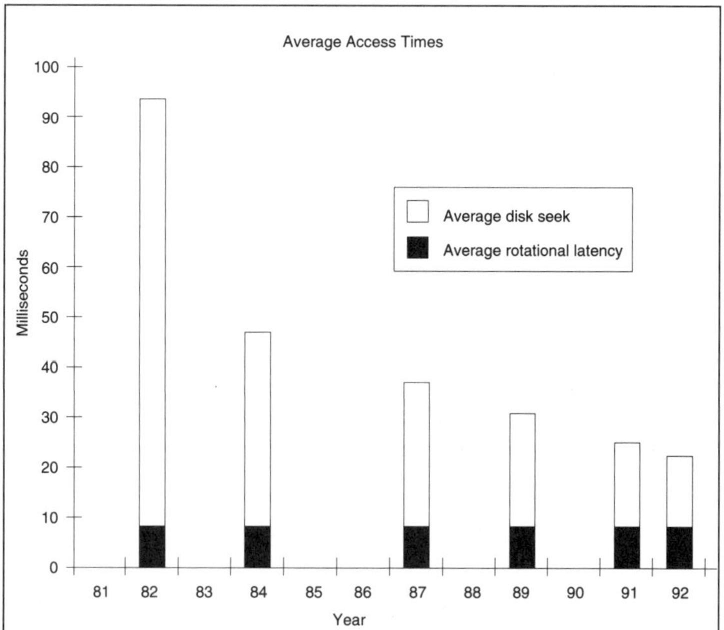

Although average seek times are improving, rotational latency isn't. So average access times are improving less and less.

On the other hand, some of the tiny drives found in notebook computers actually rotate more slowly than drives used to, spinning at 2,600 rpm, which increases the rotational latency to nearly 12ms. The slower spin reflects physical limitations: there isn't enough room to install a motor powerful enough to spin the drives at high speed. On a positive note, less power is used to spin the disk more slowly, which helps notebook computers conserve battery power. But be aware that if you're dealing with anemic disk drive performance on a notebook computer, a contributing factor may be its greater rotational latency. The fact that your manufacturer lists a reasonable average seek time can be misleading.

Overall, disk drive performance has increased approximately fourfold in terms of drive access times over the last decade. Although this 400 percent improvement in access times has certainly helped system performance, it is relatively insignificant when compared with the 100-fold increase in CPU speeds delivered during the same ten-year period.

Thus, the potential for disk drives to be a bottleneck has increased tremendously. When PCs with hard disk drives first appeared, the disk drive accessed any piece of information just as fast and, in some cases, even faster than the CPU.

Today, any time your system needs to access a piece of data from the disk drive, you're going to experience a delay 100 times or longer than if it could be accessed directly from the CPU, its cache, or main memory. Fortunately, this is a condition that can be improved and often at little cost, as we'll discuss in the next chapter.

Throughput

As we've just explored, one reason a disk drive is slow relative to the CPU and main memory is the time needed to move the actuator arm to the correct track and the wait for the platter to rotate until the correct sector comes under the read/write head. But the access time is not the end of the bottleneck that the drive introduces into the system. Once the access time has elapsed, you've only started the process of getting the information from the drive to the CPU. You still have to get that information off the drive platter, onto the read/write head, through the controller on the hard drive itself and then the controller in the I/O slot, and finally across the system board to the CPU.

Throughput is the speed at which information can be read from or to the drive. Two factors have a direct impact on how fast the disk subsystem can move the information on or off the drive: how fast the drive is spinning and how densely the information is packed onto the drive.

Programs that measure disk drive performance

Several programs give you a quick take on hard disk performance. Both the disk drive performance measure in Norton's SysINFO and Core International's Core Disk Performance Test Program (or Coretest) evaluate the two most important hard disk parameters, seek time, and data transfer rate.

PC Magazine's benchmarks, as always, give you more numbers than you know what to do with. The BIOS Disk Seek benchmark measures mechanical track-to-track access times. Fast times are helpful with programs such as databases, which often store and must later find data in many separate places on a drive. Both sequential and random access is tested.

PC Magazine's DOS Disk Access benchmark test measures the time necessary to perform 1,000 read requests at random locations on the disk via DOS calls.

The DOS File Access benchmark is a bit more realistic, because mechanical disk drive speed, hard disk controller function, and bus speed are all factors. The test even shows the effects of disk caching—performance changes dramatically if you run with and without a cache. You can even use this test to tune those disk cache's, like Norton's NCACHE2, for better performance when working with a particular record length, either small or large.

Finally, *PC Magazine*'s Variable File Access via DOS benchmark is very similar to the DOS File Access benchmark. It simply runs through a variety of record sizes and file sizes. It also measures the impact of a disk cache.

Perhaps the best way to see what the impact of upgrading a system with a particular drive is by running the BAPCo SysMARK92 on the same system before and after installing the new hard drive. This way you can measure the impact of a faster disk drive on the most popular word processing, spreadsheet, database, desktop graphics, desktop publishing, and software development programs.

Why does the speed at which the drive platter is spinning matter?

If there is a fixed amount of data on a track—that is, a fixed distance between each bit of data—the faster the disk drive spins, the faster the read/write head moves the data on or off it. Data can only be moved to or from the drive surface one bit at a time. The faster the drive spins, the more bits travel under the drive's head in a given time. The slower the drive spins, the fewer bits travel under the drive's head in a given time.

Why does the density with which the information is packed matter?

For a given drive speed, the more data packed onto a track—that is, the closer together the bits of data—the more bits of data rotate under the drive head each second. The more information packed onto a particular track of the drive, the faster it comes on or off the drive.

In other words, drive throughput, which is measured as a data transfer rate, is a function of the rpm of the drive and how much is packed onto a particular track. As noted in the previous section, today's disk drives generally spin at about the same speed as drives built 10 years ago. On the other hand, the data density, or the amount of information packed on a particular track, has increased considerably.

Most PC hard drives store 512 bytes of data per sector. As drive manufacturers have been able to increase the density of data stored (this density is called the *areal density* and it is measured in bits per inch), they have been able to put more sectors per track. The first PC disk drives held only 17 sectors per track. A single track with 17 sectors of 512 bytes each could hold a total of 8,704 bytes (17 x 512 = 8704).

If the drive's platter is spinning at 60 revolutions per second (3,600 rpm = 60 rev/sec) then at most a total of 500,000 bytes can be read or written in a second (8704 x 60 = 522,240). However, if higher recording densities let you put 34 sectors per track instead of only 17, you double the transfer rate to over 1 MB per second (34 x 512 x 60 = 1,044,480). In fact, today's typical high performance drives have about 70 sectors per track and deliver data transfer rates of about 2 MB/second.

Today's most advanced drives available have almost 100 sectors per track and spin at 5,400 rpm, which provides throughput of about 5 MB per second (512 x 100 x 90 = 4.6).

Another disk alternative: removable drives

While performance is always a factor, another key consideration with disk drives is capacity. One alternative strategy to consider, if you simply can't get by with the capacity of even the largest fixed disks, is to go with magneto-optical disk drives, which come in capacities as large as 1 Gigabyte per removable platter. When one platter is full, just insert another, knowing that the first drive's contents may be offline but can be accessed with a simple platter swap.

Magneto-optical (MO) technology involves a laser that heats up a spot on the disk while an electromagnet switches the polarity to either positive or negative. These bits of data are frozen into position when the polymer disk surface cools.

Alternatively, a practitioner of desktop publishing who often has to transport large files to a service bureau to be typeset or separated should look into Bernoulli drives. You get lower capacity than magneto-optical (Bernoulli tops out at about 90 MB per 6 ounce, $229-list disk), but great durability and the promise that many service bureaus can accept them.

One consideration with both MO and Bernoulli technology is speed. For example, MO drives take a little longer to write data because three passes are used—one to erase the section of the disc that will be written on, one to write the data, and one to verify, although you can set the drive to skip the verification pass. At best, MO drives resemble ST506 drives in performance.

But one thing to consider is how much you can boost their performance with disk caching. For example, Bernoulli's latest drives include a 32K on-drive memory cache and Central Point Software's PC Cache Plus. As a result, effective average access time falls all the way to 9 milliseconds.

The bottom line is that typical hard disk throughput has increased by a factor of 10 over the last 10 years, from the typical 178 KB of information per second for an XT drive in 1982 to a typical fast drive today that gets information off the platter at over 2 MB per second.

To summarize, the two most important factors in drive throughput are the number of sectors per track and the rpm of the drive. Since most PC drives spin at 3,600 rpm, the number of sectors per track is usually the most important factor. To a certain extent this statement is misleading because it is possible to change the size of a sector from 512 bytes to another size, either larger or smaller. But this requires that the number of sectors per track must also be changed in proportion. For example, a drive with 34 sectors per track and 512 bytes per sector could also have 68 sectors per track and 256 bytes per sector but would end up with the same number of bytes per track and, thus, the same transfer rate. So although this chapter refers to the number of sectors per track as the most important number in reality, the number of bytes per track is the most important number.

Interleave

There's a third factor at play in the apparent performance increase shown in disk drive throughput over the last ten years: interleave.

Back in the early days of the PC/XT and then later the AT, there was a big problem. Systems weren't disk-bound, they were compute-bound and memory-bound. The data funnel for an 8-MHz 286 system looks different from today's data funnel.

With the 8-MHz 286, the disk drive might deliver a data transfer rate of close to 5 MB per second, but the rest of the system wasn't able to accept or transmit the data that fast. In fact, if you tried to read data continuously, you could only read a single sector of data per disk rotation, as explained later in this chapter. To solve this problem, a technique called interleaving was introduced. *Interleaving* is a technique that intersperses what is written to or read from the sectors of the drive track, reading and writing, say, only one out of three sectors.

Without an interleave, the read/write head attempts to read all of the information off of a track in one pass. In other words, as the platter rotates under the head, every track is read sequentially.

If the system can't deal with data that fast, however, there is a delay before it can accept the next sector. Unfortunately, that means the head must rotate past the desired sector, and the system waits for a full rotation (1/60 of a second) before the desired sector passes under the head again.

To handle the problem, disk drive sectors were interleaved. In other words, the read/write head reads or writes a sector, then skips a few sectors before reading or writing another sector, as shown in Figure 5-5.

Figure 5-5.
Disk interleaving

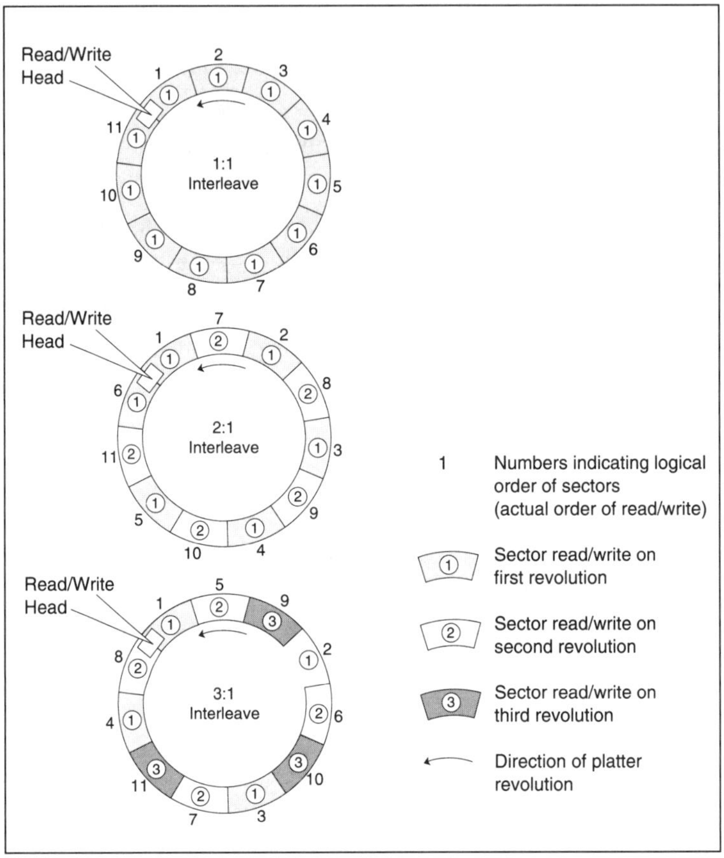

If after reading a sector the system is ready to handle data again after two more sectors rotated, it's most efficient to set the interleave to a 3-to-1 ratio. Thus, instead of a full 1/60 of a second delay for all 17 sectors to rotate past, only two sectors pass the head before the next read takes place, resulting in a delay of only about 1/500 of a second.

If the system is only fast enough to read or write one out of five sectors, that drive is most efficient when set up with a ratio of 5-to-1 interleave.

As a result of interleaving, drives spin the platter three, five, or perhaps even more times before the platter can get a full track of information on or off one track of the drive. However, that's still a major improvement over the 17 rotations needed to read or write a full track if the interleave was set too low and the controller has to wait a full rotation before reading or writing each logically successive sector.

With new systems, interleave is a moot point. If your disk drive is IDE (Integrated Device Electronics) or if you have a very recent generation of PC, you probably don't need to worry about interleave. Most of the current generation of disk drives are already set for and perform most efficiently with an interleave ratio of 1-to-1. Today's systems are fast enough to be ready to read or write the next sector of data before the next physical sector on the disk can spin under the head.

On the other hand, if you've had your disk drive for quite some time, you should definitely check the interleave. Remember, while you can gain some efficiency by setting the interleave lower, if you set it too low (so that your system fails to keep up) you'll be waiting a full disk rotation between each successive sector of data read or written. Most systems with a 16 MHz or faster CPU should use a 1:1 interleave.

A drive's interleave is not an inherent characteristic of the drive itself but merely a result of how the drive has been formatted.

If you've got a disk drive from that earlier era (until 1988 or 1989), it's possible that your disk drive has an interleave set for less than a ratio of 1-to-1. If your computer is running at a clock speed of 16 MHz or higher, then it is capable of receiving information from the disk drive with the interleave set at a ratio of 1-to-1. There's a performance increase in terms of throughput waiting for you right there—you can take advantage of it immediately by changing the interleave.

However, if you have purchased your disk drive within the last couple of years, it is likely that the interleave is already set for a ratio of 1-to-1. If you purchased your hard disk drive four or five years ago, you probably will want to improve its interleave. Unfortunately, if you also purchased your controller four or five years ago, the controller itself may not be able to accept information at that speed. If this is the case, you'll have to replace your controller.

You should also note that if you purchased your hard disk drive four or five years ago, it's probably time you replaced the drive anyway. It's probably not only slow but also limited in its storage capacity. The typical disk drive of four or five years ago had a storage capacity of only 20 to 40 MB.

Changing the interleave of your drive

One way to change the interleave of your drive is to do a low-level reformat of it. To do this, you should refer to either your computer's user manual or to the installation instructions for the hard disk drive or its controller. Of course, before you do a low-level format, or any drive format, you must perform a complete backup of the contents of your hard disk drive. When you undertake a low-level format, all the information on your drive will be wiped out.

To give you an idea of the maximum (1-to-1 ratio of interleave performance of various drives), you can run a data transfer test program like the CORE test and compare your results to Table 5-1 on page 80. To use the table, you must know what drive interface you are using (for example, ST-506 MFM, ST-506 RLL, or ESDI), and then compare the data transfer rate you obtain with the maximum results from the table. Disable any disk caching before running the test; otherwise the numbers will be misleading.

If you find performance much worse after you lower the interleave, you've

Programs that check and change interleave

As we've discussed in this chapter, it used to be that many hard disks were shipped with a non-optimal interleave, which bogged down performance unnecessarily. More recent disk and controller combinations tend not to have this problem, but it never hurts to check. Among the programs that will test the interleave and optimize it for you are Gibson Research's SpinRite II and Prime Solutions Disk Technician. They also provide some protection against hard disk failure.

(Unfortunately, the versions of these programs I've used will not work with controllers that use sector translation, as discussed in Chapter 6.)

Although these two programs are proven safe performers, they're often working with your data in the most intimate way, so it's an absolute necessity that you back up your data before using them for anything other than diagnostic purposes.

Besides changing the interleave to improve performance, SpinRite II and Disk Technician both track down potential trouble spots by doing extensive reading and writing to your disk and then make stabs at repairing them—in effect, by eliminating bad spots—with a nondestructive low-level format. In other words, the electronic markings on the disk that indicate to the controller

probably exceeded the rate at which your system accepts data off the drive and gotten into a one-sector-per rotation scenario.

The best way to determine the interleave of a drive though is to use a disk utility program like Norton Utilities or Gibson's SpinRite. These programs not only determine what your interleave is set to, but they tell you what the most efficient interleave would be and allow you to change the interleave without having to perform a low-level reformat to your drive. However, you're strongly advised to back up your drive before performing any work at this level. Even though these utilities have been field proven, there are still some quirks. Many of these programs warn you not to use them with certain types of drives or drive interfaces. Some warn that if you happen to have certain terminate-and-stay resident (TSR) programs installed, data could be lost. There are always a few "gotchas" lurking in the dark corners of documentation. Unfortunately, many

where the boundaries of sectors lie are rewritten on the fly without disturbing your files.

This is necessary because a hard disk drive does show signs of wear and tear, particularly after repeated heating and cooling cycles as the drive is turned on and off. Over time the alignment of the drive drifts, so that the position of the magnetic tracks that guide the read/write heads changes, causing portions of the disk to become unreadable. When these places on the disk are just becoming bad, the drive will attempt repeated retries until a read is successful, which can have a significant impact on performance. So this repair work can bring back some of the youthful zip to an aging drive while also safeguarding your data.

A number of other programs can make such minor repairs while also speeding up disk performance with such tricks as defragmentation and setting of interleave. They vary considerably in feature sets; some are actually part of full-blown utility programs that have many other features. They include OPTune from Gazelle Systems, Vopt from Golden Bow Systems Inc., PC-Kwik Power Disk from Multisoft Corp., Norton Disk Doctor (part of the Norton Utilities) from Symantec Corp., Mace Utilities from Fifth Generation Systems Inc., and SEA Disk Utilities 1.5 from System Enhancement Associates.

Table 5-1. Compare the results of running a data transfer test program on your drive with those listed below. By matching your drive interface type with the data transfer rate, you can get an indication of how your drive's interleave is currently set. The transfer rate you get for a drive with a 1:1 interleave may not be as high as those in the table, but they should be higher than the numbers in the 2:1 column.

	1:1	2:1	3:1	5:1
ST-506 MFM	500 KB/sec	250 KB/sec	167 KB/sec	100 KB/sec
ST-506 RLL	750 KB/sec	375 KB/sec	250 KB/sec	150 KB/sec
ESDI/SCSI	1000 KB/sec	500 KB/sec	330 KB/sec	200 KB/sec

people don't bother to read the fine print until they've lost all their data. Therefore, before you conduct any procedures of this nature, perform a complete system backup. (In fact, one of the principal rules of sound computing in general is to backup routinely.)

Zone-Bit Recording

A topic that is closely related to data transfer rates and sectors per track is a concept called *Zone-Bit Recording* (ZBR), as shown in Figure 5-6. (Zone-Bit Recording is a trademark of Seagate Technology. Other drive manufacturers employ similar techniques.)

While it is not necessary to understand ZBR, and in fact most drives do not use it, you may want to read about ZBR if your hard disk uses it and you are taking advantage of some of the optimization techniques mentioned in Chapter 6. Otherwise skip this section.

Assuming that your drive is already at a ratio of 1-to-1 interleave, the two factors that are going to slow throughput are how densely the information is packed on the drive and how fast the drive is spinning. As we mentioned during our discussion of average access time and rotational latency, disk drives spin at speeds of around 3,600 rpm. That's the same speed they operated when hard drives first came out a decade ago, little or no improvement has occurred there. However, in terms of how densely information is packed on the drive, significant progress has been made. The amount of data that can be packed onto a particular track has gone from 8 KB to 50 KB.

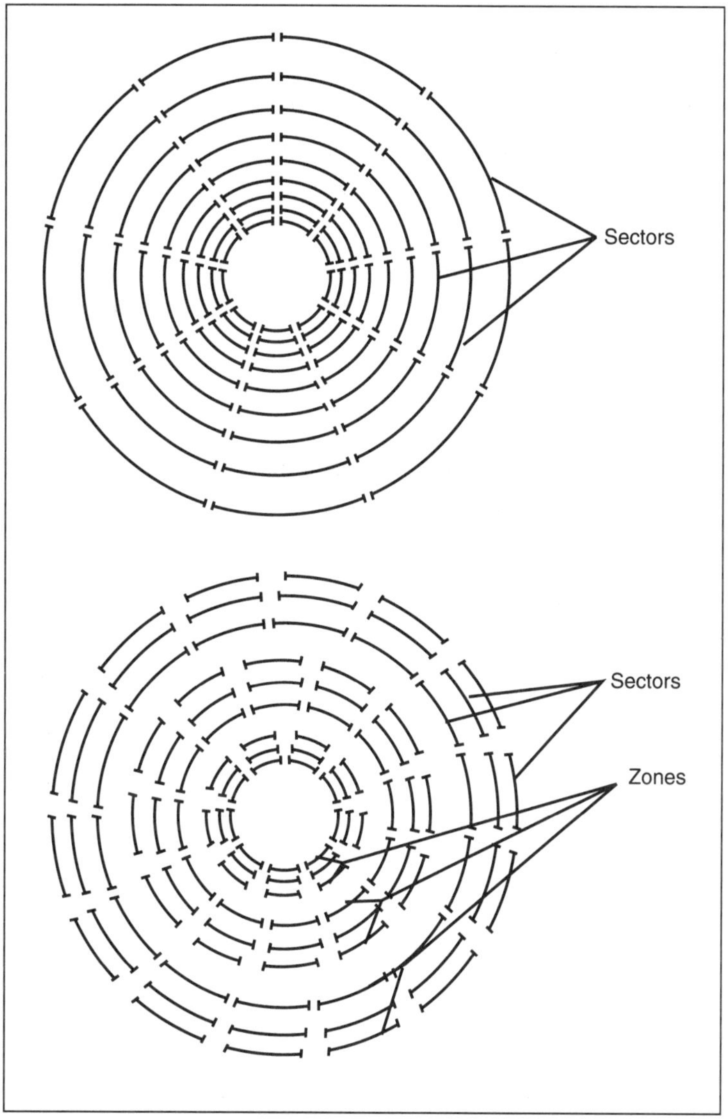

Figure 5–6. Standard sector recording (top) versus Zone-Bit recording (bottom)

As shown in Figure 5-6, the outer tracks of a drive are longer than the inner tracks. The number of sectors remains unchanged from the inner to the outer tracks, while the circumference of the tracks gets larger. But if you assume that you can pack *x* number of bytes per inch and still read them consistently, you should be able to squeeze more bytes onto the longer outer sectors than into the shorter inner sectors. Some state-of-the-art drives do just that. Drive manufacturers have taken advantage of the fact that the outer tracks have a greater circumference, and have put more sectors per track on the outer tracks than on the inner tracks. This accomplishes two goals at once. It increases storage capacity and allows for a higher data transfer rate.

The only way to determine whether or not your drive employs ZBR is to check with your computer or hard disk manufacturer. While ZBR does complicate things for the drive's electronics, your disk drive controller should handle ZBR transparently to the rest of the system or to any software you may be using.

Summary

In this chapter, we looked at the many things that cause a computer's disk drives to be performance bottlenecks. In the next chapter, you'll learn some ways around those bottlenecks.

CHAPTER SIX

Optimizing Disk Performance

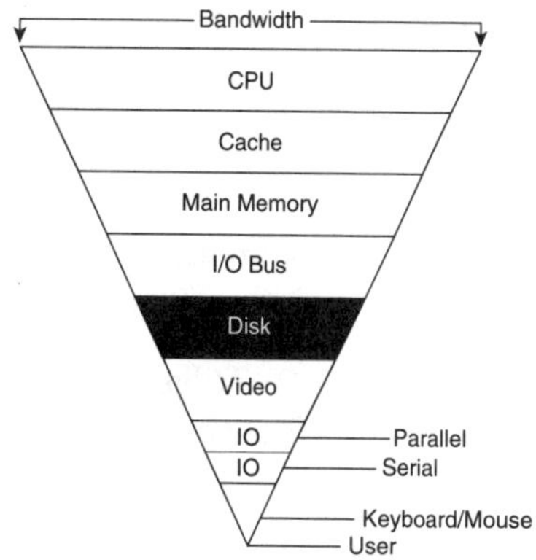

Data Funnel

Now that we have a basic understanding of disk performance, we'll concentrate on techniques to optimize it, including RAM drives, software disk caches, and caching disk controllers. (Caching is such an important part of optimizing your computer's performance—and is the subject of so much marketing mumbo jumbo, that it is also discussed in Appendix B.) Next we'll explore disk management tools and stratagems, such as defragmenting and disk file organizing. Finally, we'll look into the various interfaces drives can use and guide you in choosing drives with the highest performance.

You'll find that all of the tricks you will learn are easily implemented and extremely effective. Only the caching disk controller involves a significant cost, but in multiuser or multitasking applications, it can easily be worth the money.

Solutions to the Disk Drive Bottleneck

In the last chapter we learned that all the ways we measure disk performance—seek time, rotational latency, average access time, and throughput or data transfer rate—are affected by the need for the various mechanical parts (that is, the actuator arm and platter) of the disk drive to move into position. A solid state, electronic device like a CPU or a memory chip does not suffer such access delays.

Clearly, we can improve throughput if we can find ways to avoid these mechanical delays and take advantage of the high performance of your computer's solid-state parts. Moreover, disk drives also have a relatively low data transfer rate compared to memory or CPU. Even if they didn't, the top transfer rate a disk drive can achieve is limited by the throughput rate of the I/O bus.

You can see the cumulative result by taking a look at the data funnel. The data funnel is very narrow down at the disk drive section compared to the sections that designate the bandwidths of CPU, cache, and memory. It's clear that the hard disk can be a tremendous bottleneck if it has to be accessed a lot during normal operation. In this situation, you take advantage of the computer's tendency to use the same data over and over. As we discussed in Chapter 3's examination of memory, the PC typically accesses a relatively small piece of its data and programs repeatedly. In other words, the PC requires only a relatively small amount of information at a time and, in general, most of this information is located in the same location.

One of the most important steps you can take when optimizing your PC is to implement a disk cache that holds the information the computer needs at any given moment in very fast solid-state memory instead of the far slower mechanical memory of the hard disk. This leads to two logical questions: What if we kept all of our information in memory all the time? Why do we even need to store it in the hard disk at all?

Well, it's true that if you were able to store all your information in the wider areas of the data funnel, up in fast memory, your PC's overall performance would improve. Once again, however, the concept of the hierarchy of memory comes into play. Yes, the main memory is much faster and the CPU can access main memory much quicker than it can access a disk, but main memory costs a lot more per megabyte than a hard drive.

Backup

There is always potential for losing data stored on your disk drives, and some of the techniques mentioned in this chapter increase the risk even more. You should already be backing up your system, but before you perform any technique that involves moving your data (such as changing the interleave or optimizing the location of your files), save yourself the possibility of grief by performing a backup. Tape drive prices have fallen to the point where nearly everyone can afford tape backup. If you don't have tape, don't take a chance—you'll have to take the time to back up to floppy disk no matter how long it takes.

If you consider that a modern computer needs to store information in tens or hundreds of megabytes, you can see that having that much main memory is cost prohibitive. Besides, main memory is volatile. In other words, when you turn off your PC, everything stored in memory is lost. Main memory can only be thought of as a very temporary means of storage. In contrast, anything properly stored on a disk drive is preserved whenever you shut down the system.

Thus the disk drive is an important compromise between performance on one hand and reliability and economy on the other. The disk drive is far less expensive for any given amount of storage capacity, and the disk drive is a much more stable place to store programs and data. You can shut off your computer and come back in a few hours, days, or weeks and the information will still be there.

The need for a hard disk is clear, but can't you store the few hundred kilobytes of data that a computer is likely to to work on at any given time in fast semiconductor memory and then return it to the disk drive for safe storage? Well, in fact, you can by setting up either a RAM disk or a disk cache. We'll discuss RAM disks first, then move on to examine disk caching.

RAM Disks

If you peruse a typical book on improving PC performance or look into the documentation provided for many applications, the two suggestions that you'll come across over and over again are that you should set the interleave to 1:1 (now largely a moot point, since most drives come this way) and that you should create a RAM disk. But creating a RAM disk is probably not the best way to go.

The RAM disk concept is simple: An area of main memory is made to appear to the computer as though it were actually a disk drive—a very fast disk drive. In other words, when you establish a RAM disk, you create something that the CPU believes to be a hard disk drive but in reality is an area of main memory set aside to act as if it were a disk drive.

You can use the RAM drive to temporarily store programs and data, avoiding the need to access the disk drive. If you don't have to physically access the disk drive, your "disk access" will be much faster. In other words, you'll save yourself a lot of time. Not only do you avoid all of the long mechanical delays associated with the disk drive, you can also escape crossing over the I/O bus, another comparatively slow section of the data funnel.

It is relatively easy to create a RAM disk, as long as you have plenty of extra memory. The memory can be either expanded or extended.

Most current versions of DOS have a file for establishing a RAM disk called RAMDRIVE.SYS, while earlier versions of DOS have a file called VDISK.SYS.

Installing a RAM disk

You should already have the only software necessary for installing a RAM disk in your computer, because it comes with every version of DOS (starting with version 3.3). The procedure is simple:

1. Locate the program file RAMDRIVE.SYS. If you can't locate this file in your DOS directory, you should be able to find it on your original DOS diskette(s).
2. Copy the RAMDRIVE.SYS file to your root directory.
3. Insert a line like the following in your CONFIG.SYS file:

```
DEVICE = RAMDRIVE.SYS 64
```

4. Save your CONFIG.SYS file.
5. Reboot your computer.

You should now have an additional drive letter beyond what was formerly your last drive. If you had C and D drives before, you should now have C, D, and E. The last number in the line DEVICE = RAMDRIVE.SYS determines how large the drive will be. Thus the RAM drive we created is very small—only 64 KB—but you can still get a sense of how fast a RAM drive is by copying some files into it and then recopying those files within the RAM disk.

If you want to create a larger RAM drive, you can't afford to do it in regular DOS memory, so try the /e parameter to create the RAM drive in extended memory. DEVICE = RAMDRIVE.SYS 512 /e will create a 512 KB RAM drive in extended memory.

By the way, if you include two DEVICE = RAMDRIVE.SYS XXX lines, you'll create two RAM drives of size XXX.

A single line in your CONFIG.SYS file will set up a RAM drive in your main memory, for example:

```
DEVICE=RAMDRIVE.SYS 1024/E
```

This command line sets up a RAM disk of 1,024 KB (or 1 MB) in extended memory. When you reboot your computer, it automatically creates a RAM drive in memory and assigns it the next higher drive letter available. If you have two floppy drives designated A and B and a hard drive formatted into logical drives C and D, the RAM drive will be designated drive E.

Even if you don't intend to incorporate the RAM disk concept as a part of your PC configuration, it might be fun to play around with creating a RAM drive to see some of the performance potential locked up inside your system.

Once you've set up a RAM drive, you've got to copy your application and its data files into it. Simply use the copy command to move the information you want to work with from the disk drive into the RAM drive, and tell the system that's where the files are. Start your application from the RAM drive itself and from within the application select the RAM drive as the location of the data files you want to access.

If you do play around with a RAM drive, you'll see a dramatic performance increase—some slow programs are literally going to scream. You can see astonishing performance increases, particularly on applications that have a tendency to be disk-bound, because they either are calling constantly for a program overlay off disk or are doing heavy disk I/O while reading and writing data. But before you get hooked on the lightening quick response of a RAM disk, you need to be aware of the problems associated with the use of RAM drives.

1. It's a nuisance to copy the application you want to run along with the data it needs over to the RAM drive every time you want to start your computer.

2. If the application you are going to run is a recently released application, it's more than likely that it's going to be very large, possibly occupying many megabytes, and the data files it will access are also going to be quite large. Therefore, you're going to need a RAM disk

that's many megabytes in size. Even though memory has been going down in price, it is still very expensive relative to hard drive storage.

3. When you shut down or reboot your PC—or worse, when a power glitch or other mishap causes your computer to shut down unexpectedly—information in the RAM drive will be irretrievably lost unless you've copied work from the RAM drive back to a nonvolatile memory storage device just the moment before. That makes frequent saving to the hard disk an important factor in most implementations of a RAM drive.

You can see that a RAM drive can be inconvenient, expensive (if it requires a lot of memory), and risky. There are ways to work around each of these problems, though.

To avoid the first inconvenience, you can create a batch file that automatically moves your application from the disk drive into the RAM drive whenever you start up the computer or application.

Assume the RAM drive is designated E. The following commands load WordPerfect into the RAM disk, move to the RAM disk, and then run the program (these commands can all be executed from a batch file).

```
COPY WP.EXE E:
E:
WP
```

(Many applications also access other files besides the primary executable, and these secondary files would also have to be copied into the RAM disk for optimum performance.)

The marketplace has helped address the second drawback, as the cost of RAM has dropped considerably over the last few years. If you've got the money to spend, the performance boost may make it worthwhile to pay $50 per megabyte for memory devoted to a RAM disk, especially if your application and its data files are relatively small.

You can address the third problem of working exclusively in volatile memory by creating a batch file that automatically backs up the RAM drive to less volatile disk drive memory. Another way to play it safe is to install an uninterruptible power supply (UPS) to prevent power glitches from causing the PC to shut down unexpectedly. There are even some UPS devices on adapter cards available now. These built-in UPS devices require a special command before they will actually shut off the power entirely. A program that can periodically save all modified files to the hard disk could also decrease the danger of data loss.

RAM drives can be very helpful in certain applications, such as databases. In fact, RAM drives can offer unbeatable performance gains.(we'll discuss the use of RAM drives for specific applications in a later chapter).

Still, there is a much easier way to get around these RAM drive hassles and still very effectively address the critical problem of the disk drive bottleneck: disk caching.

Disk Caching

Disk caching is an optimizing technique that has most of the advantages of a RAM drive with very few of the disadvantages. As does a RAM drive, a disk cache keeps frequently accessed data and instructions in memory rather than on disk, allowing the CPU to access them much faster than if they where kept on the much slower hard disk. Disk caching has been used on PCs for quite a while, and there are several sophisticated disk caching software packages as well as a wide variety of disk caching controllers available on the market.

The concept behind disk caching is the same as that applied successfully in the implementation of the RAM cache: computers tend to use a relatively small amount of program code and data repeatedly. A disk cache takes a certain section of memory and sets it aside as though it were a disk. Then, without any intervention on the part of the user, the disk cache moves information off of the disk into and out of that section of memory and returns it to the disk drive. Since the computer eventually needs to work with a different section of the program or data, the disk cache must be able to anticipate which data is no longer necessary and replace it with new data. The more intelligently it does this, the higher the likelihood that the computer will find the data or instructions it needs in the disk cache, eliminating the need to actually access the hard drive (see Figure 6-1).

It is difficult to imagine a PC, no matter what the configuration and application, that wouldn't benefit in some way from the implementation of a disk cache.

Even DOS uses a technique similar to disk caching with its standard BUFFERS command. A buffer is similar to a cache, but much less sophisti-

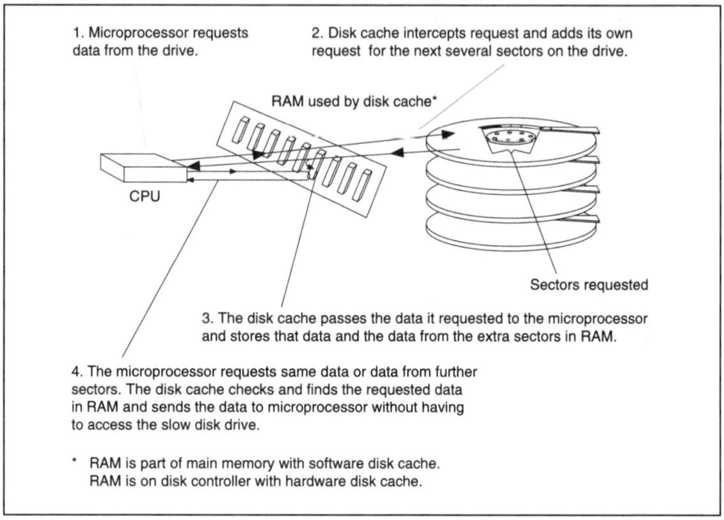

Figure 6-1. How a disk cache works

cated. A buffer is simply a brute-force method of caching. A cache makes an educated guess at what to keep and what to discard from memory. A buffer, in contrast, simply retains as much data as it can and then starts discarding things on a first-in, first-out basis.

Even though the amount of memory devoted to the DOS BUFFERS is small, the DOS BUFFERS are very successful at retaining the file allocation table (FAT), which tells DOS where files are located on disk, in memory. Because every disk access must start with a visit to the FAT, its a pretty sure thing that the FAT will stay in memory.

If you're using a disk cache, your BUFFERS = line in CONFIG.SYS can be small. If you're not, it should be fairly large, BUFFERS = 20 or more.

For the proper configuration of the BUFFERS command when using a disk cache, refer to the documentation that accompanies the software cache. For the optimal configuration when not using a disk cache, consult your DOS manual. (The optimal number of buffers varies depending on your version of DOS.)

Disk cache versus RAM drives

A disk cache avoids most of the problems associated with RAM drives. A disk cache automatically sets aside a section of relatively fast memory and moves your programs and data files into and out of that memory dynamically. In this way, you're spared the inconvenience of having to either establish the cache and direct traffic or create and maintain batch files to do so.

Most disk caches also save to disk automatically to ensure that there is always a current copy of data located on the hard disk. In this way, you can minimize accidents that result in loss of work without having to buy an expensive UPS. And because the disk cache uses the same memory over and over, it can accomplish the same amount of speedup as a RAM disk with far less memory.

Types of disk caches

You can choose from two types of disk caches: a software disk cache or a disk caching controller. The software disk cache sets aside a part of main memory and then manages the movement of applications and data into and out of that memory to and from the hard disk. The disk caching controller has its own on-board memory, processor, and firmware (firmware is software stored on read-only-memory chips) to manage the caching process. There are pluses and minuses involved in the use of either of these techniques.

Software disk caching

The software-only solution is the least expensive choice because in most cases the only hardware you need to purchase is the additional memory required for the disk cache. You may not need to add more memory, but most computers still don't have enough memory to undertake serious optimization stratagems such as disk caching. Considering that memory is now widely available for about $50 per megabyte, you can get a lot of bang for a small amount of money.

Chapter 3 reviewed the various types of memory and discussed what kind of memory you could add as well how it can be configured. It should be clear that you should opt for either 32-bit memory on the motherboard or a 32-bit memory card (if your system has a 32-bit memory expansion slot). If these options are not available—your motherboard can hold no more memory and you don't have a memory expansion slot—adding memory on a 16-bit AT-bus memory expansion card for disk caching still offers a performance improvement over uncached mechanical disk access. Even though you'd only be using relatively slow 16-bit AT-bus memory and that memory has to be accessed through the relatively narrow I/O bus, you'd still be in a wider part of the data funnel than a disk drive.

Certainly, the more memory you pry loose for disk caching, the better the results. If you're willing to purchase a few more megabytes of memory, the performance increase may be very dramatic.

This is not to imply that you'll need multiple megabytes to take advantage of a disk cache. Even if you can't or don't want to add more memory, you should have some extra memory that can be squeezed free for a disk cache. If you've got at least 256 KB to spare, installing a disk cache is going to be of some benefit to you.

Allocating memory for a software disk cache

If you have more than 2 MB of main memory and are running Windows, allocate one-third of the memory for a software disk cache and leave the rest for Windows and its applications, as shown in the table below.

Total memory in system	Disk cache	Program memory
Less than 1 MB	64 KB	all remaining memory
1 MB	128 KB	784 KB
2 MB	256 KB	1,792 KB
3 MB	1 MB	2 MB
4 MB	1.5 MB	2.5 MB
6 MB	2 MB	4 MB
8 MB	3 MB	5 MB
10 MB	4 MB	6 MB

These should be good sizes to start out with. If you want to determine the absolute optimum size for your system, you will need to experiment a little bit by gradually increasing or decreasing the cache size by 10 percent or so, and see its effect on your overall performance.

For systems that do not run Windows, start with a disk cache of about 10 percent of total memory, and then gradually increase or decrease it to determine the optimum size for your system and configuration.

Choosing a software disk cache

Here's some good news—it's likely that you already own a software disk cache program. Recent versions of MS-DOS (4.0 and 5.0) and Windows 3 include a disk caching program called SMARTDRV. While the original SMARTDRV.SYS is a very primitive disk caching program, it is still somewhat effective—and you can't go wrong with the price since it's included free. If you got SMARTDRV with Windows 3.1, you've gotten a much more advanced piece of software that competes better with other disk cache software you'd have to pay for.

It's easy to tell if you have the better version of SMARTDRV—version 4.0: It was first shipped with Windows 3.1. So if the version you're using came with Windows 3.0 or DOS 5.0, it's probably the older version of SMARTDRV.

But the foolproof way to tell is even simpler than that: version 4.0 of SMARTDRV doesn't load as a device driver in CONFIG.SYS. It's an executable called SMARTDRV.EXE that must be loaded from your AUTOEXEC.BAT or manually from the DOS prompt. When it first starts up, it displays its version number (you'll want version 4.0 or later).

SMARTDRV.EXE has a number of new features, some of which you can ascertain by typing SMARTDRV /? from the DOS prompt. If you do, SMARTDRV displays a number of optional switches, one of which is /s. If you exit to the DOS prompt after a long session of using SMARTDRV as your cache, and type SMARTDRV /s, you'll be shown the number of cache hits and misses since SMARTDRV began executing (see Appendix B).

An effective cache provides a hit ratio in the 90 percent or above range, which SMARTDRV usually achieves if you give it 2 MB of RAM. While increasing the cache to 4 MB provides an incremental improvement, the return on investment definitely declines after the first 2 MB devoted to it.

Incidentally, typing SMARTDRV /s also reveals that version 4.0 has implemented write-behind caching, which you can disable if you're the type who likes to wear a belt *and* suspenders.

Microsoft's Windows Resource Kit includes a SMARTDRV monitor that allows you to set its options with a GUI interface and track its hit ratio graphically. But the underlying monitoring capability is there in the base product; you don't have to buy anything extra to get a sophisticated disk cache for Windows. And the price—free when you buy Windows—is definitely right.

If you've got SMARTDRV.SYS, it would pay to upgrade to SMARTDRV.EXE. It even works fine with Windows 3.0 and the initial versions of DOS 5.0. And in my tests (which didn't bring out the worst of SMARTDRV because I was working with a SCSI drive, not an IDE drive for which SMARTDRV might miscalculate the track size, and also because my disk was not badly fragmented) the new SMARTDRV.EXE improved performance more than 10 percent over SMARTDRV.SYS in working intensely with Windows applications.

If you're willing to spend a little more money, you may be able to get more performance and flexibility from some of the excellent third-party disk caching programs on the market. The most popular product is probably PC-Kwik or Super PC-Kwik from MultiSoft (see Figure 6-2). There are many other excellent caches available, for example, Power Cache Plus from Intelligent Device Corp.

Most of the utility packages such as PC Tools and Norton Utilities also include a disk caching program. In fact, some versions of PC Tools include PC-Kwik or Super PC-Kwik and most recent versions of Norton Utilities include Power Cache Plus. Digital Research's DR DOS 6.0 includes Super PC-Kwik .

One way or another, it's more than likely that you already have some disk caching program in your possession, either SMARTDRV (thanks to DOS and Windows), PC-Kwik (thanks to PC Tools), or Power Cache Plus (thanks to Norton Utilities). If, for some reason, you don't have one of these software cache programs already or you want to invest in a third-party program, you'll find a list of available products among the appendices at the end of this book.

If you already have a free software disk caching program with DOS or Windows, why would you want to buy a third-party product? The reason is that the

Figure 6-2. Super PC-Kwik. Third-party caching products offer more options than are available in SMARTDRV.

```
10:50:17.25 C:\UTILIZE>superpck /?

Super PC-Kwik(R) Disk Accelerator, Version 4.10 S/N 3030339502E01
Copyright 1986 - 1991 Multisoft Corporation, All Rights Reserved.
Registered to: Stephen Dougherty

Super PC-Kwik program was previously loaded and caching is enabled.

 You can use these parameters while Super PC-Kwik is loaded:

   /D    Disable caching.
   /E    Enable caching.
   /F    Flush cache.
   /M    Display measurements.
   /P    Display parameters in effect.
   /U    Unload Super PC-Kwik.

 For a list of parameters you can use when loading Super PC-Kwik,
 first unload it with /U and then type SUPERPCK /?

10:50:23.13 C:\UTILIZE>
```

original SMARTDRV.SYS is at best a very primitive disk cache. It would be more accurate to refer to it as a kind of track buffer rather than a disk cache. The original SMARTDRV.SYS caches tracks of information. In other words, when your computer accesses tracks from the hard disk, SMARTDRV.SYS moves those tracks into memory and holds them there with the assumption that you're going to use the information again.

Installing SMARTDRV

If you are excited about the possibilities of speeding up your disk accesses, but you don't want to spend money for one of the third party products—at least until you've given disk caches a try—you can install SMARTDRV on your computer. You probably already have it anyway because SMARTDRV is included with recent versions of DOS and Windows and is very easy to install.

1. Locate the file SMARTDRV.SYS on your hard drive or on the original disks that came with your computer.
2. Copy SMARTDRV.SYS to your root directory.
3. Add a line to your CONFIG.SYS file like the following:

```
DEVICE = SMARTDRV.SYS 512 512
```

4. Reboot your computer.

(The version of SMARTDRV that comes with Windows 3.1 is actually SMARTDRV.EXE. You can activate it by putting a line in your AUTOEXEC.BAT that reads simply SMARTDRV 512 512.)

You should now have a disk cache installed. To see the dramatic difference a disk cache can make on disk operations, try running a file manager program like XTREE or Window's File Manager, both with and without the disk cache installed. The difference should be significant. (Note that the first time you issue a DIR command with a cache installed there will not be much of a speedup, but the next time you issue a DIR the files in the directory should appear almost instantly.) If you don't use a file manager program—although I highly recommend that you do—try running CHKDSK with and without the cache installed to see the impact a cache has.

The original SMARTDRV.SYS falls down in a number of ways. For one, it doesn't necessarily cache entire tracks at a time, because it makes some assumptions about how many sectors per track your particular disk has—assumptions that aren't necessarily accurate for more modern disk drives.

Nor does the original SMARTDRV.SYS provide the range of options that some of the third-party disk caches make available to you. For example, Super PC-Kwik or Power Cache Plus lets you control where in memory the cache will be installed and how it reads and writes from the disk. These programs also understand different types of disks instead of assuming that all drives are the same, as the original SMARTDRV.SYS does.

Another attractive feature of these third-party programs is that they generally have some sort of a metric that shows you just how effective they really are. You can call the program up at any particular time and it will tell you how often you're accessing the disk and how much of the time the relevant information is in the disk cache.

In general, the third-party programs are much more intelligent about the way they handle your cache. They don't necessarily cache an entire track at one time, so they can be a little more efficient and effective in their use of memory.

Still, the version of SMARTDRV.EXE that ships with Windows 3.1 and later is a much more competitive program.

Delaying writes: Dealing with the downside

SMARTDRV.SYS and many of the other disk caching programs tend to err on the conservative side. Knowing they are dealing with your data, and knowing the volatile nature of main memory, these programs make sure that as soon as you write something into the cache your disk drive is updated as well. As a result, you are protected if your computer crashes or loses power. While this safeguards your data, it also diminishes the cache's effectiveness. Whenever your computer is writing from the CPU or main memory to cache, it also writes to the disk, and the disk remains a bottleneck.

Therefore, SMARTDRV. SYS and similar programs provide a performance increase only when reading from the disk and not when writing to the disk. Fortunately, during most typical applications, the computer reads from the disk far more than it writes to the disk, so this limitation doesn't do too much damage. However, some applications perform numerous writes. And no matter what the

> **!**
>
> ### *Beware of double caching confusion*
>
> Be careful about having two software disk caches installed at one time. They can confuse each other and lead to loss of data. Remember that Windows automatically installs the SMARTDRV disk cache when it is installed—it may be on your system without you realizing it. The best way to check for the presence of a software disk cache is to look at your CONFIG.SYS and AUTOEXEC.BAT files.

circumstance, you're going to have to write to the disk periodically. Thus disk caching programs sometimes are far less effective at increasing write performance than are RAM disks.

Some third-party products—Power Cache Plus, for example—allow you to delay writing back to the disk. In other words, you can tell the program how frequently you want it to update the disk—anywhere between 1 and 1,000 seconds. Thus, if your application is predisposed to write to the disk frequently, you can delay updating of the disk and hold the changes in main memory. Of course, you have to keep in mind that you're doing this, so that you don't shut down or reboot the computer without having written the work to disk.

If your disk caching program provides you with a write-delay option and you decide to live a little dangerously by dabbling in extended delayed write time, you might consider installing a UPS in your computer. Having a UPS would safeguard you from disaster brought on by some external force beyond your control, for instance, somebody inadvertently tripping over your power cord.

Disk caching programs that allow delayed writes will greatly improve performance of applications that demand a lot of writes to disk. The downside of disk caching programs that allow delayed writes is that there is more risk of losing your data.

So many of the third-party caches leave it up to you. If you don't mind living somewhat on the edge, or if you're very aware of what you're doing, go ahead and write to disk infrequently. If you get nervous thinking about your data remaining in volatile main memory for too long rather than being saved to disk, you can increase the frequency of the writes. It's your decision.

If you do get a third-party cache, make sure that you get the very latest version available. As DOS and Windows have evolved, the way they write to disk has changed as well. Applications also change over time. The latest version of any software disk cache product will more than likely be aware of recent changes in DOS or Windows or the various applications.

How much memory should you devote to a software disk cache? If you can afford it, 2 to 4 MB of memory. This is far more memory than is typically recommended for a disk cache, but most of the recommendations for disk caching size were made back in the days when a 1 MB of memory could cost as much as $500. Back then, memory was precious and expensive. Now, memory is cheap and available. On the other hand, your time certainly hasn't gotten any cheaper or less precious. It's a fair trade-off—you spend a little money on some inexpensive memory and free up some of your own valuable time.

Install a 4 MB disk cache on a 386/20 or a 386/16 and you'll find that it is going to outperform a 386/33 with no disk cache on most popular applications. You'll be able to feel the difference when you sit down at your computer that doesn't have a disk cache installed.

Disk Caching Controllers

A second kind of disk caching is implemented with a disk caching controller. A disk caching controller has its own memory and its own CPU (although that CPU is normally less powerful than the computer's CPU). A disk caching controller also has its own disk caching program (in firmware) that directs the entire process (Figure 6-3).

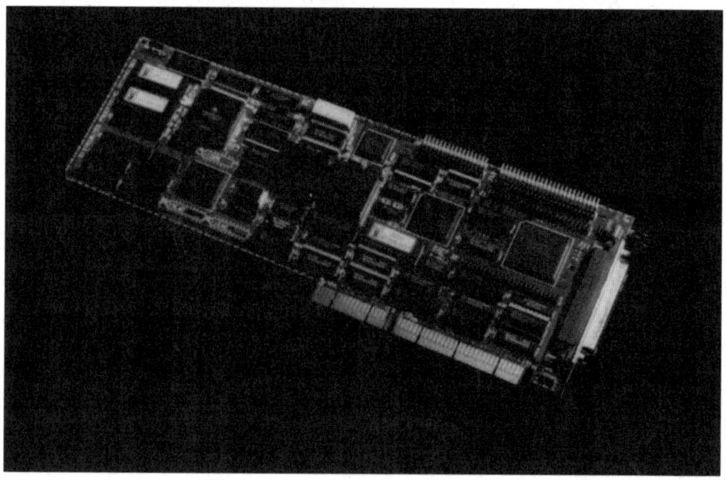

Figure 6-3. The DTP Smart Connex is one of the more popular caching hard disk controllers.

Disk caching controllers differ from software disk caching in a couple of ways: First, because a caching controller doesn't depend on the PC's CPU, it decides what it's writing to cache, when and how it's writing to cache, where things are in the cache, and all the rest. Second, a disk caching controller has its own memory.

Although the fact that disk caching controllers have their own memory is often stressed, it's usually the controller's intelligence—that is, the firmware caching program's intimate knowledge of where files are stored on disk—that makes a caching controller outperform a software disk cache.

If you've already got a software disk caching program, like SMARTDRV.SYS, and you could buy a third-party caching program with a few dazzling features for under $100, why would you want to spend over $1,000 for a disk caching controller? Well, perhaps you don't have any room left to add more memory in your system. But this is unlikely since a 16-bit memory expansion card on the AT bus is acceptable for disk cache memory. Another consideration might involve the unpleasant fact that some software disk caches suffer compatibility problems with certain applications and/or disk drives. SCSI drives and removable media drives can be tricky.

What is the cause of most of these compatibility problems? Software developers sometimes design their programs to bypass DOS and the system's BIOS when reading and writing files. That is, they write directly to and from the hard drive without going through channels. But a software disk cache expects the application to be well behaved and use DOS or the system's BIOS. It intercepts calls to DOS and the BIOS to read or write the disk, and doesn't even know if an application writes directly to the hard drive. Therefore, if your application throws it a curve with a direct write, you may experience compatibility problems between the software disk cache and that particular application. Some software disk caches also tend to have problems with removable media.

In a well-implemented hardware disk caching scheme, the caching controller should be much more transparent to the application or operating system. Why? If the application decides to write directly to the hard disk, it's bypassing the software disk cache, but it really can't bypass a hardware disk cache. So the hardware disk cache offers more compatibility than the software disk cache.

Another advantage that the hardware disk cache offers is that it comes with its own memory. Thus, a disk caching controller provides a place for additional memory that you may not have room for if you have a fully loaded system or if you need all other available memory for a specific application.

Let's say you have a computer that can address only 16 MB of main memory (which is the case with many 386s and certainly all 286s) and you're using all that memory with your applications, but you still want to set memory aside for disk cache. A hardware disk cache will accommodate whatever additional memory it requires.

Finally, a software disk cache demands greater user intervention, at least when it comes to the initial configuration. You must choose its size, its location in memory, and a lot of other parameters.

A hardware disk cache requires less work. In many cases, you can plug it in and forget about it. You don't have to do too much fine tuning.

Trade-offs in choosing between hardware and software caches

Of course, there are some obvious drawbacks to using a disk caching controller. For one, the memory that comes on a hardware disk cache isn't free. Then there is also the cost of the caching controller itself. They range from $200 at the very low end to over $1,000 at the high end. The price also varies with the amount of memory loaded on the card.

These days, many such cards can be populated with standard memory. If you buy such a card, you can probably save money by buying a relatively depopulated controller card and adding standard $50 per megabyte memory. But some caching controllers require proprietary memory. In other words, you have to buy the memory from the caching controller manufacturer. If you went with such a controller, you'd undoubtedly end up paying more than you would for non-proprietary memory.

But even if you're able to buy ordinary SIMMs to populate the controller, any memory you load onto it can only be used for that disk cache. In contrast, any additional memory loaded onto the system board's main memory for use with a software disk cache can be used in other ways if desired.

Another critical element to factor into your evaluation of disk caching options is the I/O bus. If you establish a software disk cache, you're going to keep most of your information in the memory on the fast side of the relatively slow I/O bus. If you have a hardware disk cache, you're going to have to go back and forth over that relatively slow bus every time you access the caching controller.

Trade-offs of software versus hardware disk cache

Software Disk Cache	Hardware Disk Cache
❖ Less expensive	❖ More expensive
❖ Faster for DOS and Windows	❖ Potentially higher performance with UNIX
❖ Limited or no write caching	❖ May allow write caching
❖ Memory can easily be used for other tasks	❖ Memory can only be used for disk cache
❖ More flexible	❖ Generally more compatible
❖ No need to format drive when installing	❖ May need to format drive
❖ Very easy to disable if necessary	❖ Nearly impossible to disable (without physically removing the board)

Even if your system has one of the newer 32-bit buses (MCA or EISA), crossing the bus is still going to be slow relative to main memory. Of course, if your system has an ISA bus (which most systems do), the situation is worse. This factor alone seems to point to an advantage for the software disk cache (see Figure 6-4).

Your system's I/O bus is typically going to reach its limits somewhere between 1 MB and 8 MB per second in terms of data transfer rate. When you compare this speed range with that of main memory, which can move somewhere between 20 MB to 80 MB per second, the advantage of having your disk caching done on the memory side of the I/O bus should be obvious. The bus is a significant bottleneck to the transfer of information.

So, on the one hand, you have fast 32-bit main memory for the software disk cache. On the other hand, you have relatively slow (8 MHz or 10 MHz) bus-based memory for the hardware disk cache. But before you decide it's a clean sweep in favor of software disk caching, there are still other factors to consider. Remember, a disk caching controller has its own intelligence, which

Figure 6-4. The data funnel with disk caching

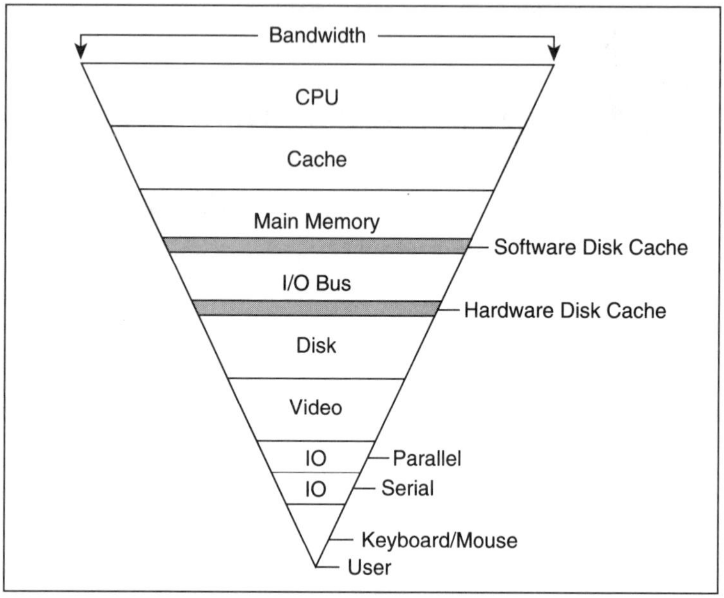

means it's capable of doing certain things that a software disk cache can't. This factor comes into play in multitasking environments, such as UNIX or NetWare. The disk caching controller can access, read, and write information to and from the disk drive independent of the CPU. In other words, while the CPU is off doing something else, the caching controller can be reading from or writing to the disk drive. In this way, some CPU cycles are freed up. Score an advantage for hardware disk caching in the multitasking realms of UNIX and NetWare.

Elevator seeks

Another advantage of the hardware disk cache is that a caching controller often applies much more intelligence to the way it reads from or writes to the hard disk. Since the hard disk cache is also serving as the system's disk controller, it has a much more intimate knowledge of what's on the disk drive and how it's organized than a software disk cache could ever have.

Typically, when the CPU is asking for information from a hard disk, it asks for it in a somewhat random order. A standard controller, in turn, asks the disk drive for the information in the same random fashion. However, a disk caching controller with sufficient intelligence can exercise its intimate knowledge of the way in which the drive is organized and bring a concept called elevator seeks into play.

Imagine three people getting on an elevator on the ground floor of a building. The first person presses the button for the tenth floor, the second person presses the button for the third floor, and the third person presses the button for the seventh floor. The elevator doesn't go to each floor according to the sequence in which the buttons were pushed. Instead, the elevator reorganizes the requests and fulfills them in numerical order. It moves from the third floor to the seventh floor to the tenth floor. Of course, this method is much faster than filling the requests in the random order they were received.

In the same way, a sophisticated disk caching controller can employ the concept of *elevator seeks* to achieve more efficiency in how it performs its disk reads and disk writes. The disk caching controller intercepts the CPU's requests to write sectors to the disk, and reorders the requests so they can be written in a more efficient manner, from the outer tracks to the inner tracks (see Figure 6-5).

Remember, too, that the hardware disk cache can do elevator seeks independently of the CPU, so there's even a greater potential performance boost. The CPU can be elsewhere doing something unrelated while the caching controller is performing the reads and writes.

So the advantages provided by the disk caching controller aren't limited to just having its own memory—it also has intelligence that can read and write from a disk more efficiently. It can often do these reads and writes while the CPU is busy doing something else.

However, in a single-tasking environment like DOS, the CPU is going to wait if information has to come from the disk drive, so the advantage of having a separate processor on the caching controller to go find the files and bring them back into memory is lost.

Moreover, a typical computer's CPU is faster and more powerful than the little microprocessor found on an intelligent disk controller. A typical caching controller has an 80186 chip operating at 8 or 12 MHz and capable of delivering perhaps 1 MIPS of processing power. A typical current CPU a 386 or 486 operating at 25 or 33 MHz, can perform at speeds 10 or 20 times faster.

Bottom line: If you're running DOS (or even Windows on top of DOS), the fact that your disk caching controller has freed up the CPU from reads and writes only to relegate the task to a relatively slow processor may be

Figure 6-5.
Elevator seeks

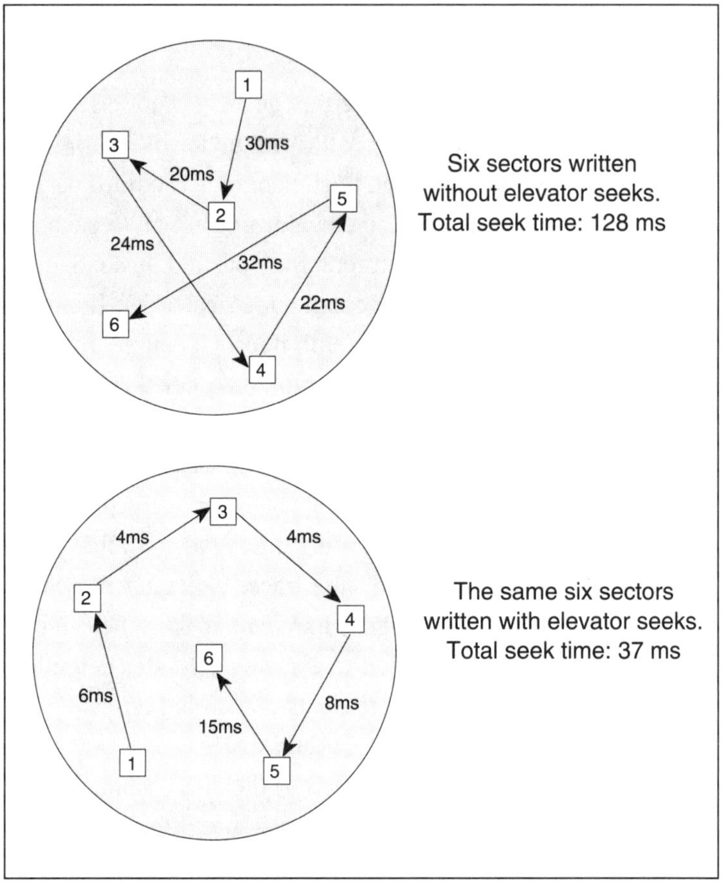

somewhat meaningless if the CPU is extremely fast to begin with and would have to wait anyway. You might even hurt performance by going with such a controller. For most DOS applications, you're probably better off with a software disk cache.

On the other hand, in a multitasking environment it may make sense to have both software and hardware disk caches. Actually, both UNIX and NetWare include disk caches as a fundamental part of the operating system, which can give you the benefit of very quick reads and delayed writes, while the hardware disk cache can give you the advantage of elevator seeks and the processing of reads and writes while the CPU is off servicing some non disk-related request.

You will want to use one of the disk caching techniques outlined in this chapter, unless you have some unresolvable compatibility problem, you physically can't add more memory, or you're using one of the more advanced disk technologies such as a solid-state drive.

Disk Optimization

Whether or not you use a disk cache, other disk techniques can improve disk performance.

Compared to semiconductor memory, a disk drive is very slow because of the physical movement required to seek the correct track and wait for the desired sector to rotate underneath the read head. As it turns out, the situation is worse than implied by the average seek times and throughput times listed for disk drives. Those times apply only under ideal circumstances. The reality is that files end up spread all over a disk, meaning multiple seeks and multiple periods of rotational latency are often required to read a single file or even part of a file. This is a result of how DOS and other operating systems work.

Fragmentation

When DOS writes a file to the drive, it has to choose an empty space to write it to. On a freshly formatted drive, DOS writes files in order to the very next set of empty sectors, say, four sectors for the first file, then 20 for the next file, and so on, as it slowly fills up the drive. Generally, however, some files are erased as you go along. You also increase the length of files that are already on the disk.

What happens to that first four-sector-long file when you come back a few days later and add records, pages, or cells, so that the file is now 8 sectors long? Remember, other files have been written in the interim on the sectors imme-

> **How to tell if your disk is fragmented**
>
> What's a quick way to see if your disk is fragmented? If you've been using it for a few months or more and have not defragmented it, your disk is almost certainly fragmented. But to convince yourself, try typing CHKDSK *.* in any directory you use frequently. If the computer returns a list of filenames that include the phrase "noncontiguous," you know for certain that you have fragmented files.

diately after the first four sectors it occupied. DOS will leave the original four sectors where they are and write four sectors more on the next available sectors. That means the file's data is fragmented—it's now in two noncontiguous (unconnected) places on the disk. Depending on how much other disk activity transpired between when the first and second parts of the file were written, the two parts of the file may be close or far apart.

The other phenomenon contributing to disk fragmentation is that as you erase files, you leave "holes" in the disk. DOS, not wanting to waste any space, fills these holes. Sometime it will even try to fill these holes with files that are bigger than the holes themselves, which means it might actually use several holes and that a file can be fragmented from the very first time it is written to disk.

Imagine, for example, that you have erased 10 four-sector files that are all in different areas of the disk, and then you save a file that's 40-sectors long. DOS is liable to spread that 40-sector file out over those 10 four-sector gaps. This relatively short file (a 20 KB file only 40 sectors long) now has parts spread out over 10 different sections of the drive. Larger files can be fragmented across dozens of different sections of the drive. And when we go to read or write to one of these files, it's not a matter of moving the head to a single track and doing a continuous read or write. Instead, the head may have to move back and forth over many tracks. This slows down data transfer considerably.

This problem of noncontiguous files gets worse the longer a drive is in use. As DOS sees gaps from erased files it fills those gaps. Moreover, increasing and decreasing file sizes creates more gaps.

The net effect is that a relatively small file can take a long time to load as the head moves back and forth to the correct cylinders, and you must wait for the relatively long rotational latency to take place as the platter spins to the right position and reads the correct sectors (see Figure 6-6).

Fragmentation seriously degrades your computer's performance. Disk fragmentation is something that's insidious and not noticed when the drive is either brand new or recently formatted. Eventually you'll notice it when sitting at someone else's computer that's supposed to have similar performance but seems much faster that your computer. Or one day a relatively small file seems to flash the disk access light on and off a lot and you have to wait a long time for the file to load. Fortunately, disk fragmentation is fairly easy to correct.

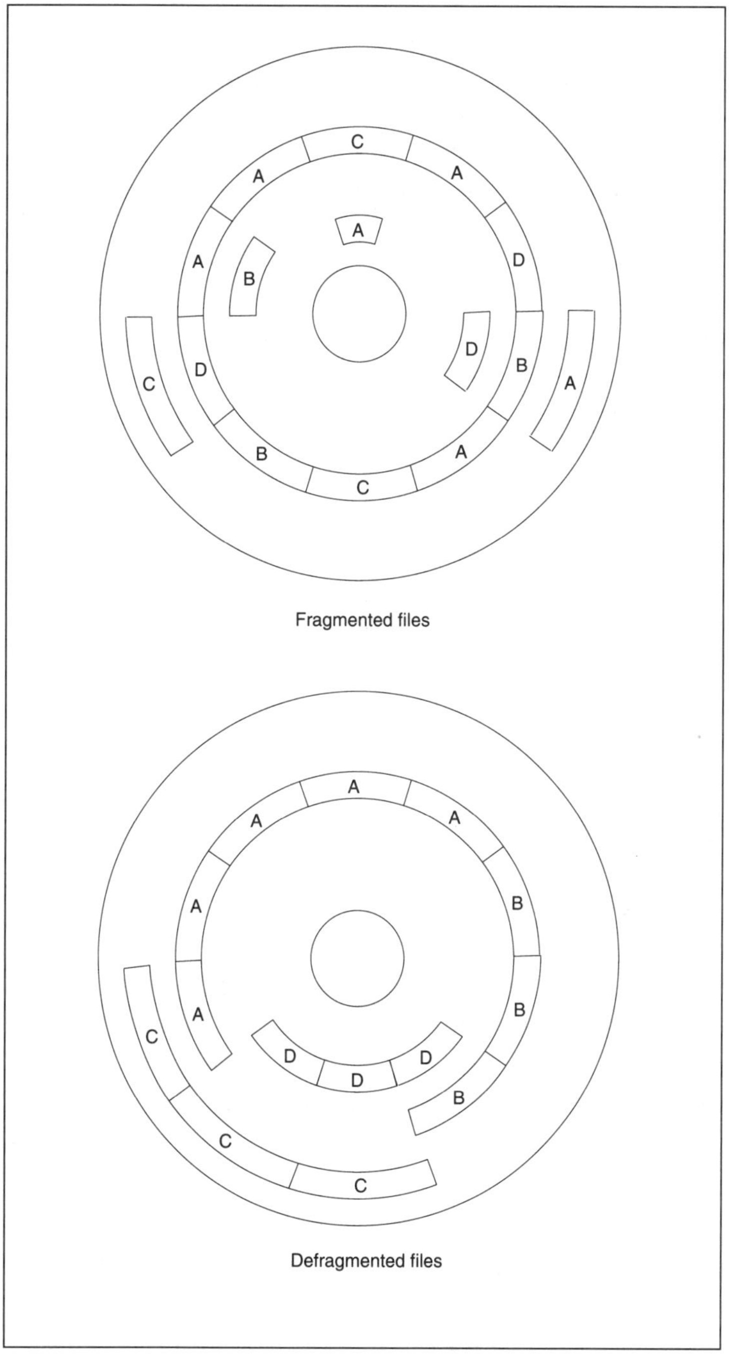

Figure 6-6. Fragmented files (top): Various sectors from one file spread throughout disk. The result is a delay in reading or writing.

Defragmented files (bottom): All sectors from each file lie close together. The file can be read or written much quicker.

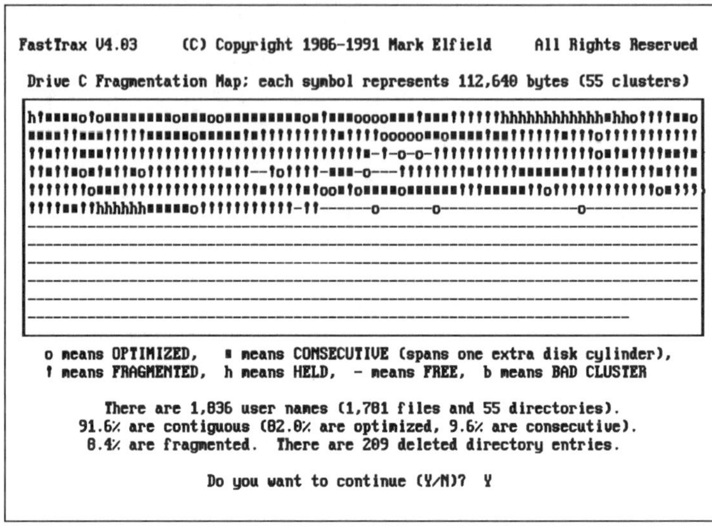

Figure 6-7. Fastrax defragger menu. It doesn't have the most beautiful user interface, but it works very well.

There are programs called disk defragmenters, defraggers, or disk optimizers that reduce fragmentation and make your files contiguous. Two of the products available are Fastrax (see Figure 6-7) and V-Opt. There are many others on the market. One also comes with most of the utility program collections, like the Norton Utilities or PC Tools. Norton Desktop for DOS, for example, comes with Speed Disk.

You should proceed with caution, however, when defragmenting your disk. Even though these products are reliable, they can't know everything about your computer, your terminate and stay ready programs (TSRs), and your operating system. Therefore, be sure to back up your drive before you use one. This is not to say that defragmenters are dangerous and that you have a high probability of losing your data, but even a low probability of data loss is significant.

The defragger programs are easy to use. They provide a visual indication of how fragmented the drive is before and after the process, and most of them even provide a percentage readout of just how fragmented the drive is.

Documentation to the defragmentation programs goes into what is an acceptable amount of fragmentation, what is not, when it's time to do defragmentation, and when it isn't.

Most defragmentation programs are flexible enough to do either limited or complete defragmentation, depending on how much time you have. Some of them recommend including the program as part of the boot-up sequence so that defragmentation occurs every time you reboot your computer.

In general, the longer the time between defragmentations, the longer the defragmentation process is going to take. The first defragmentation could take hours, and you may wonder if you're going to have to do this every time you boot up your computer. The answer is no. If you defragment the drive on a regular basis it will go much quicker. Also, some of the defragmentation programs ask if this is daily defragmentation or weekly defragmentation.

A question that may come to your mind immediately is, "If I am using a good disk cache, do I need to use this defragmentation program?" The answer is a definite yes.

Recovering lost drive space

Sometimes programs, especially those that use DOS extenders, crash and leave large file fragments on your drive. These fragments are hidden from your normal file utilities (DIR, File Manager, XTREE, and so on). The way to recover these file fragments is to run CHKDSK with the /F parameter (for example, CHKDSK /F) and then answer Y (yes) when CHKDSK asks if you want to recover the "Lost allocation units" or "Convert lost chains to clusters?" If there were lost allocation units or chains and you answer yes, they will be converted to files with the .CHK extension. These files could then be found with a normal file utility and deleted. Sometimes this process can free quite a bit of disk space. If you have programs that are prone to crashing then there is a chance that you have some of these files on your drive.

Note: If you were trying to recover some of the information in these file fragments then don't delete them; use a file utility like Norton or PC Tools to recover them. The fragments, however, are typically from some long forgotten file that you no longer want.

One thing to be careful about, though: do not run CHKDSK /F from within the MS/DOS prompt provided by Microsoft Windows. Many Windows-related files will appear to be lost allocation units when you issue CHKDSK /F from within Windows, but they really aren't and recovering them will lead to a minor disaster.

No matter what type of cache you're using, or if you're using a RAM disk, ultimately your files all have to be read from or written to the physical disk and you'll still want this to occur as fast as possible. With a disk cache, the defragmentation that's taking place on your disk drive is not nearly as apparent. But a disk cache must physically read and write information from the hard disk multiple times each session. Even a RAM disk requires a read at the beginning of the session and at least one write at the end of each session. Thus, defragmentation is still recommended.

Defragmentation is especially important if your disk cache is the original version of SMARTDRV. Since that version of SMARTDRV only buffers tracks,

Sector translation

Another critical issue to consider in our evaluation of disk drive optimization techniques is drive translation—sometimes referred to as sector translation. One of the inherent limitations of DOS (any version of DOS) is that it can't recognize anything higher than 1,024 cylinders on a hard disk. You're faced with a couple of choices when you're using a disk with more than 1,024 cylinders (and many of the higher-performance drives now have far more than 1,024 cylinders).

First, you could ignore this fact and start using your drive, but disaster looms if you do. When the drive gets full enough to move to cylinders higher than 1,024, DOS won't recognize that the drive is on cylinder 1,025. DOS may direct your disk drive to use cylinder 0 when it should be using cylinder 1,025. The results can be disastrous since cylinder 0 generally holds important formatting information. Overwriting cylinder 0 can cause the drive to crash and all data to be lost. That's not a very pleasant scenario. Moreover, it's insidious because it doesn't occur until you've been using the drive without any problems for a considerable length of time.

With an IDE drive, this limitation can be overcome because the drive is intelligent. Although it has X number of heads and some number of cylinders higher than 1,024, say 2,000, it can report to the computer that there are 2X heads and 1,000 cylinders. This fools DOS quite nicely. The same is also true with some ESDI and SCSI drives that allow sector translation. Sector translation is a technique used by some drive manufacturers that tricks DOS into properly using a

it's going to have a hard time with files that are fragmented over multiple tracks. Imagine a 2 KB file consisting of four sectors that's spread out over four tracks. That means four entire tracks, occupying 128 KB, would need to be read into cache just to access that single 2 KB file.

The other reason why it makes sense to do defragmentation has to do with on-board caches—another development that's come about in drives. Drive manufacturers have realized that cache increases performance. Because they want their drives to perform well so that you'll prefer their drives over the competition's, most of the higher-performance drives include a certain amount of disk cache on the disk drive itself. These types of disk caches typically are about

---

drive with more than 1,024 cylinders. This is accomplished by telling DOS that there are more heads or sectors an less cylinders than there actually are.

The downside to this approach is that some software bypasses DOS and writes directly to the disk drive. If the software is not aware that the drive is doing that translation, serious incompatibilities can result.

Yet it's advisable to do sector translation in a DOS environment because, well, what choice do you have? You certainly don't want to lose your data when you reach cylinder 1,025.

The translation software will not improve performance, but neither will it degrade performance to a noticeable degree. The only performance degradation is really just a roadblock to one kind of optimization: when you use a disk optimizer program to put related files together on a single cylinder, the software may think it has succeeded when in fact the hardware has actually put your files on a couple of cylinders because of the translation.

On the other hand, be aware that the hidden translation that goes on with many IDE drives is the reason why some drives will have compatibility problems with certain software. For example, Windows has an ability to set aside its own partitions on the drive, which it calls a permanent swap partition, to obtain higher performance. However, Windows does this by bypassing DOS and writing directly to the drive. Thus Windows can sometimes experience problems on drives that use translation. On the other hand, you can avoid the problem by choosing the temporary swap file option as opposed to the permanent swap partition.

one track in size (32 KB is a common size, although some have 64K and some are even as large as 256 KB in the bigger, more expensive drives). A one-track disk cache is more correctly called a disk buffer because it's reading just one track at a time and it can only store one track at a time on the drive. Many of the better ESDI controllers now include a 32 KB track buffer also. So the previous argument applies whether or not the drive itself has a track buffer.

Consider a situation in which the on-board cache, which can be extremely fast, can hold only one track at a time, and if a single file is spread out over multiple tracks. You're not even going to be able to cache that single file on the hard drive's on-board cache because that file is spread out over four tracks. All you're going to have in the drive's on-board memory is the last track.

This affects not only reads but, more importantly, writes. Writes often escape a software disk cache and can escape a hardware disk cache, depending on the type you have. All of your writes have to be written to the drive, but if your drive has a track buffer on it, that track buffer could have accepted the write information and freed up the CPU to go on to other things, while the drive controlled the update.

If that one file is spread out over multiple tracks, you lose most of the benefits of on-board track buffering because the drive's on-board buffer can't free up the CPU (or the rest of the system) until it's gotten to the part of the file that is on the last track. To take full advantage of a modern drive it is critical to perform defragmentation on a routine basis.

File Organization

One of the side benefits of buying a defragmentation program is file organization. When the file defragmentation program is defragmenting the file, it also gives us the choice of where to locate that file on the drive. This can be of benefit in several ways.

Chapter 5 discussed how information is stored on the various tracks of the drive and how some of the more advanced drives can store more information on the outer tracks than on the inner tracks. In other words, you can actually read and write to the outer tracks at a faster rate than you can to the inner tracks. A file organizer can let you move your frequently accessed or larger files to the outer tracks of such a drive.

You would want to move frequently accessed files to the outer tracks of any drive, even one that doesn't differentiate between inner and outer tracks. When the computer accesses files on the drive, it first has to access the DOS file allocation table (FAT) to find out where the file is on the drive. Since the FAT table is almost always located on the first track/cylinder of the drive's partition (which is the outer track of most drives), any file located closer to that track is going to be accessed faster than a file on one of the cylinders that's most remote from the location of the FAT.

File organization also allows you to place files together in a logical manner. You could put your word processor, its document files , and your spell checker all in close proximity on the drive. Such an action would reduce your drive access times during operation.

Another technique is to place files that tend to become fragmented in an area of the disk with a great deal of free space in order to minimize further fragmentation. The user manuals for disk optimizing software normally suggest strategies for organizing your files.

Disk Drive Interfaces

No matter how many disk optimization techniques you choose to implement, you can improve performance further by buying a faster drive. You may also find yourself needing a larger drive, particularly given the huge amount of disk space taken up by the popular breed of programs emerging for the Windows environment

The central issues in selecting a new disk drive revolve around the following questions:

1. Which of the drive interfaces will deliver the best performance for my particular needs?
2. What is it going to cost?
3. What are the trade-offs?

In this section, we'll take a brief look at each of the drive interfaces currently available and address each of these critical issues.

The factor that contributes most to the performance of the drive interface is its particular recording technique (that is, how densely the data can be laid down on to the drive's track). Density varies with different interfaces, and that means performance varies with different interfaces. After all, density actually equates to transfer rate, since a disk drive can transfer no more data during the time a sector is under the disk head than a sector contains.

In other words, the biggest performance issue in a controller or a drive interface type is the density of the sectors per track on the drive, which varies with different interfaces.

Now we'll take a look at each of the five most popular disk drive interfaces for PCs: ST-506 MFM, ST-506 RLL, SCSI, ESDI, and IDE.

ST506 MFM and RLL

ST-506 Modified Frequency Modulation (MFM) is the oldest of the standard PC interfaces. It was first used on the original IBM PC/XT systems and later on the PC/AT systems. Being that ST-506 MFM is the oldest, it is not surprisingly also the slowest of the popular standards.

ST-506 MFM is slow because drives employing ST-506 MFM have very low density relative to more modern drives: only 17 sectors per track (SPT), with 512 bytes per sector. With the platter spinning at 3,600 rpm, which is 60 revolutions per second, 17 SPT times 512 bytes is 8 KB. Multiplying 8 KB times 60 revolutions per minute we get 500,000 bytes per second. This may seem like a big number, but relative to our memory and CPU speed, it is very slow.

ST-506 MFM drives also are typically lower-capacity drives. At this point in the history of PCs, ST-506 MFM drives usually are offered as close-outs or liquidations. So, if you're trying to put together a system as cheaply as possible, ST-506 MFM might work for you. But if you want high-performance, ST-506 MFM won't be able to deliver.

ST-506 Run Length Limited (RLL) is quite a step up from ST-506 MFM. ST-506 RLL increases the data density to about 50 percent more sectors per track than ST-506 MFM. Instead of 17 SPT ST-506 RLL has 26 SPT. The increased data density provides 50 percent better data transfer rates, which means ST-506 RLL drives transfer data at 750 KB per second. Similarly, an ST-506 RLL drive has almost 50 percent higher capacity than an ST-506 MFM drive with the same number of platters.

At the time the RLL variation came out, these were respectable numbers, but relative to today's drives, an ST-506 RLL is slow and low in capacity. You'll see many of them in close-out sales but it's probably wise to avoid them.

Don't be tempted to reformat an ST-506 drive with MFM recording into a drive with RLL recording by replacing the MFM disk controller with an RLL controller. Although it is often possible to do so, and in the process increase both the data transfer rate and the capacity of the drive by 50 percent, it is very risky. Data stored on such a drive is in jeopardy of being lost or corrupted because the drive was never designed nor tested for the necessary higher recording density.

ESDI

Enhanced Small Disk Interface (ESDI) is a relatively high-capacity, high-performance interface. ESDI is at a minimum twice as fast as the old ST-506 MFM style. It doubles the performance with at least 34 SPT and 512 bytes per sector at 3,600 rpm. The ESDI data transfer rate is typically upwards of 1MB per second, and more advanced, higher performing ESDI drives are available that will transfer data at twice that rate. Those numbers are more than respectable, particularly if you consider that the AT bus is at best able to transfer data at speeds of 2 MB per second.

In the world of ESDI drives, there are two other predominant factors at work. First, ESDI drive capacity is always much larger than the earlier generations of ST-506 MFM or ST-506 RLL drives. (It's unusual to see an ESDI drive less than 100 MB, and its not uncommon to see one that's 300 MB or 600MB.)

Second, drive manufacturers make sure that ESDI drives achieve fast access times as well. The older ST-506 MFM and ST-506 RLL drives had access times as slow as 100 ms and at best of 28 ms. ESDI and the more modern drive interfaces have drives with seek times of less than 28 ms (often far less).

ESDI drives and megahertz

The performance of most ESDI drives is measured in megahertz. Although this may seem odd, it shouldn't pose a problem. Simply remember that every time one cycle occurs, one bit can be transferred. So all you have to do is is change megahertz into megabits. One megahertz equals one megabit, which must be divided by eight to get a megabyte. Since a typical ESDI drive operates 10 MHz, that translates into a respectable 1.2 MB per second data transfer rate. The fastest ESDI drives operate at 24 MHz or 3 MB per second.

Compared to the ST-506 MFM and ST-506 RLL interfaces, the ESDI interface delivers higher density, which means larger storage capacities as well as faster data transfer rate. And although the interface has nothing to do with access times, manufacturers typically make sure such drives offer very high performance access as well.

SCSI

Although ESDI is currently the most popular interface for high performance PC setups, two other standards also get a lot of attention. One of them, Small Computer System Interface (SCSI), is a standard that's been around for some time and always seems to be on the verge of breaking through as the major drive standard (Figure 6-8).

Technically, SCSI is a bus standard rather than a device interface standard. When you plug an SCSI host bus adapter into your PC, you're essentially adding another bus. This bus, like the AT bus, has its own command language, which is highly flexible

An important advantage of SCSI over ESDI is that, as a bus, SCSI can accept many more devices than an ESDI disk controller can. An ESDI controller can usually take no more than two drives, while it is theoretically possible to plug up to 63 devices (plus the PC) onto the SCSI bus. In practice, this is limited to no more than 7 devices connected in what's called a "daisy chain," although it is rare to find seven devices on a single SCSI host adapter.

Figure 6-8. The Seagate Elite SCSI Drive. Because this drive spins at 5,400 rpm, it provides a high transfer rate and a low rotational latency.

The problem with SCSI is that there has never been a strictly defined standard. The earlier drive standards (ST-506 MFM, ST-506 RLL, ESDI) were all introduced by one manufacturer and then quickly copied by other drive manufacturers. They were copied very closely so that drives were interchangeable—you could take out one ST-506 MFM drive and put in an new ST-506 MFM drive without a lot of problems or compatibility issues.

SCSI drives had much more loosely defined standards. Part of the reason is that the SCSI standard is not just a disk drive standard, but is also a standard for tape drives and scanners and all sorts of peripheral devices. After all, SCSI stands for small computer *system* interface, not *drive* interface. The standard is therefore broader and has never been as formalized as were the earlier interfaces. Thus you'll have to be careful when you try combining a number of different SCSI devices on the same bus. If you stick to daisy chaining a number of the same kind of drives together, you're not going to have problems.

SCSI is also noteworthy for being intelligent. With ST-506 MFM and ST-506 RLL drives, the PC's CPU has to direct all drive activities—in effect, the CPU has to tell the drive controller what to make the drive do. With ESDI, the drive gained more intelligence and was able to locate most sectors and tracks, which meant the PC's CPU and the disk controller didn't have to expend as much effort.

The SCSI drive has even more intelligence. The intelligence normally found on the controller is instead built into the SCSI drive's on-board electronics. This onboard intelligence locates the data, moves the heads to a particular track, and reads from the correct sector. What's often called the SCSI controller, in fact, is not really a controller at all—it's a host adapter. Its function, as the name suggests, is simply to connect the host (the PC) to another bus (SCSI).

At first glance it may appear that a more intelligent drive should be a higher-performance drive simply because the PC's CPU doesn't have to do as much work. Unfortunately, the SCSI bus does add some of its own "command" overhead. Measured strictly in terms of access times, SCSI is not necessarily faster than an ESDI drive, particularly when accessing small files (which makes access time more important than data transfer rate).

SCSI drives do provide benefits in a couple of areas. One is that manufacturers tend to use the SCSI interface for their highest-performance drives. In other words, a state-of-the-art drive will come out first with an SCSI interface and later with one of the other drive interfaces. So if you want to get the highest-performing drive on the market, you'll have to get an SCSI drive.

The on-board intelligence of an SCSI drive also adds value in a multitasking environment where the CPU of the computer system is doing many tasks at once. In a traditional DOS single-tasking environment, the CPU can do only one thing at a time. If a CPU is waiting for information from a drive, nothing else can be going on anyway, so there's not a lot of benefit to the drive doing its own seeks. In a multitasking environment—for example, in a NetWare or a UNIX environment—the CPU can perform multiple tasks at once. In this case, there is something to be gained by the CPU sending a request for particular data out over the SCSI bus and then simply going on to the next waiting task. When the information requested from the SCSI drive is returned, the CPU can come back and process it without having wasted any time just sitting there waiting.

The bottom line is that the inherent intelligence of an SCSI drive can make it a higher-performance drive in a multitasking environment.

In terms of throughput, SCSI does very well indeed. While ESDI drives typically operate in the 1 MB to 2 MB per second data transfer range, SCSI drives typically operate at between 1 MB and 2.5 MB per second. The highest-performing, state-of-the-art SCSI drives can deliver up to 5 MB per second, exceeding the data transfer rate of the AT bus.

In addition, the new SCSI-2 standard allows a drive to operate at as much as 10 MB per second. Finally SCSI drives have another advantage in a multitasking environment, since the drives on-board intelligence makes it possible for multiple drives to be performing seeks simultaneously. We'll see how we can put that feature to work as the next chapter explores some advanced optimization techniques.

IDE

Intelligent Drive Electronics (IDE), first introduced in 1987, is the most recent disk standard. Like the SCSI interface, IDE puts the intelligence on the drive. Indeed, the necessary electronics are minimized because IDE uses the same command language as the AT bus. In other words, the drive's write command is the same as the bus's write command. Thus the electronics on the disk need only interpret the AT commands and perform the transfer operation. And unlike the SCSI, which needs a full-blown host adapter, the IDE drive's natural host adapter is the AT-bus itself because they speak the same language.

Because of IDE's inherent cost savings (no controller is necessary), IDE drives are often found in very low-cost applications. Lots of entry level PCs these days are using low-capacity, low-performance IDE drives because of cost.

On the other hand, that doesn't mean there aren't high-performance IDE drives. IDE is certainly a standard to look into when you're shopping for high performance. For now, however, the very highest capacity drives aren't yet available in IDE. One-gigabyte IDE drives are just now coming into the market, for example, while SCSI and ESDI 1-gigabyte drives have been around for awhile. But, if your capacity requirements range from 100 to 500 MB, there are a large number of IDE drives from which to choose. Most of the high-capacity IDE drives offer very high performance, typically with seek times under 20 ms per second. And the data transfer rates of some of these drives can be eye opening, reaching as much as 4 MB per second (see Figure 6-9).

Not all IDE drives are compatible with each other. Some IDE drives cannot coexist with different IDE drives on the same host adapter, especially if they are older IDE drives. When using two IDE drives, it is best to use two of the same drives, or at least two drives from the same manufacturer.

Figure 6-9. Despite their small size and relatively low prices IDE drives can deliver very good performance.

Drive interface summary

If you are interested in high performance, at a minimum you should have an ESDI drive. You can probably get still higher performance with an IDE drive or an SCSI drive.

If price is a factor, remember that, generally, ESDI and SCSI are about the same price for comparable capacities, while IDE will be less expensive (at least for drives up to about 500 MB in capacity).

And despite all this discussion of drive interfaces, it's far more important for you to look carefully at the statistics for a particular drive than it is to worry about interface. There are relatively slow drives available in all drive interface categories. In other words, just buying an SCSI or ESDI drive doesn't mean you've gotten a high-performance drive.

Take a look at the average seek time and the data transfer rate. If you're dealing with many small files, the seek time is going to be the most important factor to you. If you're dealing with larger files, the data transfer rate becomes more important. In nearly all cases, you'll want both seek time and transfer rate to be as high as you can afford.

The disk interface itself is not nearly as important as the underlying characteristics of the drive to which the interface is connected. Try to get a very fast seek/access time or data transfer rate.

Of the three high performance drive interfaces, the ESDI has the fewest compatibility problems. SCSI is the trickiest to deal since the SCSI interface usually requires some sort of device driver before the operating system will recognize the drive. IDE is the most straightforward of all the drive interfaces, but in some cases software is completely fooled by IDE drives. Table 6-1 summarizes the features of all disk drive interfaces we have discussed.

Table 6-1. Summary of Drive Interface Features

Disk Drive Interfaces	Interface Speed	Capacity	Compatibility	Price	Best Used for
ST-506 MFM	.5 MB/sec	20-80 MB	Very High	Cheap	Homemade Clone
ST-506 RLL	.75MB/sec	30-120 MB	High	Cheap	Homemade Clone
ESDI	1-3MB/sec	90-8 MB	Very High	High	Single-Tasking
SCSI	1-5MB/sec	40-1,600 MB	Medium	High	Multitasking
IDE	1-2MB/sec	20-500 MB	Good	Full Range	Single-Tasking

Average seek time is not as important as track-to-track seek time

Few people realize that when choosing a high-performance disk drive, the track-to-track time is normally more important than the average seek time. Average seek time is actually more a theoretical number than a practical one. It does not necessarily indicate how long on the average it will take to reach a particular track *while actually computing*. The reason is simple.

Computers normally access the same general vicinity of a program or file for a period of time before moving to another area. This phenomenon is called *locality of reference*. (You took advantage of this fact before by implementing a cache, a small area in memory in which you stored your most frequently used data.) Because of the locality of reference, you know that you will rarely need to access data that is located very far from where the data you are currently using is located. This means that on average the data that the computer will access on the drive will be located relatively close to the data that was last accessed on the drive.

Comparing the amount of time necessary for various drives to access nearby data is more important than it is to compare the amount of time it takes various drives to access data located on any cylinder on the entire drive. Because the average access time and average seek time are measures of how long a drive takes to access data irrespective of where that data is located, they are not nearly as important a measure as the track-to-track seek time, which more directly reflects how long it will take the drive to seek nearby data.

Perhaps an example is in order. Consider two drives, one with 500 cylinders and the other with 1,000 cylinders, both with average seek times of 20 ms. Because of the way in which seek times are calculated the drive with 1,000 cylinders must be able to move its actuator arm past 500 cylinders in 20 ms in order to qualify as a 20ms average access time drive. But the drive with 500 cylinders need only move its arm past 250 cylinders in 20 ms to qualify as a 20 ms average seek time drive. If the drive with more cylinders had to move its arm over only 250 cylinders instead of all 500, it would calculate out as a much faster drive. That extra speed actually shows up, on the other hand, in a faster track-to-track time.

Will the 20 ms average seek time measure ever be meaningful? Yes, if the data we are using is spread out randomly over the entire surface of the drive. This occurs only in the case of a database that always made completely random accesses of a database that was the same size as the drive, which is a very rare occurrence.

When evaluating a drive for performance, the drive with a faster track-to-track time will probably be faster in practice than the drive with the faster average seek time.

Because drive customers have become so fixated on the drives average seek time as the primary means of performance measurement, some manufacturers actually offer the same drive in two versions: one with a faster average seek time and the other with a higher capacity. How can they do this? Simple. They format the drive that they want to have a faster average seek time with fewer cylinders. This reduces the total distance that the arm will have to travel and thus reduces the amount of time it takes the drive

Beware of advertised access times

When it comes time to buy a new hard drive or a new computer that includes a hard drive, be careful about claims for average access times. Most of the ads are written by people who don't know the difference between access time and seek time. The ad writers tend to confuse average seek time with average access time and end up listing the seek time as the access time. While this is often simply due to ignorance it can also be done as an intentional deception since by calling the seek time the access time the drive will appear to be considerably faster than it really is. The true access time is always considerably slower than the seek time (because access time includes both the seek time and the rotational latency).

This wouldn't be such a problem if everyone substituted the seek time for the access time, but there are honest, knowledgeable dealers that correctly call seek time seek time and access time access time.

Most computer manufacturers and computer dealers and many hard disk dealers misuse the term average access time. Most disk drive manufacturers avoid the use of the term access time entirely and stick to listing the drive's

on average to move from the outermost cylinder to the innermost one. Reducing the distance also reduces the time, and thus the average seek and access times are also reduced. The trade-off, of course, is that with fewer cylinders, the drive will have a lower capacity (there are fewer cylinders to store data on). While this seems like a crazy way to boost drive "performance," it will continue to make sense to some manufacturers as long as customers are hung up on average seek time as the primary means of drive performance.

Of course, you can perform the same "performance enhancement" yourself. Simply reformat your current hard drive with fewer cylinders (this must be done at the physical format stage before you partition or logically format the drive). Will your drive operate any faster now than it did before? No. But the drive will show a better average seek or access time (whichever one you measure) than it did before.

---

average seek time and average rotational latency separately. The best way to determine the true performance for a drive that you are thinking about purchasing is to contact the drive manufacturer. (The names, addresses and phone numbers of most of the major drive manufacturers are listed in Appendix H.)

If you are dealing with someone selling a drive who doesn't know the difference between seek time and access time (in fact most dealers don't know there is a difference) then you should assume that the advertised average access time is actually the average seek time and the true access time is about 8 ms slower (8 ms being the typical rotational latency for most hard drives). This 8 ms may seem like a small amount but it can be a relatively significant amount of time when you consider that a drive being advertised with a 16 ms "access time" actually has a seek time of 16 ms and the real average access time is probably 24ms (16 ms seek time plus 8 ms rotational latency). That is 50 percent slower, and 50 percent is a significant amount.

If an ad for a drive claims a certain access time it is probably the seek time that is being advertised not the access time. The real access time is most likely 8ms slower than the number claimed.

Things to look for when buying a new hard drive

1. **Capacity.** You will always need more capacity later. Don't be shortsighted and buy only enough for present needs

2. **Interface.** Avoid ST-506 (both MFM and RLL)—a low-performance drive interface that is going to be disappointing in a PC tuned for performance.

   - IDE is the right choice for most users. IDE drives are generally low cost and can be very high performance.

   - ESDI is a good choice if you can't get an IDE drive with a high enough capacity or you already have a big ESDI drive that you would like to keep and just want to add another drive to the system.

   - SCSI is best used in multitasking systems (for example, UNIX or Netware) or if you need very high capacities or ultrafast performance on a standard DOS system.

3. **Seek time, both average and track-to-track.** While average seek time is the most commonly advertised drive performance figure, track-to-track performance is often more indicative of actual performance. Don't be fooled into thinking that the average access time is actually the average seek time. If you will be performing tasks with lots of random activity, like database management, then a fast seek time is a must. For most users, drives with average seek times below 20 ms and track-to-track seek times of less than 5 ms will be good. The fastest drives have average seek times approaching 10 ms and track-to-track times of less than 2 ms.

4. **Data transfer rate.** This normally is a function of the drive interface, but it can also be affected by the number of tracks per cylinder. If you will be working with large files, a high data transfer rate is a must. Look for at least 1 MB per second.

5. **Best transfer rates.** The drives with the best (lowest) seek times also tend to have the best data transfer rates. You shouldn't have to compromise one to get the other.

6. **Rotational latency.** For most drives, this will be the standard 8.3 ms, but beware of drives that have less than 3,600 rpm and thus higher latencies. If you are looking for the ultimate in drive performance look for a drive with a high rpm and thus a low latency.

7. **Number of data heads.** If the choice is between two drives that have similar specs, but one drive has more data heads (or data platters), then the drive with the larger number of data heads will probably deliver higher performance.

The drive with more data heads will be faster

When you are trying to decide between two drives that appear to be equal in all performance specifications except the number of data heads, you should probably choose the drive with the higher number of data heads. Why? With more data heads there are more tracks per cylinder and thus a greater likelihood that the data the computer must access is on the same cylinder as the current cylinder. If required data is on the current cylinder, the computer doesn't have to wait for the drive's actuator arm to move to the next cylinder. The drive can usually access different tracks within the same cylinder much faster than it can access tracks on a different cylinder.

To access data on another cylinder, the drive must move the actuator arm, which is a mechanical operation. To access data on another track on the same cylinder, the drive must only switch tracks, which is an electronic operation. This is also the reason why the best disk optimizing programs allow you to place files on the drive in relation to both track and cylinder, not just cylinder.

8. **Price.** For most users, price will be at the top of the list. The best price performance drives are normally IDE drives. Compare drive prices on both an absolute basis and a dollars-per-megabyte basis. Lower-capacity drives may seem cheap until you look at how much they cost per megabyte. When buying SCSI or ESDI drives, don't forget to include the price of a host adapter or controller. A SCSI host adapter or ESDI controller can easily cost 50 percent of the price of a 120-MB drive or 30 percent of the cost of a 200-MB drive.

9. **The dealer.** Possibly the most important part of the entire drive purchase is the dealer from whom you buy the drive. While it is unlikely that a good

MTBF Numbers

Don't place too much faith in claims about extraordinarily high mean time between failure (MTBF) numbers. There are probably more ways to measure MTBF than there are drive manufacturers. The marketing departments of the drive manufactures are locked in an ever-escalating war to raise their MTBF numbers. (Fortunately the engineering departments of most of these companies are trying to improve the reliability of the drives as well.)

I think that any MTBF number over 100,000 hours is pretty meaningless. Consider that many of the MTBF numbers are based on power on hours (POH). To put a 100,000 POH MTBF number in perspective, consider that at 10 hours a day, 5 days per week, 100,000 hours is roughly 40 years. Not only is it hard to believe that a drive could last for 40 years, it is also silly to give much weight to the difference between a drive that has an MTBF of 100,000 POH and a drive with an MTBF of 150,000 POH. Are you really concerned that your drive may fail in 40 years instead of 60 years? (The MTBF rating of drives can be important when evaluating drives for use in drive arrays. For more on this see the next chapter.)

For systems with one or two drives, don't be concerned with the manufacturers claimed MTBF rating. It is more important to consider the warranty (look for at least one year, and two years is becoming more common) and the likelihood that the drive's manufacturer will be in business long enough to make good on the warranty should it become necessary.

quality drive will fail before its warranty expires, it is quite likely you will have some questions about configuring or installing your drive. Make sure that your drive dealer is willing and able to answer your support questions and willing and able to replace your drive in the event that it fails prematurely.

Common drive measures and rates

Term	Abbreviation	What it stands for	Equivalent to
Milliseconds	ms	Thousandths of a second	0.001 seconds
Kilobytes	KB	Thousands of bytes*	0.001 megabytes
Megahertz	MHz	Millions of cycles per second	megabits per second**
Megabits	Mb	Millions of bits	0.124 megabytes
Megabytes	MB	Millions of bytes	8 megabits
Megabits per second	Mb/sec	Millions of bits per second	0.125 megabytes per second
Megabytes per second	MB/sec	Millions of bytes per second	8 megabits per second
Gigabyte	GB	Billions of bytes	1,000 megabytes
Terabyte	TB	Trillions of bytes	1,000 gigabytes

* The usage of KB and MB when applied to disk drives is somewhat different from its meaning when applied to the computer's memory. When we use KB or MB in reference to drive capacity, we mean 1,000 or 1,000,000 bytes. When KB and MB are applied to main memory, they refer to 1,024 and 1,048,576 bytes, respectively.

** This is true when applied to serial devices, which most disk drives and controllers are. It is not the case for other system components like the CPU or memory.

Summary

Improving the performance of a PC's drive subsystem is not difficult. It is largely a matter of releasing the potential performance that is already in the system. You are likely to get a much larger performance boost by optimizing the drive you already have than by replacing it with a faster drive. Even if you do elect to replace your drive with a faster one, all of the disk optimization techniques will still apply.

Because so much of your computing is dependent on your disk drive, anything that you do to improve drive-related performance will probably improve your PC's overall performance.

CHAPTER SEVEN

Advanced Disk Optimization Techniques

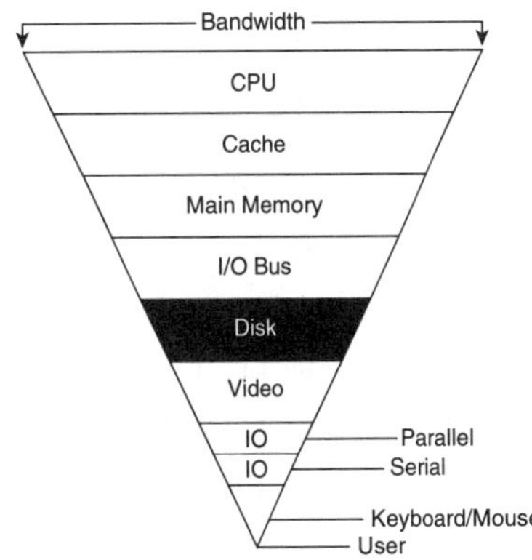

Data Funnel

In general, advanced disk optimization techniques do not apply to the typical PC user. Although they can be quite effective, most people won't try them because they're either relatively difficult to implement or expensive—very expensive. Before you read further, be warned that you could replace the word *advanced* with the word *expensive,* and the title of this chapter would still be valid. Most of the techniques mentioned in this chapter cost thousands of dollars. Proceed at your wallet's own risk.

Disk Arrays

The first advanced disk optimization technique we'll discuss is the disk array. The primary interest in arrays is not so much a matter of the performance level they can deliver but the amount of differentiation they can offer the various computer manufacturers and drive disk array suppliers.

As PC prices fall and PCs become more and more a commodity item, PC manufacturers and marketers have to think of every trick in the book to differentiate their products. One of the hottest differentiators these days is the disk array. If you are interested in performance on a PC sooner or later you'll be hearing about drive arrays.

Let's take a close look at arrays and see where they're appropriate, where they aren't, and what they really can and cannot deliver. A disk array is a group of disk drives that are connected together in such a way that they deliver higher capacity, availability, or performance than a single disk drive. In this chapter we will discuss four disk array techniques: disk mirroring, disk duplexing, multiple drives, and RAID.

Before we look at any of these array techniques I think it's important to note that in many cases the reason for having a disk array is security (in the sense of greater data availability) rather than performance. And certainly techniques implemented for the sake of increased data availability may or may not improve performance.

As the life insurance industry found long ago, however, it's much easier to sell products with a positive outlook (life insurance) than by dwelling on the negative (death insurance). Indeed, it's easier to sell life insurance based on the potential investment return than it is to sell based on the possibility of catastrophic failure.

Similarly, it's much easier to sell disk arrays based on high performance than on reducing computer down time; everyone likes higher performance, and no one wants to think about down time. So as we go through the various disk array techniques, keep in mind that most of them are designed to maximize data availability and not necessarily to optimize performance. Indeed, keep in mind that these two goals are often at odds. Greater data availability almost always comes at the expense of performance.

Disk mirroring

The simplest drive array technique is called disk mirroring. Disk mirroring involves attaching two disk drives to one controller and writing the same information to both drives (see Figure 7-1).

The increase in data security and availability gained from disk mirroring is obvious. If something happens to the primary drive, you hope to be able

Figure 7-1. Disk Mirroring

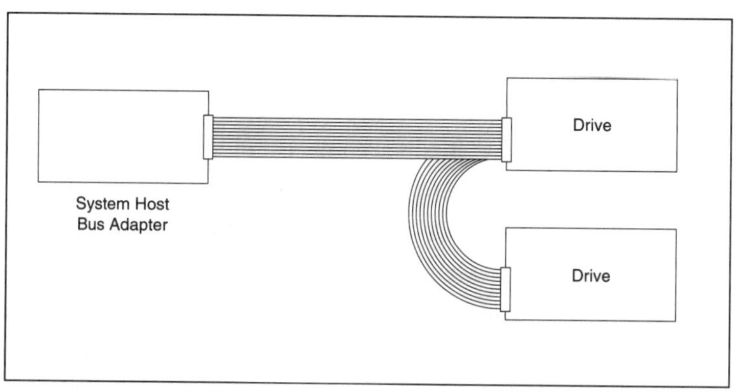

to recover all of the data from the secondary drive. Disk mirroring is supported directly by some operating systems, such as NetWare. It can be implemented on other operating systems, including DOS and UNIX, by using the appropriate drivers.

Why do disk mirroring? Why not use a traditional form of backup, like tape? After all, tape storage costs cents per megabyte, while disk drives cost dollars per megabyte. But tape backup is slow and therefore only practical at intervals—say, once a day. Thus, tape tends to miss data representing at least part of a day's work. Moreover, tape takes a great deal of time to restore—it takes hours to restore hundreds of megabytes of data. For some "mission-critical" situations, hours is too long. A business may not be able to function without some of its computers for that long.

Of course, the hope is that when a mirrored disk fails, the computer can be shut off, the failed disk removed, and the computer brought up again using the second drive. This will not always be the case, however, so any time disk mirroring is implemented, you should also continue doing regular backups.

The risk with disk mirroring is that whatever accident befell the primary drive is likely to affect the secondary drive as well. If a voltage spike zaps the main drive, it's likely that the second drive will also be corrupted. If a controller goes wild and screws up the main drive, it's more than likely that the second drive is faithfully mirroring that screwed up data.

It's also possible that drive data is lost not due to a mechanical or electrical failure but due to operator error. A file can be inadvertently deleted, written over, or modified when it shouldn't have been. Or files may be erased intentionally by a virus or disgruntled employee. In either case, disk mirroring is not going to help because whatever was done to one drive is also done to the second drive simultaneously. Nor will disk mirroring help when a computer is stolen, because of course both drives are going to be stolen at the same time. Nor will disk mirroring be of use if a fire wipes out both drives at the same time.

Disk mirroring is not only less than perfectly secure but also expensive since it uses two drives to provide the capacity of one.

Despite these lacks, proponents of disk mirroring cite a potential performance advantage. Disk reads on a mirrored system should be faster, the argument goes. Once your information is on both drives, whichever disk can provide you with the data you need first is the disk you read from.

On the other hand, at least some of the improvement in read time is offset by a similar slowdown when you attempt to write, because you can't complete the write operation until you finish writing to both drives. And writes are definitely slower in a mirrored environment; contrary to what you might think, the single disk controller can't write just once and have both disks "listen." Rather, every bit of data has to go over the drive channel twice: once to the first drive and once to the second drive.

Disaster insurance: removable media backup

No technique involving fixed disk drives is a substitute for removable media backup. Your data is only secure when it is stored in a different location from your computer. Using multiple drives for data security only lets the data be restored quicker than it can from tape. Only removable media can protect your data from fire, theft, viruses, disgruntled employees, or inadvertent deletion.

How can you be sure your data is perfectly secure from any kind of disaster? Well, of course, you can't be. But if you do something along the lines of the following you'll never lose more than a few days worth of data:

Once a week, do two complete backups to tape of your hard disk. Store one tape onsite, so you can do a quick restoration of data if someone erases a file inadvertently or if disaster strikes and a disk head crashes. But go the extra mile and store the second tape offsite. While there are services that do nothing but store electronic media and guarantee them against damage, it would be fine if you just took the tape home and stored it someplace where it's safe from the kids and the dog.

Then, as you do your incremental backups on a nightly basis, take the extra time to make two, storing one tape at work and the other at home. If you do, it's highly unlikely that even a flood, earthquake, fire, or disgruntled employee can wipe out more than eight hours worth of new data. While this kind of procedure is usually reserved for the shared data stored on a file server, it pays to take similar care of your personal data. If you think about what it would mean to lose everything on your hard disk, you'll take the time. The question isn't whether you'll eventually lose hard drive data: the question is when.

Still, the net result should be a slight performance improvement, because a computer typically performs more reads than writes.

Disk duplexing

One level above disk mirroring is disk duplexing, at least for operating systems that support it, such as UNIX and NetWare. (DOS does not support duplexing.)

The disk duplexing concept is similar to disk mirroring in that there are two drives, but disk duplexing employs two controllers as well (see Figure 7-2). This gives you a total of two drives, two disk controllers, and two disk channels. Thus, disk duplexing eliminates the bottleneck we referred to of data having to go through the same single controller channel twice. By having two controllers, data can pass through both channels at once so there are greater performance advantages than with mirrored drives.

The other advantage of duplexed drives over mirrored drives is that if a controller fails it's unlikely (although possible, if failure is caused by something like a power surge) that the same failure would also affect the second controller. Duplexed drives are thus a lot more secure than mirrored drives, and they offer better performance.

The performance gained by having duplexed drives is still not tremendous, however. The cost of the nominal increase in performance is significant because you have twice as much hardware to support the same amount of disk storage.

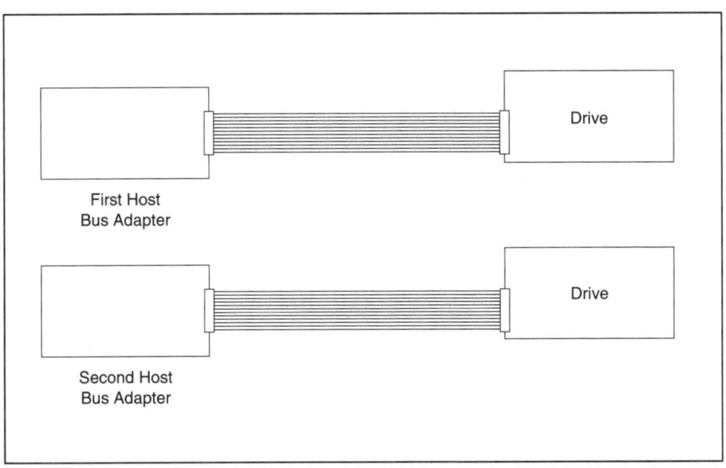

Figure 7-2. Disk Duplexing

From a performance standpoint, you're going to be better off spending money on a much higher performance drive. And you can certainly take the money you spent on two drives and get a much higher-performance and capacity drive. So unless you happen to have two drives and two controllers lying around, disk mirroring or duplexing is an expensive solution. While you may feel the additional security achieved by having mirrored or duplexed drives is worth the expense, don't do it for performance.

On the other hand, there is something to the idea that you can use multiple drives to increase performance. It's just that there's not a big benefit to writing and reading all the same information to both those drives at the same time.

Multiple drives

Administrators of large database systems have known for some time that dividing their database over two or more drives could decrease drive access times and increase data transfer rate. In multitasking environments, each drive and controller can operate independently of the other drives and controllers. Thus these database administrators were benefiting from multiple disk drive heads seeking or transferring data at the same time.

This is a pretty obvious win. If the computer needs to perform two different read operations, one from a file on one drive and the second from a file on the other drive, both reads can occur simultaneously. In the case of a single drive system, the CPU must wait for the first disk read to be completed before it can start the second. If the bus is an SCSI bus, one controller can run multiple drives. If it is an ESDI or IDE environment, you're going to need multiple drives and multiple controllers to see the maximum benefit.

If the system already has multiple drives, the cost of achieving this performance improvement is nominal—it is a matter of spending the time to disburse your data files over multiple drives. It's important to remember that merely dividing your files over the two drives may not achieve the desired effect. What you need to do is distribute similar data files over the two drives. For example, if you put all of your operating system and application program files on one drive and your data files on another, it's likely the computer is going to be looking for one or the other but not both simultaneously. Therefore, make sure to disburse both types of files on both drives. Ideally, the database files need to be spread out over more than one drive. This technique can be very effective; indeed, it's application is something of a science as it is applied by database administrators to improve the performance of database applications.

To review, the first two techniques (mirroring and duplexing) cost a lot of money relative to drive capacity (you essentially double the cost per megabyte of disk storage) and offer little in the way of performance. In contrast, the third technique—disbursing files over multiple drives—can be very effective with a nominal impact on cost. Even if you have to buy more drives, the additional expense is recouped because your storage capacity increases in proportion to the money you spent. (In a mirrored or duplexed environment, you have only half the capacity you paid for.)

There is a slight reduction in drive capacity versus what you pay for if you opt for implementing redundant arrays of inexpensive drives (RAID). There's

Networked PCs versus mainframes and disk I/O

One of the reasons that PCs are able to offer better performance than mainframes is often overlooked. The big iron guys (mainframe supporters) generally concede that a network of PCs has far more CPU power than a typical mainframe. (For example, a typical PC has about 3 MIPS (millions of instructions per second) of performance per machine while a typical mainframe has between 3 and 20 MIPS.) Thus a 10 person network would have over 30 MIPS and a hundred person network could easily have over 300 MIPS. But, say the mainframers, the mainframe has far better I/O—especially disk I/O—than the PC. They are quick to mention the multiple 12 MB per second disk drive channels that a high-end mainframe might possess.

But if you consider the total disk bandwidth available on all the PCs on a network, the picture changes. Many PC drives have about 1 MB per second throughput. Thus a 10-node network has a total disk bandwidth of 10 MB per second and a hundred person network has a combined bandwidth of 100 MB per second. That means a network of PCs outperforms the mainframe in CPU and disk bandwidth. The challenge facing today's information system (IS) directors is how to take advantage and control all of this computer power.

a lot of misinformation being spread about RAID by certain marketing and sales departments, but we can clear up that misunderstanding right now.

RAID

Originally the idea behind disk arrays was this: Computer users realized that they needed increased drive capacity and better drive performance. They saw that very high capacity drives sold for multiples of the cost per megabyte of lower capacity drives. In other words, the price/performance of six 100-MB drives could be better than that of a single 600-MB drive; similarly the price/performance of three 1-GB drives could be better than that of one 3-GB drive. The idea was to buy redundant arrays of inexpensive drives (RAID) and take advantage of the fact that there could be more heads active at any one time than there could be with one single large expensive drive (SLED).

However, RAID had a downside. Computer administrators realized that if you ran three drives simultaneously, each with a mean time between failures (MTBF) rate of 50,000 hours, those drives combined would have an MTBF rate of something less than one-third of 50,000 hours. (The "something less" part comes from increased temperature, the increased strain on the power supply, the extra complexity of cabling, and so on.) Since increasing the number of drives to three increases the likelihood of a drive failure by slightly more than three, adding lots of drives to a system did not seem to be the most desirable way to improve drive performance times, particularly since those looking for very high capacity tend to be interested in high availability as well. Thus, buying lots of relatively inexpensive drives involved a major compromise of data availability compare to buying a single large expensive drive.

What saved the idea of using multiple inexpensive drives is the introduction of a way to compensate for the reduced reliability of having many components that can fail. A series of papers came out, the most widely known of which was "The Case for Redundant Arrays of Inexpensive Disks (RAID)" published by David A. Patterson, Garth Gibson, and Randy H. Katz of the University of California (Berkeley) in 1987. This paper outlined a series of techniques that resulted in five different levels of redundancy.

RAID Level 1 was really nothing new: disk mirroring (see Figure 7-3). But the additional RAID levels all implement a technique referred to as *striping.*

The concept behind striping is that instead of writing all of a file to a single drive, a file is split into smaller pieces that can be written to multiple drives simultaneously. One obvious impact of the striping technique is an improvement in the data transfer rate, since we are no longer dependent on the transfer rate of a single drive but can take advantage of the combined transfer rates of multiple drives.

RAID Level 2 actually goes beyond striping (see Figure 7-4). Files that are broken into bits and stored on multiple drives do reduce the time to read or

Where's the **inexpensive** *in RAID?*

Most PC publications have lots of 100 MB drives listed for about $350 each and many 200 MB drives for about $600 each. Compare this to 600 MB drives for $1,300 and 1,200 MB drives for $2,000.

The relative cost per megabyte of these drives is as follows:

- 100 MB at $350 is $3.50 per megabyte
- 200 MB at $600 is $3.00 per megabyte
- 660 MB at $1,300 is $2.00 per megabyte
- 1,200 MB at $2,000 is $1.70 per megabyte

So while the "inexpensive" in the RAID acronym might lead you to believe otherwise, there is actually a cost per megabyte penalty from using multiple lower capacity drives instead of a single large drive. And while the seek times of the lower capacity drives are roughly 15 to 17 ms, the 1,200-MB drives have 13-ms seek times. The data transfer rate is presumably higher on the high capacity drives as well since one of the ways they achieve higher capacity is by using more sectors per track.

So it would appear that there is currently no cost advantage to using multiple lower capacity drives versus a single high capacity drive. This is especially true if the high cost of a fancy disk array controller is included with the cost of the so-called redundant array of inexpensive drives.

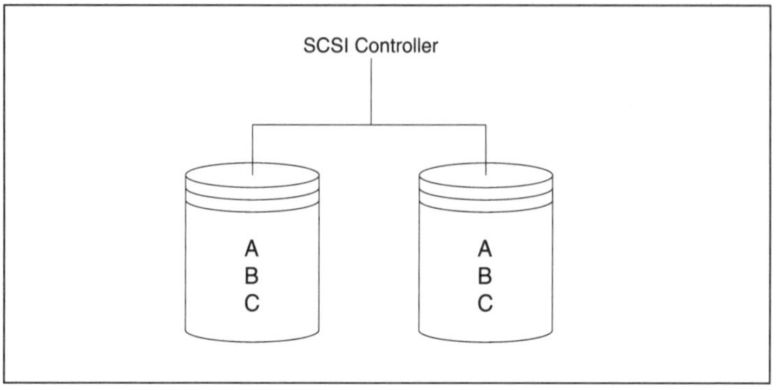

Figure 7-3.
RAID 1

write the file, but at the cost of reduced reliability. Should any one of the drives fail (and remember, there is a greater likelihood of a failure in a multiple drive system than in a single drive system), all our files would be lost since every drive would be storing parts of every file.

It turns out this problem can be overcome by adding additional drives to store extra information that can be used to reconstruct the original data should a drive go bad. This extra information is actually a kind of error correction code (ECC), called a Hamming code. Hamming code associates even-parity bits with unique combinations of data bits. In the RAID Level 2 scheme, data segments are striped across data disks bit by bit, and enough additional disks are used for ECC to ensure superb data protection; it can actually survive two simultaneous drive failures. If one of the data drives fails, the data on that drive can be reconstructed by using the parity information stored on the parity drives.

On the other hand, the cost is rather dear. For example, in a seven-drive Level 2 array, the first four drives hold data while three more are required to store parity information. Level 2 outperforms a single drive in large write transactions but falls slightly behind in doing large reads. But a single drive far outclasses a Level 2 array in all small data transfers, due to Level 2's need to access all disks in a group to modify part of a sector.

The desire to avoid the reduced capacity penalty of RAID Level 2 lead to RAID Level 3 (see Figure 7-5), in which data is striped by bytes and the number of drives necessary to safeguard the data is reduced. Instead of the multiple drives used for ECC in RAID Level 2, RAID Level 3 uses a single drive to hold the ECC information. RAID Level 3 is less expensive than Level 2 because it requires fewer drives and is somewhat faster since less data need be written.

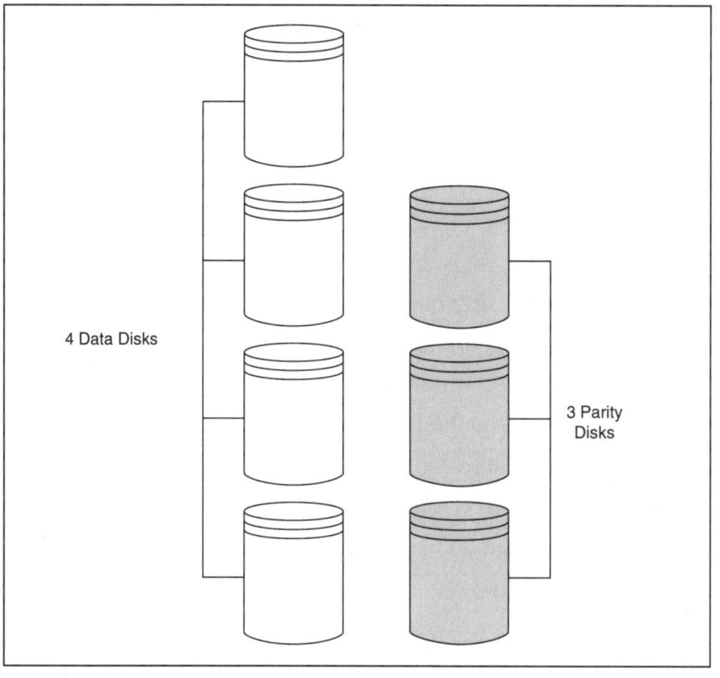

Figure 7-4.
RAID Level 2

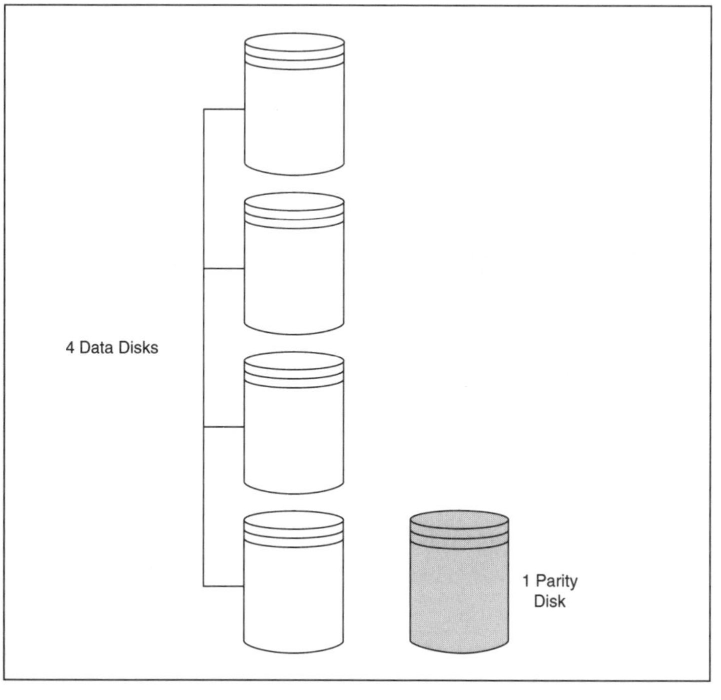

Figure 7-5.
RAID Level 3

But it has the same performance trade-offs as Level 2, with the additional trade-off that RAID Level 3 can only recover from a single drive failure. Of course, in most cases that should be sufficient. But the inability to do more than one I/O at a time, because even a single sector I/O involves all the drives in the array, handicaps Level 2 and level 3.

Level 4 takes striping to the sector level, enabling multiple data reads to take place simultaneously on the disks in the array (see Figure 7-6). Additionally, a single read requires accessing only one disk. On the other hand, small writes are slow, requiring a reread of the old sector of data and old parity bit in order to write the new data sector and new parity. All writes must access the check disk, so this clearly becomes the bottleneck.

RAID Level 5 is the highest level mentioned in the paper (see Figure 7-7). It delivers the highest level of performance for both reads and writes. In Level

Figure 7-6. RAID level 4

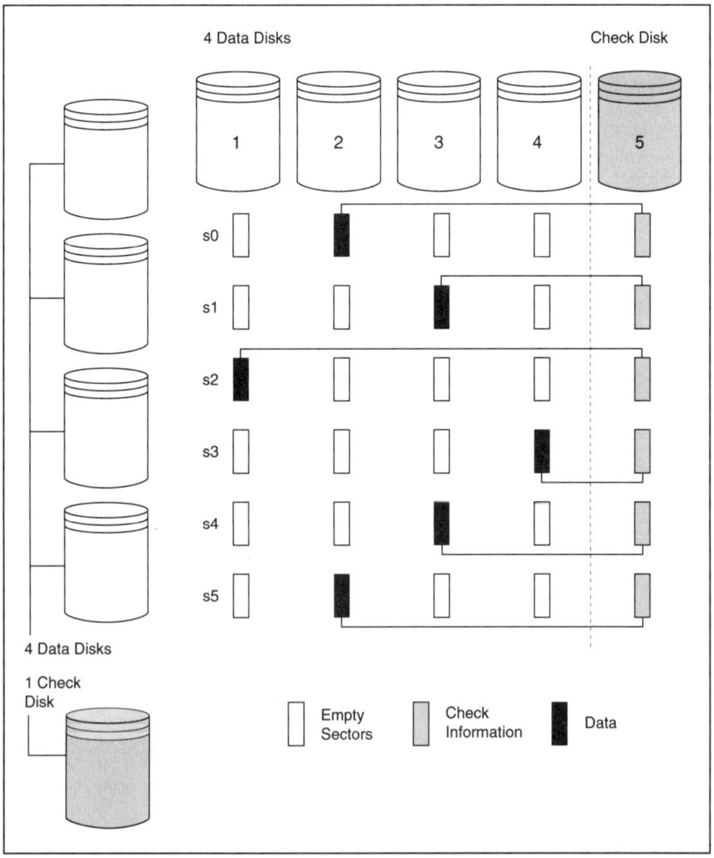

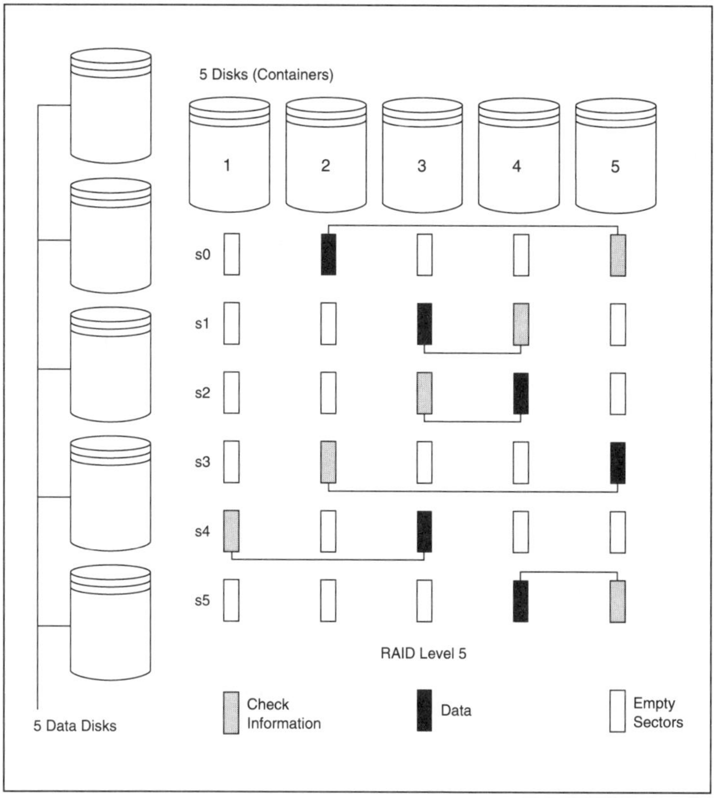

Figure 7-7.
RAID Level 5

5 files are striped by sectors as in Level 4, but unlike Level 4, no dedicated drive is required to hold ECC data. All drives serve to hold both data and ECC information. Files and their ECC information are spread over all the drives without any one drive serving as a parity drive. This eliminates the check-disk bottleneck for disk writes that the RAID 4 parity scheme introduces. Both transfer rates and accesses in a Level 5 array are higher than those of a single-drive configuration. The capacity efficiency is relatively high in RAID 5 as well, approaching 85 percent—that is, only about 15 percent of the storage is taken by ECC codes. RAID Level 5 also provides the opportunity for the disk information to be reconstructed "on the fly" should one of the drives fail.

The downside to RAID Level 5 is that it requires a special high-performance controller to be implemented. At the present time, these controllers are expensive and are typically only sold with complete drive subsystems. As a result, a 1 GB RAID Level 5 drive subsystem can cost over $10,000. That's three to four times what a single 1 GB drive costs. So while a Level 5 disk array does provide most of what the marketing guys are touting with disk arrays, that performance and reliability comes with a steep price.

A key point to keep in mind with all of these arrays is that very little of their theoretical performance gains can be realized in a DOS environment. Only a multitasking operating system such as UNIX or Novell will see any appreciable performance gain from these fancy techniques. Also, only a few of the arrays on the market are Level 5 arrays.

Also keep in mind that unless your PC includes an EISA or 32-bit Micro Channel Architecture I/O bus, your I/O bus will most likely limit your data throughput.

Now, it's clear that RAID is a wonderful idea. It allows many inexpensive drives to be substituted for a large, very expensive drive. It also introduces gains in performance because of the additional read/write heads that are brought into play, but it trades some of those performance advantages back because of the need for ECC to implement redundancy and make up for the fact that more drives means more chances for failure. (Actually, the multiple inexpensive drives versus the single large expensive drive analysis only holds up in the case of *very* large drives, for example, over 3 gigabytes, since large drives now cost less per megabyte than multiple medium-size drives. See the "Where's the *inexpensive* in RAID?" sidebar.)

But when this information got to marketing departments, a couple of things happened. Computer marketing departments realized that performance sells, so they started touting the performance advantages of RAID Levels 1 through 4, even though these drives delivered only very nominal performance increases. Also, marketing departments, not knowing the history of RAID, grasped the whole redundancy aspect and began talking about the increased reliability of these drives. Ironically, the redundancy is required merely to make availability of the system as high as it would be for a single drive. This is one of the ways that computer innovations can be twisted to the needs of the marketing and sales departments.

When implemented properly, arrays can provide better drive performance. But an effective array is an expensive array. Only RAID Level 5 delivers both better access times and higher throughput. Lower-level RAID optimizes certain aspects of disk performance while actually slowing down other aspects. Levels 2 and 3, for example, might be very good in certain scientific applications but would perform terribly in transaction processing applications. Before implementing any of the disk array techniques, it would be wise to consult further with someone who has successfully implemented that level of RAID for an application similar to yours.

Solid-State Drives

The next advanced disk optimization technique we'll discuss is one that can provide extremely high disk performance. This is the solid-state storage device, which appears to the computer as a conventional disk drive but uses semiconductor memory for storage instead of magnetic media (see Figure 7-8). The concept of the solid-state storage device (often referred to as a solid-state disk drive, even though no disk is involved) is not new—it has been around for some time.

You may ask, "Isn't this what were talking about when we referred to a RAM disk? Weren't we using memory chips to replace or imitate a disk drive?" True, but in this case we're actually installing a physical device that might as well be a standard disk drive, albeit a very fast one. The only difference is that it's comprised of memory chips as opposed to a mechanical device of a spinning plat-

Figure 7-8. This solid state drive from Imperial provides extremely fast access times.

ter with read/write heads. A RAM disk, in contrast, is only a logical device—a portion of the computer's own memory set aside to act like a drive.

What slows down hard drive performance is the fact that it's a mechanical device. You have to wait for the head to move over the proper cylinder and for the rotational latency of the drive. If you can eliminate these mechanical delays, you'll get a big gain in performance.

Why is it then that we use hard drives at all? Why don't we just use high-speed solid-state DRAM entirely? There are two reasons. DRAM storage costs far more than hard disk memory. Consider that a 100-MB hard drive costs about $400, whereas 100 MB of DRAM costs $4,000 to $10,000. The second issue is that once you shut off power to the computer, everything stored in DRAM memory is lost due to DRAM's volatility. A hard drive isn't volatile, you can shut off the power and come back weeks or months later and your data will be intact. So although DRAM is very fast, it has some major trade-offs.

Expense is a matter of how much you're willing or able to pay. If performance is what you're after and you can pay the price for that higher performance, then solid-state may be cost-effective for the task you're doing. If your work is slowed down so much by the hard disk and your time is valuable, the additional cost may be offset quickly. The problem of DRAM's volatility can be overcome either by the addition of more hardware or by additional user or software intervention. The volatile memory can be connected to a battery supply so that even if the main power is turned off, the memory still has power. Batteries have a limited life, and DRAM uses relatively large amounts of electricity, so you're looking at best at hours or days of backup.

Another way to back up solid-state memory is to use a hard disk. If you copy everything from volatile DRAM memory to nonvolatile hard disk memory, the computer can be shut down. This requires a more sophisticated system or a lot more user intervention than you may be used to. As we said at the beginning of this advanced optimization chapter, these are not techniques recommended for everyone. But sometimes there is just no other way to deliver the level of performance your system requires. Make no mistake that a solid-state disk drive can deliver very high performance in certain applications.

Let's be clear about what those applications are. The primary disadvantage of hard disk drives are the latencies introduced by its mechanical aspects. In applications or in environments that require a lot of random accesses to the drive, these mechanical delays slow users down considerably. If you have an application that's bogged down because of lots of random accesses, the solid-state disk drive could be an ideal solution to that problem. If you are looking for a higher transfer rate, then a solid-state drive is probably not the answer. Many of the solid-state drives currently available use a SCSI-1 bus. This limits their data transfer rate to 5 MB per second, which is a rate that some of the fastest mechanical drives can achieve at a far lower cost. Besides, keep in mind that 5 MB per second is probably faster than the AT bus can sustain, so you'll need to use an EISA or 32-bit Micro Channel Architecture machine.

The types of applications that best benefit from a solid-state disk drive are database and transaction processing applications where there are many random accesses to the file. Computer graphics and other types of programs that need such large amounts of main memory that even a machine equipped with the maximum amount of RAM is going to do a lot of paging to disk are also likely candidates.

Most PCs don't support more than 32 MB or 64 MB of main memory. It might seem crazy, but it's not unusual for computer graphics users doing three-dimensional modeling or rendering to exceed the 64-MB limitation of their main memory. As soon as they exceed that limitation, their machine starts paging to disk. That slows down their performance considerably because they are reading and writing small amounts of random information to and from the disk. Solid-state disk drives could help considerably.

Actually, any sort of paging environment induced by lack of main memory, is a potential candidate for solid-state disk drives.

One of the areas where solid-state drives are also used, but not for their performance, is in "hostile" environments. These environments usually include lots of vibration or dust that wouldn't be conducive to a delicate head flying incredibly low over a fast-moving platter.

What are the trade-offs of a solid-state disk? The cost. The cost of a solid-state disk drive is considerable relative to a standard drive. It may not be considerable, though, relative to the cost of the overall system if you include the cost of all the peripherals and software (some high-end software can run into the tens of thousands of dollars). Also, it may not be expensive when you consider the amount of time that you could save by having the solid-state disk drive. Finally, if a PC is being used to replace a far more expensive minicomputer system, the relative cost may not be great.

What about volatility? We mentioned there are two ways to deal with the volatility. One is battery backup, but that will only solve the problem temporarily. You can't plan on leaving information in a solid-state disk drive for an indefinite period. If you have battery backup (and typically backup on solid-state drives lasts only a matter of hours), all you're looking for is protection from power failure or intermittent shutdown of the system. You still have to save information from the solid-state drive back to a nonvolatile device.

In an environment where you're working with lots of different databases and it's only important to have fast access to a particular database at a particular time, it may be fine to store all of the data information back onto tape because you don't need fast access once you've finished a particular job. For example, a company that administers mailing lists needs to do a lot of sorts and indexes on a particular mailing list database, but then when the job is finished they can store it on tape and go on to work on the next list. Most people are uncomfortable with tape; it's relatively slow compared to disk backup. The beauty of tape, though, is that you

Flash drives

A few words about Flash memory are appropriate here, since Flash memory can be confused with the solid-state drives mentioned above. Flash memory is a technology that is very similar to standard EPROM technology. The primary difference though is that Flash memory is electrically erasable while a standard EPROM is erased by shining an ultraviolet light source on it. EPROMs and Flash memory are available in capacities of 1 MB per chip and even higher.

Flash memory is being used in applications in which data should be stored in a nonvolatile format but a disk drive is not desirable. For example, Flash memory has been used to create credit-card-size cards that store a particular program for notebooks and palmtop computers. It is also being used on special adapter cards to hold DOS and diagnostic software, as well as for special-purpose PCs.

Although Flash memory can be reprogrammed without removing it from the system, it is not attractive as a replacement for standard disk drives because it cannot be reprogrammed (that is, made to store different data) at random, as standard DRAM or a standard disk drive can. Like an EPROM device, it can store data

can turn your solid-state drive into a drive with endless capacity by off-loading the information you don't need from the solid-state drive to inexpensive tape. In contrast, if you use traditional hard disk drive as a backup to a solid-state drive, you're going to limit your capacity to how many hard drives you can afford.

If you're using your solid-state drive for the type of graphic work mentioned earlier, you may not have to back up that drive at all. It may be sufficient that you have battery life for a few hours (in case of a power failure) and that you can use your drive capacity to do some file swapping while you do some calculations or data manipulation.

Once you're finished with the application, all that memory may have been erased anyway. For example, when a program that pages to disk is finished, it erases from the disk all the data that it was paging back and forth, so you do not need to back up everything when you use this type of program.

When is a solid-state disk drive not appropriate? Whenever you can't afford it, for one. Also be aware that solid-state drives are not going to buy you any

---

only a whole chip at a time. This means that to update a single byte on the Flash memory chip, everything on the chip must be erased and rewritten. This requires special file handling and is much slower than a randomly programmable device like a DRAM chip. As a result, Flash memory is not a good choice for use in a solid-state disk if performance is the goal.

Bottom line: Flash memory is appropriate when you don't intend to change what you're storing. For example, it's fine for the boot disk of a dedicated computer in a security system or a point-of-sale terminal. In these cases, the computer accesses the contents during boot, an operation Flash can perform relatively quickly, and you won't have to worry about an inexperienced user inadvertently overwriting the memory (by accidentally formatting the hard drive).

Flash memory is becoming popular for use in PCs instead of a standard EPROM for holding the system BIOS. By using Flash memory in this application, you can update BIOS at any time without having to remove and replace the EPROM chip(s) that normally store the BIOS. The new BIOS can be distributed on a floppy disk or by modem. So Flash is an interesting and useful new technology, but it probably doesn't have a place in improving system performance.

---

performance gain in an environment that requires a lot of large file transfers—your performance will be limited by the data transfer rate of the drive interface. Even though there are some solid-state drives coming out with a SCSI-2 interface, which allows for data transfer rates of up to 10 MB per second, the same transfer rate that can be achieved by the highest-performance mechanical disk drives at a far lower price. In general, if you're looking for high data transfer rates, mechanical drives can probably serve you just as well as solid-state drives, at far less cost and with fewer problems.

Parallel Transfer Drives

What if you're looking for high-speed data transfers without a lot of random accesses? This situation is commonly found in applications of medical imaging, for example, where you have very large image files of 20 MB or higher that you need to manipulate fast. Geologic work also requires wholesale manipulation of large files. As mentioned, solid-state drives are not the answer because, as fast as they are, their throughput is still limited to the throughput rate of the disk interface.

There are two solutions to high-data transfer: the RAID configurations we discussed, or parallel transfer drives (Figure 7-9).

Parallel transfer drives are leading edge technology. And, unless you have very large files and a very large budget to move those files around, parallel transfer drives are not for you. However, if you need to move very large files at a very

Figure 7-9. A Seagate parallel drive. This exotic drive provides the highest transfer rate possible in a single drive at 27 MB per second.

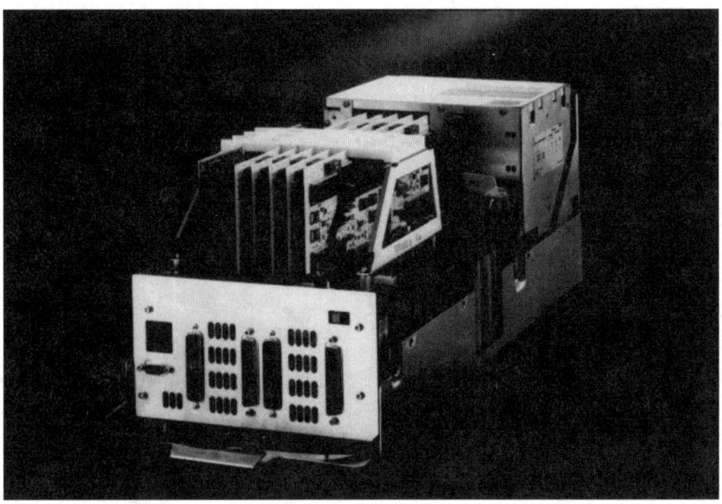

high rate of speed, then a parallel transfer drive, or a drive array that emulates parallel transfer drives, can be useful.

If you think back to the limitation of your disk drive transfer rate (it's the size of a sector times the number of sectors on a track times the speed that the drive spins), you can see that it's a pretty solid limit. One head simply cannot transfer more data at a time. Making the drive spin faster or getting more sectors per track would achieve a higher data transfer rate, but the practical limit here is about 5,400 rpm and 100 sectors per track.

On the other hand, the construction of a typical mechanical drive includes multiple heads and multiple platters. If it could read from some or all of those heads at the same time, you could increase the data transfer rate considerably. And that's the concept behind a parallel transfer drive. A parallel transfer drive reads from multiple heads at the same time. Reading from two heads should be twice as fast as one, reading from four heads should be four times as fast, and reading from eight heads should be eight times as fast.

The highest-performing drive currently available reads from nine heads at once to achieve a data transfer rate of 27 MB per second. This is not a typical PC drive; it's a large 8-inch drive that has a lot of exotic electronics and uses an IPI-2 bus (a nonstandard interface). Some parallel transfer drives include an SCSI-2 interface, and some drive configurations imitate a parallel transfer; for example, Storage Concepts has multiple drives configured together that can achieve a 10 MB per second data transfer rate (see Figure 7-10).

Figure 7-10. This Storage Concepts array can sustain transfer rates of at least 10 MB per minute.

Summary

If you're performing a large number of relatively small accesses, the highest-performance method would be the solid-state disk drives. If the expense or additional work of a solid-state drive isn't appealing, you should choose a very fast access drive (one with both a low seek time and low rotational latency). If you're moving very large files, you can use a parallel transfer drive or one of the disk arrays, but they may not have fast random access.

Before you invest big money on a solid-state disk drive, a parallel transfer drive, or a drive array, keep in mind what you're trying to accomplish. All of these techniques can improve your performance, but they're very expensive, so make sure you're applying them to an application where you'll get some bang for the buck.

For example, you could spend $5,000 for a solid-state disk drive and notice that your Windows application runs at the same speed it did on your $1,000 disk drive with a large disk cache. Alternatively, you can spend $20,000 for a disk array system only to realize your database is running at the same speed or even slower than it did on your fast $1,000 drive. Therefore, make sure you're using the appropriate optimization technique for your task.

In some cases, disk caching will handle the problem without the need for anything exotic, but remember that disk caches typically cache disk reads and not disk writes. To the extent that your program is bottlenecked by disk writes, solid-state disk drives or parallel transfer drives are going to be a big improvement over cache.

Because these advanced techniques are high-ticket items, you can usually get a considerable amount of support from vendors. They probably have no interest in sending you down the wrong track, so if you discuss your particular application with them, they should be able to tell you the most appropriate method for solving your problem. Chances are they've dealt with other individuals who have had similar problems, and they can point you in the right direction. Seek additional advice, however, before investing thousands of dollars in exotic drive solutions.

CHAPTER EIGHT

Video Performance

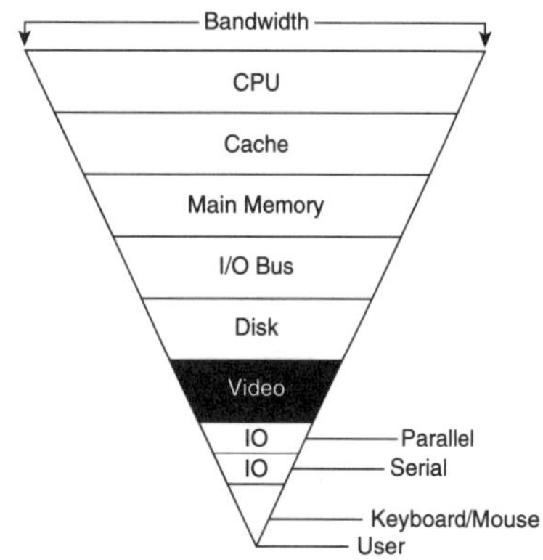

Data Funnel

Although normally only a fraction of your PC's time is devoted to video output, its video subsystem's performance has a disproportionately large effect on how fast the computer feels. After almost every operation, the computer responds with some visual cue. No matter how long the operation took, if that visual cue appears slowly, the computer will feel slow. Conversely, if the cue is displayed quickly, the computer will feel fast.

The PC's video performance is slow relative to the rest of the system, as a glance at the data funnel will tell you, in part because video is normally connected to the slow I/O bus and in part because the computer must translate data from its native, low-level format of bits and bytes to a much higher-level set of symbols that humans can understand. The amount of information the computer must manipulate to draw the symbols we choose to display has a significant impact on the PC's video performance.

The best apparent video performance is achieved when a limited number of prestored monochrome characters are displayed on the screen. This traditional display mode consists of 80 columns by 25 rows of alphanumeric characters. Most PCs can display such a screen rapidly; even adding colors doesn't appreciably slow a character display. Far slower is a *graphical user interface* (GUI), which consists of a complex mix of boxes, characters, and icons composed in multiple colors from hundreds of thousands, even millions of pixels. Drawing a wire frame of a complex image is even slower than a GUI, and slower still is a three-dimensional rendering of complex objects (such as shadows and reflections created by multiple light sources).

The word *apparent* at the beginning of the last paragraph is very important. To improve video performance, we must first make sure the bottleneck is in fact in the video system. Indeed, when the computer is rendering a complex model with many light sources, the bottleneck is not in the video subsystem at all. In fact, the video system could display the image in a fraction of a second, but it's receiving the image very slowly from the CPU and the math coprocessor (which is determining what the image should look like).

Character Mode Versus GUI

If we ran all our programs in character mode, the mode in which most programs operated until the acceptance of GUIs, we wouldn't need faster video. Character mode is a relatively efficient way for the computer to display information because the screen is divided into an invisible framework of boxes called *character cells*. These cells represent the only places characters can appear on the screen. The most common framework for a character display is 80 columns by 25 rows—in other words, 25 lines with up to 80 characters per line (see Figure 8-1).

While that may seem like a lot of space, it only amounts to 2,000 characters on the screen at one time. Also, video output is relatively fast when confined to characters; even a slow PC can display characters on the screen faster than we can read them, so character displays are rarely a significant system bottleneck.

Figure 8-1.
An 80-column-by-25-row display

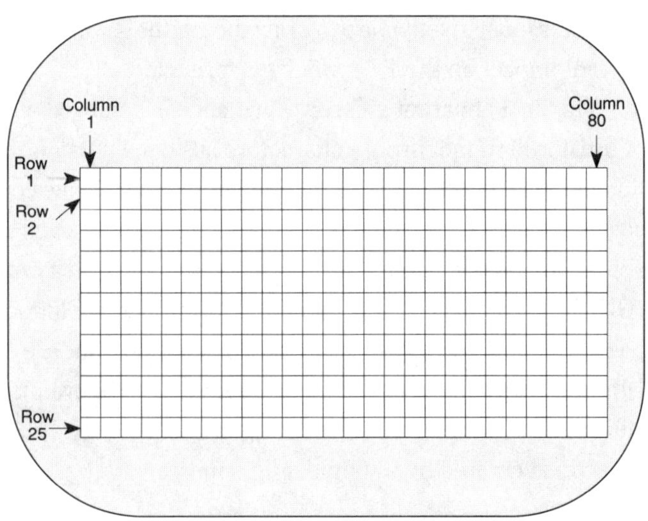

Figure 8-2.
A simple polygon. (One drawing is worth how many words?)

If you think character-mode video is too slow on your system, try using shadow ROM (discussed later in this chapter).

The problem with character mode is that it isn't always the best way to display information. It's much easier to understand a concept by looking at an image than by reading text. Imagine how much text it might take to explain a simple polygon like the one in Figure 8-2. The polygon is five-sided with three sides of equal length but one side is, well, sort of shortened by a segment that crosses at an angle and....You get the point.

The more complex the image, the more difficult it becomes to explain with text. That's why having a way to view images as well as text on our displays is desirable. The earliest PC display adapters did have a way of displaying graphics on the screen—the original IBM Color Graphics Adapter (CGA) for low-resolution color displays and then the Hercules Graphics Card for monochrome displays. The fact that the Hercules card quickly replaced the IBM character-only Monochrome Display Adapter to become the de facto monochrome standard for PCs was an indication of the demand for the ability to display graphics as well as text. The low-resolution CGA card was later replaced by the Enhanced Graphics Adapter (EGA), which offered higher-resolution color graphics display.

This movement from character displays to graphics displays introduced a bottleneck into the PC's video system. While the character display was normally limited to 2,000 characters on the screen at a time, the graphics adapters had to display many thousands of separate pixels. In fact, the EGA display had to display and control as many as 224,000 individual pixels at once. The image on a graphics screen is composed of individually manipulated pixels, while the character screen is composed of blocks of pixels. Moreover, those blocks are prestored and ready to be displayed, while in graphics mode each pixel must be individually placed in the display buffer before being displayed.

In other words, video adapter cards like the EGA are *frame buffers*; that is, they contain memory where an image is stored prior to being displayed. Most of the work involved in creating the image stored in the frame is done by the CPU itself. The video card's responsibility is to get the stored image onto the screen after the CPU has helped it create the image in its buffer.

EGA was eventually superseded by VGA, which had slightly higher resolution and many more colors. When manufacturers introduced super VGA cards with higher resolutions (1,024 x 768 and even more colors), that meant more bytes for the display system to deal with. But until users started taking advantage of the graphics abilities of their cards, there was still relatively little need to speed graphics performance. There were exceptions, of course. For example, expensive cards were developed to speed video performance for graphic applications like CAD and desktop publishing. But the average user continued to use the graphics adapter in text mode except for the occasional chart or graph.

The popularity of GUIs has changed all that. With GUIs, users spend most of their time in graphics mode rather than character mode, and the bottleneck brought on by the need to manipulate all the pixels of the graphical display becomes significant.

Unlike text mode, with its constraints on the number and types of characters that can appear on the screen, a GUI requires the computer to manipulate the pixels in an infinite variety of ways. But most of the manipulations actually involve moving blocks of pixels and drawing lines, which a normal CPU has no special optimized instructions to perform. Yet the CPU must still perform the work.

The CPU

After the preceding discussion, you won't be surprised to learn that one of the most effective ways to boost PC video performance is to upgrade to a faster CPU. Once again, the video subsystem is a storage place for video information—a frame buffer—and a channel through which the video information flows and is ultimately displayed. It depends heavily on the CPU to fill the buffer with properly arranged data. That is, the faster the CPU, the faster the data is ready to be displayed.

Thus I'd like to point out that video performance can be improved dramatically by going from, say, a 286 running at 12 MHz to a 386 running at 33 MHz. If that seems a little drastic just to improve video, keep in mind that a faster CPU will also contribute to higher performance in other areas of the system. It can even improve disk subsystem performance if you're using motherboard memory for a disk cache or RAM disk.

But you can get an even bigger performance boost—even if you already have a 386- or 486-based system—by going to a special-purpose video coprocessor.

Graphics Coprocessors

Because a standard microprocessor like a 386 or 486 is designed to be general-purpose, it's proficient at many kinds of operations but not a speed burner for any particular specialized function. One of the functions it's not especially adept at is the creation of screen images. Besides, when the CPU is tied up performing various display duties, it can't be doing any other type of computing. If we had another processor to help the CPU perform its graphics functions, it could improve our video display speed while simultaneously freeing up the CPU to do more of the tasks it's better at.

A coprocessor is designed to enhance the processing power of the CPU. Because coprocessors are designed specifically to optimize certain types of operations, they can outperform the CPU at certain tasks. In Chapter 2, we discussed specialized coprocessors designed to enhance mathematical operations. In this chapter, we'll look at specialized coprocessors designed to assist the CPU with graphics functions. These graphics coprocessors have been incorporated in PC graphics cards to speed up the PC's video display.

It's important to be aware that a PC graphics card may include a coprocessor and run a particular piece of software without the software being able to take advantage of the coprocessor. Before buying an expensive graphics adapter that you hope will run a particular application faster, ask the retailer how much faster program X will run while executing operation Y if you add card Z to your system. Just as disk arrays are often positioned as disk performance enhancers when they're really disk availability enhancers, graphics cards can appear to enhance performance when they actually enhance resolution or some other feature but run the application at the same speed as before. Nothing is wrong with spending money on a card to get higher resolution or some other feature; if you're buying for performance, however, make sure that's what you're getting.

The Texas Instruments 34010

The most commonly used coprocessor for PC video cards is the Texas Instruments 34010. This coprocessor was designed specifically to off-load graphics functions from the CPU. Because it was designed to optimize a limited number of instructions, it can execute those instructions faster than the general-purpose CPU it assists. In most versions, the 34010 runs at a higher clock speed than the CPU (as fast as 60 MHz).

The 34010 also has a big brother, the 34020. The 34020 is similar to the 34010 but is considerably faster. Its cache is twice the size of the 34010's, and it has a 32-bit data bus compared to the 16-bit data bus of the 34010. Because the 34020 is more expensive than the 34010, expect to see it only in the more expensive ($1,000 and up) graphics adapters.

Considerable controversy exists over whether the 340x0 family is as good a graphics accelerator for Windows as some of the other graphics accelerator chips. The 34010 and 34020 deliver very good Windows performance in all areas except text scrolling.

Be aware that the 34010 and 34020 don't include VGA support, which means if you use an accelerator card based on a 340x0, you still have to use a VGA adapter when you're not running a program that card supports. You can plug a special VGA card into some of the 340x0-based cards, while others have a special connector, called a *VGA passthrough*, for connecting a standard VGA card and letting it take over when a program doesn't have a software driver that enables it to take advantage of the 340x0-based card.

The i860

Intel's i860 is a strange beast. This very high-performance processor can deliver both integer and floating-point performance at levels even higher than the 486 itself.

The i860 also has been used as the basis of many high-performance graphics coprocessor boards. Although it has many graphics-specific instructions, it's generally used for its extremely high floating-point performance rather than its special graphics capabilities. Most of the graphics cards that use the i860 are expensive, and all require that software be written specifically to take advantage of it. If your applications can take advantage of the i860 as a coprocessor, you may want to take a serious look at a card that uses it.

However, don't assume that just because a particular video adapter's literature claims that the adapter will support a particular program that it will make the program run any faster. To see if the adapter will really speed up a particular program's performance, check with the technical support department of either the developer of the program or the manufacturer of the adapter (or both). As mentioned previously, a technical support department is much more likely to give you a straight (and knowledgeable) answer than the marketing department.

Graphics Accelerators

A certain class of increasingly popular graphics accelerator chips can be thought of as graphics coprocessors even though they don't fit the true definition of a processor. To be a true processor (or coprocessor), a device must be programmable. The 34010 and 34020 are programmable. The i860 is programmable. IBM's 8514/A chip and its clones are not programmable; they're designed to function only under the tight control of the CPU.

Until recently, it wasn't feasible to design and manufacture such a chip. In addition to making a chip that allowed the CPU to perform graphics operations faster than the standard VGA chips, it was also desirable to design chips that could support higher resolutions than the standard VGA or the older EGA. Because chip designers had no standards to follow, there was no way to ensure that a new chip would be compatible with other similar chips that provided higher resolutions.

It might seem that some of the gross characteristics of higher resolution versions of VGA have been collected together under the super VGA (SVGA) banner, but even when resolutions are the same there are still differences in the underlying hardware. (In actuality, any VGA-compatible adapter with resolutions higher than the highest standard VGA resolution of 640 x 480 is referred to as *super VGA*.)

These differences must be masked with software, called a *driver*, which sits between the video adapter and each particular piece of application software, translating generic graphic descriptions into the specific instructions understood by the video adapter.

Creating a driver was an arduous programming task because one had to be written for nearly every piece of software. And as each new version of the software came along, the drivers had to be updated. This was a major hindrance to advancing video standards with specialized graphics accelerator chips.

The wide acceptance of Windows has changed all that. Programs written to run under Windows must conform to Windows' method of displaying the

What is super VGA?

The term super VGA is frequently seen in advertisements, articles, and even books like this one; yet, it is rare to see a definition of super VGA. That's because there is no such thing as a super VGA standard.

The VGA standard, like the EGA standard before it, was set by IBM. When IBM introduces a new product, it generally becomes a de facto standard. IBM's market presence is sufficient to make almost anything it produces into a standard. This is not a formal process, and in fact, IBM usually tries to delay the proliferation of its de facto standards as long as possible. That's because as soon as a product becomes a standard, other companies try to make a compatible product that sells for less than the IBM version. In fact, not only do such products sell for less, they usually include additional features. This was exactly the case with the so-called super VGA standard.

When IBM introduced the PS/2 line of computers in 1987, it also introduced a new graphics standard called Video Graphics Array, or VGA. Because the new VGA standard provided higher text resolution than the previous EGA

screen image, leading to the creation of a standard. The graphics card manufacturers now can cope with a high percentage of programs for which users want high performance video by making their products work with the Windows environment; all software designed to run under Windows is then supported. Not only did this simplify life for the card manufacturers, it enabled computer users to use a graphics adapter without having to worry about drivers for all the programs they wanted to run.

Of course, there are still a few major programs that need video acceleration but don't run under Windows (the non-Windows version of AutoCAD is the prime example), but manufacturers are usually able to deal with the major exceptions by continuing to write special drivers for them.

standard (640 x 480 pixels vs. 640 x 350 pixels with EGA) and a larger color palette (as many as 256,000 colors), the VGA standard quickly began replacing the EGA standard.

In order to differentiate their products, the third-party card manufacturers immediately set about extending the new VGA standard. They offered higher resolutions and a larger number of colors. Some of them began calling their cards super VGA, and many other manufacturers followed suit and the name stuck.

But what does the super VGA label mean? Simply that a card is capable of VGA display with additional resolutions beyond the standard VGA pixel or color resolutions. So while one video card manufacturer's idea of super VGA is 800 x 600 pixels resolution with 16 colors, another's is 640 x 480 pixels resolution with 256 colors, and a third might claim that 1,024 x 768 pixels with 256 colors is super VGA. And they are all right, because the term super VGA is essentially meaningless.

When a computer seller claims a computer or card or monitor supports super VGA, all you really know is that it supports resolutions beyond the standard VGA shipped by IBM. This means that nearly every VGA card that is being sold these days is a super VGA.

PGC

IBM's engineers realized early on that there was a need for accelerated graphics on the PC so they developed the Professional Graphics Controller (PGC). While this adapter, which was introduced in the mid 1980's, did offer improved PC graphics performance it was extremely expensive. The adapter was a three-card set which cost nearly $3,000 and the special monitor required to accompany the adapter cost almost as much. Application developers were required to write special drivers in order for their software to be able to take advantage of the adapter. These facts combined with the fact that the resolution of PGC was not particularly high, it's maximum was only 640 x 480, prevented the PGC from ever catching on as a popular standard.

The 8514/A

IBM's second effort at accelerating PC graphics was the 8514/A adapter, introduced in 1987. The 8514/A, now called simply the 8514, is probably much more important for its clones than it will ever be in its own right. It had two major shortcomings: it didn't support standard VGA resolutions (640 x 480, 16 colors), and its high-resolution mode could only support an interlaced display.

The fact that the 8514 didn't include VGA support meant that a PC would need both a VGA adapter and an 8514 adapter. It couldn't have an 8514 alone because that adapter didn't support DOS. The reasoning was clear enough. This was 1987 and IBM expected everyone to purchase a PS/2 computer, which already had VGA support built in on the motherboard, so there was no need to buy two graphics cards, as IBM saw it. The fact that 8514, as originally implemented by IBM, only included an interlaced 1,024 x 768 resolution was the more serious oversight.

These two shortcomings, combined with the relatively high cost of IBM's 8514 adapter and its accompanying monitor, prevented the IBM 8514 adapter from being adopted as a standard. In mid-1991 IBM announced that it would no longer make or market the 8514 adapter. However, the fact that IBM's version of the 8514 did not catch on doesn't mean the 8514 didn't have an impact on the market. The graphics adapter manufacturers saw that the 8514 did have some desirable features. The 8514 adapter offered a significant performance boost to software that had drivers for it.

Interlaced versus noninterlaced

Why is a card that displays in noninterlaced mode preferable to one that uses an interlaced display? An interlaced display has a slight flicker because only half of an image is displayed at a time. In other words, a 1,024-line display has 512 odd lines and 512 even lines; in noninterlaced display, all the lines are displayed in one pass, starting at the top and going down the screen. In an interlaced display, the odd and even lines are sent to the display in alternating passes. While the entire screen is visible at one time, our eyes can discern a slight flicker as the two sets of lines are alternately displayed. An interlaced display is most obvious when thin horizontal lines are present on the screen—they'll actually seem to vibrate slightly.

The flicker is barely noticeable when the image has no horizontal lines, but you might notice a small amount of ghosting when any image moves on an interlaced display. An interlaced display's phosphors (the material on the screen that glows when excited by the beam of the display tube's "guns") are designed to glow longer between excitations to allow the alternating images of the odd and even lines to blend into one.

Nearly all display adapters and monitors are noninterlaced in resolutions below 1,024. At 1,024 and above, only some adapters and cards will operate in noninterlaced mode.

The graphics adapter manufacturers developed cards that bettered the performance of IBM's 8514, in part by including noninterlaced display at 1,024 x 768 resolution and VGA support. A few of these adapters are shipped as 8514 clones, but most manufacturers of 8514 clones have dropped the 8514 name and any attempt to be compatible with it, and they have repositioned their products as GUI accelerators.

8514/A clones and work-alikes

A number of cards on the market based on graphics accelerator chips have been specifically designed to speed graphics performance under Windows (see Chapter 11 for more detail). These chips are being made by many companies, including S3, Weitek, ATI, Western Digital (Paradise), Chips and Technologies, and others.

Fortunately for users, the intense competition and the sudden increase in the size of the market for video acceleration brought on by the popularity of

S3 '911 Accelerators

Among the fastest of the video accelerator cards are the ones equipped with S3's 86C911 chip. Yes, S3 is the name of the company, but people usually call them S3 cards because who can remember 86C911, although the Porsche-like number may help. Indeed, the chip's code name was Carrera.

The first notable product based on S3's 911 was Orchid's Fahrenheit 1280 board, but now S3 claims that more than 60 vendors are using their chip.

An S3 card routinely runs ten times faster than a video card that relies solely on the main CPU for graphic manipulations. While you won't get a ten-times overall performance improvement by just speeding video, it will certainly make a difference in the how fast an environment like Windows feels.

The S3 chip includes a so-called hardware blitter (a blit is a block of pixels), and thus can move blocks of pixels (like a window, for example) around the screen very quickly.

Not only does the S3 chip free up CPU time, it avoids moving lots of data through that relatively narrow point in the data funnel, the I/O bus.

What should you expect to pay for S3 cards? About $100 more than an ordinary super VGA card, although with the huge volume of Windows users that will install some sort of Windows accelerator and the clear emergence of the S3 as a performance leader, it's possible that the price differential could fall.

Another factor in prices is the amount of on-board video memory. You need a full megabyte of VRAM (which is faster than DRAM) to handle 32,768 colors at 640 x 480, and to achieve best performance at 800 x 600 or 1,024 x 768 modes. One thing to remember, too. If you need to be able to display colors with photo realism, the S3 boards aren't for you. For that you need a 24- or 32-bit color board and a lot more than 1 MB of video memory.

Windows has caused the price of boards based on these chips to be reasonably priced. In fact it is now possible to purchase graphics accelerator cards for about what a good VGA card used to cost, that is $250 to $450.

The cards, which are usually called Windows accelerators or GUI accelerators, are available from all major PC video card manufacturers as well as many minor ones.

If you are considering buying one of these cards, you need to be aware that not all of them include standard VGA support. This is not an issue if you already have a VGA adapter in your system. But if you are configuring a new system or are using an EGA or monochrome system, you'll need to make sure that you have VGA as well as accelerated graphics support. Otherwise, you won't be able to run non-Windows applications.

The relative merits and features of these cards will continue to be one of the most popular subjects of product reviews in PC publications over the coming months. But beware of buying products based on reviews in magazines. Make sure the reviewer is using a card configured for the same resolution and number of colors that you intend to use. Magazine reviewers have a tendency to review graphics adapters in the highest resolution modes, while many readers will be buying the cards for use in lower resolution. This is because most reviewers have access to large (expensive) monitors that can take advantage of the high resolution modes, while most users don't.

Even more important, beware of benchmark results. The benchmark results for many of these accelerated graphics cards are going to be unbelievably fast. Some of these cards can run the benchmarks as much as 20 times faster than a VGA card. Does that mean that Windows will run 20 times faster if you install one of these cards? Absolutely not. Certain Windows' operations will run much faster, but it's highly unlikely that a graphics card alone could speed Windows up even two or three times. On the other hand, certain operations will be much faster, and, most important, your perception will be that Windows is running much faster. These cards can make Windows "pop" onto the screen instead of being slowly painted on.

XGA

In 1990, IBM introduced yet another accelerated graphics standard for PCs—the XGA, which offered more color depth than the earlier 8514 and made up for the 8514's lack of VGA support. Although IBM has announced that it's interested in making XGA a graphics standard for all PCs, not just IBM's PS/2s, it seems unlikely that XGA, as implemented by IBM, will become a widespread standard.

Besides not supporting noninterlaced monitors in 1,024 mode, the original implementation of XGA was designed specifically for 32-bit Micro-Channel–based computers. And while IBM has stated its willingness to work with third parties in developing XGA for PCs that aren't Micro-Channel–based, it's unclear when that will happen. For those with 32-bit Micro-Channel–based computers, XGA may be a good (albeit expensive) accelerated graphics solution. For those with a PC based on the AT or EISA bus, one of the other accelerated graphics solutions would be a better choice.

VGA Adapters

Even though VGA cards are heavily dependent on the CPU for their operation, they nevertheless have a noticeable impact on video performance. The latest generation of VGA chips uses a number of tricks to allow the CPU to work faster. The CPU still does most of the work, but the best VGA cards let it work more efficiently.

Cards that incorporate the ET-4000 VGA chip from Tseng Labs generally outperform the other VGA cards. The ET-4000 includes on-board cache memory. Caches, as we've seen, can be very effective at improving performance.

A VGA card frequently cited as having high performance is the Speed STAR from Diamond. This card is widely available, inexpensive, and includes good driver support. Like most of the cards based on the ET-4000 chip, the Speed STAR can support resolutions as high as 1,024 x 768 with 256 simultaneous colors. (All VGA cards, regardless of brand, will require 1 MB of on-board memory to support the 1,024 x 768 modes with 256 colors. Most VGA cards allow you to buy the card with 512 KB and add another 512 KB later.)

8-bit versus 16-bit VGA cards

One of the more confusing aspects of PC graphics is the reference to the number of bits the card supports. For example, you might hear about a 16-bit VGA card that supports 8-bit color. Two aspects of a graphics adapter can be measured in bits: the bus interface, which is either 8 or 16 bits, and the color palette or pixel depth, which can be 4, 8, 16, or 24 bits. We'll discuss the bus interface first.

The first VGA cards, like the EGA cards before them, were designed with 8-bit bus interfaces. That means that although these cards could be plugged into the standard 16-bit AT bus, they could only send and receive data over the bus 8 bits at a time. This 8-bit bus interface soon proved to be a bottleneck to video performance and, as second-generation and later VGA cards were introduced, was redesigned to support the entire 16 bits of the AT bus. If you're using an EGA or VGA card with an 8-bit bus interface, you should notice faster video performance if you upgrade to a VGA adapter with a 16-bit bus interface.

Bits and color palette

Where do these color bits come in? The number of bits in the color palette refers to how many colors the card can display, generally two to the power of the number of bits. For example, a card with a 4-bit color palette has 2^4 (16) colors. A card with 8-bit color would have 2^8 (256) colors. Those are the typical numbers of colors found on VGA cards, but some cards have higher resolutions as well.

Many of the latest VGA cards can now display as many as 32,768 or 65,536 colors, a huge advance over the original maximum of 256 colors. This new support is known as *hi-color.* These cards can display the additional colors thanks to an enhanced version of a special chip called a *RAMDAC* (a digital-to-analog converter with RAM). The VGA card uses a RAMDAC to translate digital information from the computer to analog information that the monitor can display. The RAM holds a lookup table, which the card needs to translate the colors from digital bits into analog colors. The availability of low-cost RAMDACs that support the hi-color modes and require little, if any, modification to existing VGA designs enables manufacturers to offer cards that support hi-color for only a slight increment over the cost of standard 256-color VGA cards.

Cards with a 16-bit color palette have 32,768 colors, and cards with 24-bit color palettes have 16.7 million possible colors. These hi-color cards have 16-bit color. Cards with 24-bit color are called *true-color.*

(If you're quick with math, you might have blanched at the above paragraph when you realized that 2^{16} is actually 65,536, not 32,768. The reason for the discrepancy is that the standard for 16-bit color is 15 color bits and one bit for overlay. Therefore, a card with 16-bit color actually devotes 15 bits to color.)

Some of the very high-end graphics adapters actually have 32-bit color depth. The Truevision Targa 16/32+ is an example of this type of card. These cards don't actually display any more colors than the 16.7 million colors of a 24-bit card. They use the additional 8 bits for something called the *alpha channel.* This is special transparency information used by certain programs when compositing images on top of one another.

Remember, don't confuse 8- and 16-bit color with references to a graphics adapter as an 8- or 16-bit card, which will usually have to do with the bus interface. Unfortunately, there is no widely-accepted manner of determining from name alone whether 8-bit or 16-bit refers to the interface bus width, or

Which monitor do you use?

There are two primary concerns when choosing a monitor: compatibility with your video card and the quality of the display.

If you're satisfied with standard VGA displays, you can get a fixed frequency monitor cheaply. If you want to use super VGA and other higher-resolution cards, you'll need a multiple frequency or multiscan monitor (although there's a technical difference between the terms, the bottom-line difference is insignificant in practical terms).

In general, high-frequency monitors are better, and there are two frequencies to worry about: the frame rate and the line rate. The frame rate (the number of images that appear on screen per second) has an impact on whether you'll perceive flicker or not. Especially in the paper-white backgrounds common when running Windows, you'll find anything lower than a 70-hertz (Hz) frame rate seems to flicker.

The second frequency, line rate, determines how high a resolution the monitor can display at a given frame rate. Displaying regular 640 x 480 VGA resolution at a 70-Hz frame rate requires a line rate of only 31.5 KHz. However, the line frequency goes up with resolution, so you'll need 48 KHz to achieve a 72-Hz frame rate at 800 x 600. That same 48 KHz monitor will achieve 1024 x 768 resolution at a 60-Hz frame rate, but at this lower frame rate you'll begin to notice flicker. Raise the refresh rate to a steadier 72-Hz image, and a 58 KHz line rate is required to handle a 1,024 x 768 display.

the color depth, or both. Also, don't infer that because a card with a 16-bit bus interface is faster than a card with an 8-bit bus interface that a card with 16-bit color is also faster than a card with 8-bit color. There's actually a slight performance penalty for displaying the extra pixels that increase the number of available colors.

1,024 x 768 resolution

The driving force behind the move toward more features in PC products is the manufacturers' need to differentiate their products from each other. This has led to better performance and more memory, colors, and pixels. It also has

Be especially wary of achieving higher resolution by going to an interlaced display, in which lines 1, 3, and 5 are drawn in one pass while a second scan draws lines 2, 4, and 6. An interlaced display has an intense flicker.

Another specification to consider, dot pitch, depends on the resolution displayed and the screen size. Putting more dots on screen requires either a tighter pitch or a bigger screen. For VGA on a 14-inch monitor, a dot pitch of 0.31 mm will be sharp; putting a 800 x 600 super VGA image on the same monitor will require 0.28 mm to seem sharp. Keep dot pitch in mind, because it's not uncommon to find inexpensive VGA monitors with dot pitch courser than 0.50 mm.

Remember that as the size of a monitor increases, so does the size of the character it displays (and the fineness of details it displays) in a graphical environment like Windows. In other words, higher resolution boards squeeze more small characters onto your display—they don't simply make the same image crisper. But if you increase the size of your monitor, as resolution increases you can compensate for that shrinking of the size of characters displayed on screen. It turns out that a character stays approximately the same size if you match a standard 640 x 480 VGA card to a 14-inch monitor, an 800 x 600 super VGA card to a 16-inch monitor, and a 1024 x 768 display on a 19-inch monitor.

From strictly a performance standpoint, a monitor has no effect on performance. The performance terminology that is associated with monitors applies only to ergonomics, not to how fast your application will run.

lead to higher and higher resolutions. The original EGA standard had 640 x 350 resolution. The first EGA clone cards offered 800 x 600. The first VGA clones had 800 x 600 resolution, but some soon offered 1,024 x 768 resolution. Now some cards offer 1,280 x 1,064 resolution and better.

But bigger doesn't always mean better. When we increase the screen resolution from 640 x 480 to 800 x 600 and then to 1,024 x 768, our applications decrease the size of what is displayed on the screen. The block of bits that made up a character in 640 x 480 mode might be 0.25 inch high, while in 1,024 x 768 mode only 0.15 inch is necessary to display the same block of pixels.

If when we increase resolution we also increase our monitor size from 14 inches to 19 inches, that's a different story. If we're staying with a standard 14-inch monitor, however, I don't think there's any advantage in going to 1,024 x 768 resolution. Some might argue that it allows us to display more applications under Windows at the same time. Sure—but you generally only work with one application at a time anyway, and don't you want to be able to read it?

Also consider that to support the higher resolution we need more memory on our graphics adapter—at least 1 MB—and probably a new monitor as well.

Finally, don't forget about the performance hit you'll probably experience as you increase resolution. A 640 x 480 display has 300,000 pixels to move around, while a 1,024 x 768 display has more than 780,000 pixels.

Shadow ROM

We have seen that one way to improve computer performance is to move data and instructions from the lower part of the data funnel into the higher, faster sections. One of the bottlenecks of standard video is the slow read-only memory (ROM) chip(s) on video adapter cards. These chips, which hold the video BIOS, slow the CPU's access to the video software. Access is further slowed because the software on the adapter cards is continually sending and receiving instructions over the slow I/O bus to and from the CPU.

(Hold it. What does BIOS stand for? BIOS stands for Basic Input Output Software. This special software controls low-level operations of the system or its peripherals. The video BIOS contains many of the instructions the CPU uses to control the video adapter and display information on the screen. Technically speaking, the video card doesn't have a BIOS; it has what's known as *firmware*. Firmware is software that is stored in nonvolatile memory like ROM.

Since most people refer to the video firmware as the video BIOS, I'll adhere to that convention.)

If you could store the BIOS in fast motherboard memory, much of the bottleneck caused by the slow speed of the video ROM would be alleviated. We can do this in a couple of ways. Some PCs have a feature that allows you to "shadow" this video BIOS—that is, move it from slow ROM memory into fast motherboard memory. PCs that include built-in support for shadow video ROM normally have a provision to enable this feature in the system's setup software. Those that don't have built-in support for shadow video ROM—in other words, most PCs—might be able to use software that came with the video card. One of these special programs, normally called something like RAMBIOS.SYS or RAMBIOS.COM, must be included as a line in your CONFIGSYS file (if it has a .SYS extension) or in your AUTOEXEC.BAT file (if it has a .COM extension).

Once shadow ROM is enabled, most of the video BIOS instructions the CPU requires are called from fast motherboard memory instead of slow ROM on the video card. Enabling this feature can have a noticeable effect on some of the video operations. Ordinary DOS commands, such as a DIR command issued from the prompt, should run much faster. You should see your screen scroll much more quickly than before, and some of the graphics operations should speed up. Video benchmarks usually show impressive gains from this shadow ROM.

Be aware that most of the performance gain you see when running a DIR or video benchmark won't translate to increased video performance when you run your applications. Software developers realized long ago that the video BIOS was a performance bottleneck and tried to bypass it whenever possible, controlling the video from within the application in order to take advantage of the performance gain from running in main memory rather than from the slow BIOS memory. Therefore, the video ROM bottleneck may already have been removed, and moving the video BIOS into RAM won't change anything at the application level, although DOS itself may seem much faster than before.

Be aware also that these shadowing programs may incur some cost in terms of compatibility issues. Certain applications expect to find your video adapter's BIOS in a certain location; if you've moved all or part of it using one of these techniques, the application may become confused and put strange characters on the screen or hang the system entirely. The shadow ROM program shouldn't cause any permanent problems, however, even if it does have compatibility problems; if it doesn't work, you can always disable it.

The other cost of shadowing is the small amount of system memory the program will steal. If memory is tight, this could be a problem. I use a shadow video program with my PC even though the only things it has sped up are DOS operations that write to the screen and certain video benchmarks.

Summary

The PC's video display system is one of the areas most difficult in which to improve performance without actually replacing the video adapter itself. While certain display operations are sped up by using shadow ROM, most operations require a faster display adapter for significantly improved performance. Graphical user interfaces have placed a much greater burden on your PC's video display than the character-only displays of the past. The good news is that the price of video accelerator cards is dropping rapidly and it is now possible to purchase an accelerated display adapter for what a standard display adapter cost previously.

CHAPTER NINE

Printers, Plotters, and Modems

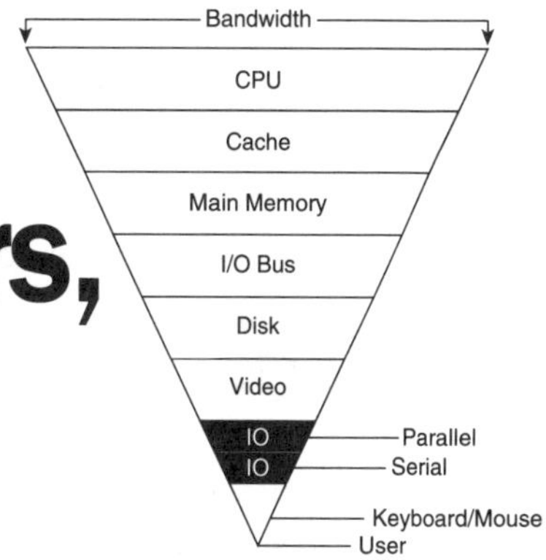

Data Funnel

If you take another look at the data funnel, you'll see that the parallel and serial interfaces are near the bottom at the slowest, narrowest end of the funnel.

A typical PC parallel port operates at a maximum of about 100,000 bits per second (bps). A typical high-speed serial port operates at 9,600 bps, though speeds of about 2,400 bps are not uncommon. If you contrast these speeds with the typical performance levels of your PC's memory (20 to 100 MB per second) and CPU (up to 200 MB per second), you can see that the serial and parallel ports are an extreme bottleneck.

If you regularly have to wait for information to move through the serial or parallel port, a little time and money invested in minimizing this bottleneck will result in a significant performance boost. Fortunately, it is relatively easy to get around the slowdown I/O creates. In this chapter, we'll look at a few easy and relatively economical ways to do this.

The Parallel Port: Printers and Plotters

The devices connected to your PC via the parallel port are usually printers and plotters. Because these are mechanical devices, they're slower than the electronic components found inside the system. Thus, not only is the parallel port very slow, the external devices attached to it are even slower. This particularly acute system bottleneck gives us another opportunity to implement the caching principles we've discussed in relation to memory and disk drives.

Print spoolers

To avoid having the rest of the computer wait for data to be sent over a slow parallel port to an even slower printer or plotter, you can set up a *print spooler* as part of main memory. A print spooler is a software program that sets aside part of the computer's memory as a buffer to hold data on its way to a printer or plotter. It then sends the data to the printer as a background task while your other applications continue to work.

Managing these operations in the background frees up most of your CPU's resources. However, the key phrase is "most of your CPU's resources." If you've ever used the Windows print spooler, you know that printing a file in the background can have a severe negative effect on foreground performance.

Far more advanced third-party products are now on the market. For example, Print Cache from Laser Tools not only manages your print spooling (without robbing so many CPU cycles from the foreground task) but accelerates the speed at which information is sent over the I/O port (see Figure 9-1). Both features alleviate the I/O bottleneck.

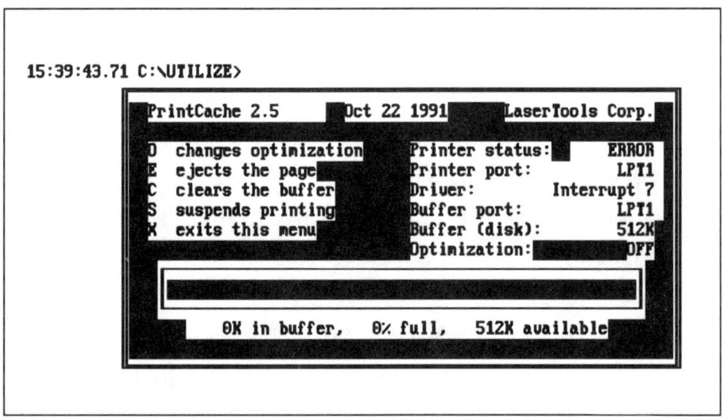

Figure 9-1. The Print Cache from Laser Tools can be very effective at speeding up Windows printing.

External print buffers

Another common way to alleviate this I/O bottleneck is to install an external device called a print buffer or plotter buffer. An external print buffer is similar to a print spooler except that it is on the other side of the I/O port (see Figure 9-2). The print buffer uses memory to store data while it waits for the printer or plotter. It may also store the data while someone else is using the output device. Some sophisticated print buffers even let you change the order in which files are printed or print multiple copies of a file.

The amount of memory a printer buffer must have depends on the kind of printer you're printing to. If you're printing an 8 page newsletter with large pieces of art to a PostScript printer, for example, the amount of data you're sending is going to be at least hundreds of kilobytes in size. For PostScript printing, then, an external print buffer must be very large or you have to resort to other techniques to alleviate the bottleneck.

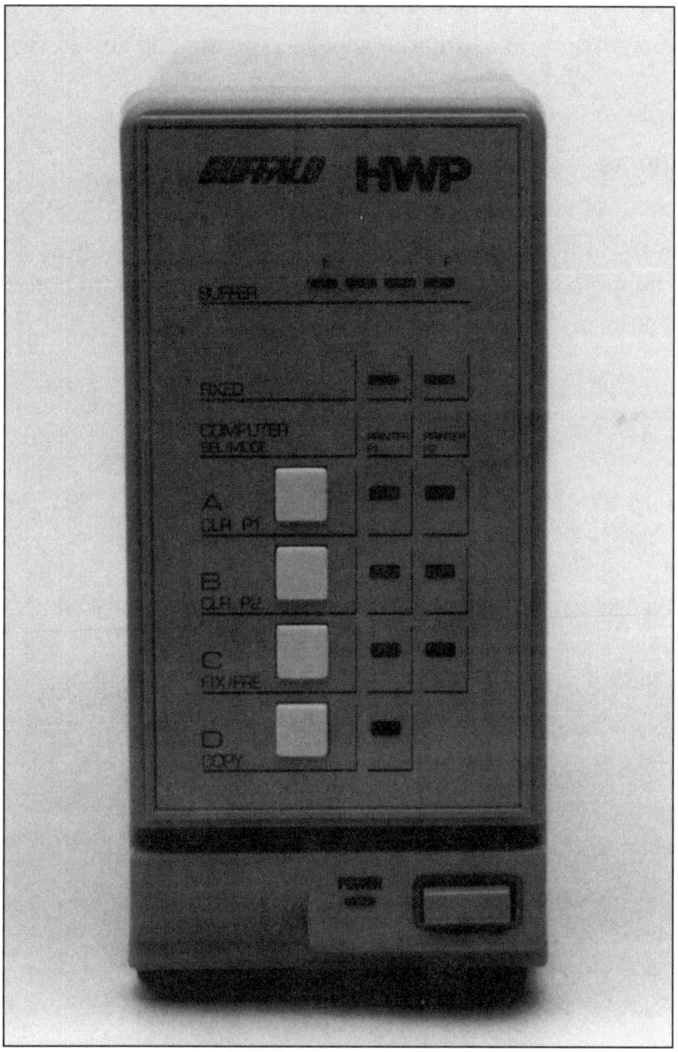

Figure 9-2. This device includes a print buffer as well as provides for printer sharing.

Most printers include at least a small buffer of their own. The advantage of an external print buffer is that, although you still have to send information over the parallel port, you can send the full print job to a device that stores the data in its own memory. It then parcels out the job at the printer's or plotter's pace; meanwhile, you can be working on something else at your computer.

In other words, installing an external print buffer means you no longer have to rob CPU cycles to manage the printer's or plotter's spooler; you also don't need to tie up the computer's memory by storing the files to be printed. Of course, you still have to go through the parallel port bottleneck, but at least you're not held up by the speed of the printing device.

The ideal solution may be to use a print spooler program and an external print buffer.

The Serial Port: Modems

We've talked about printers and plotters in regard to the parallel port connection; however, some printers and most plotters use the serial port. The techniques outlined in the preceding section for the print spooler and print buffer also apply to these serial devices.

Speeding up PostScript printers

In general, you can speed up a PostScript printer the same way you speed up a computer: get either a faster processor or more memory. You can't upgrade a printer's processor, but you can add memory, so your choice is easy.

What do you do with the extra memory? Well, fortunately, you don't have to do anything to get some benefits. One thing PostScript has to do each time it prints is create bit maps of fonts from what's known as a *font outline* (a mathematical description of the font). If your PostScript printer has enough memory, a font's bitmap is likely to stay in an area set aside for font cache until the next time you need it.

You can speed a PostScript printer that's going to print documents from the same application over and over again by downloading the *laser prep file* permanently to the printer, rather than making the application load it each time it

The serial port is relatively slow, although it can be configured to exceed its typical output of 9,600 bps. Adding a data or fax modem, the most common device found on a serial port, only aggravates the problem.

Although some of the faster modems operate at 9,600 or even 14,400 bps, the modems owned by the majority of people operate at 2,400 bps. You don't even achieve that rate, however, if you're using an error-detection program like X-modem or Y-modem (normally used when sending executable files or files in which an error involving even a single bit could cause a problem, such as financial data). To correct the errors, these protocols send a check sum along with each packet of data, and if the receiving end calculates a different sum for the packet, the data is retransmitted. Such schemes safeguard the integrity of data transmission but cause a further bottleneck.

Keep in mind that these numbers are in bits per second, not bytes per second. In other words, you need to divide those speeds by 8 to get the speed in bytes per second. Bytes per second, in turn, translates to characters per second if you happen to be sending an ASCII text file. No matter how you measure modem speed, it boils down to painfully slow data transfer. Let's look at a couple of techniques for improving modem performance.

prints. Most sophisticated applications for drawing or desktop publishing include such an option.

Downloadable fonts benefit from similar treatment. It can take as much as 20 seconds to download a soft font from your PC's hard disk to your PostScript printer's font memory. Thus PostScript allows you to download a font to the printer's memory, where it will remain until you turn the printer off.

Another approach is to move the disk drive full of soft fonts to the printer's side of the cable, thereby avoiding the parallel or serial port bottleneck. Thus, some high-end PostScript printers include an optional hard drive. Storage on such a drive is usually devoted half to storing font outlines and half to caching font bit maps. While retrieving a font bit map from a cache on the hard disk is not as fast as getting it from RAM cache, it is far faster than recreating the bit map from the font outline.

MNP Protocols

The reason there is so much confusion surrounding the term MNP, (is it for error correction or data compression?) is that it can be both. MNP Class 1 and MNP Class 2 are both protocols for error detection and correction. They are not particularly efficient, so they have a lower actual throughput than their data rate. The MNP Class 3 is more efficient than Classes 1 and 2 . In fact the MNP Class 3 is so efficient that the throughput is actually a little higher than the data rate. A 2,400 bps modem using the MNP Class 3 protocol has a throughput of about 2,600 bps. The MNP Class 4 protocol has an even higher efficiency, so a 2,400-bps modem with MNP Class 4 can have an effective throughput of nearly 3,000 bps.

The MNP Class 5 protocol includes data compression in addition to error detection and correction. Although the efficiency of the data compression varies with the type of data being sent, a modem using MNP Class 5 can deliver a throughput of twice its data rate. Thus a 2,400-bps modem using MNP Class 5 can potentially deliver 4,800 bps.

V.42bis

The V.42bis standard is another data compression standard. V.42bis compression is very efficient: it can increase the throughput of a modem by as much as four times over its data rate. This means that a 9,600 bps modem has the potential to send and receive as much as 38,400 bps. Achieving this extraordi-

Data compression

One technique implemented by most modem manufacturers to improve performance is to build in a data-compression facility to squeeze information into as small a package as possible. Of course, modem on the other end must be able to decompress the files you've sent.

Modem manufacturers use several levels of data compression: modems that run at 9,600 bps using the V.32 MNP5 standard for compression can transmit at up to twice that speed, while those with V.42bis can transmit at nearly four times the rated speed (that is more than 38,000 bps). This compression

narily high throughput requires the appropriate file types (text files and CAD .dwg files are particularly susceptible to high compression), very clean phone lines, and relatively large file sizes. It is more reasonable to expect an effective throughput of around 20,000 bps from a 9,600-bps modem using V.42bis and transmitting a typical file.

Why do V.42bis modems often mention MNP5?

V.42bis and MNP Class 5 are two completely different standards that do much the same thing. Even though V.42 is the more efficient standard and has been accepted by the CCITT, it is not yet widely implemented. In contrast, the MNP Class 5 protocol has been around for a number of years and has an installed base of well over a million modems. Modem manufacturers often include MNP Class 5 as a "fall-back" mode, in case the modem must communicate with one that does not have V.42bis. So a modem advertisement that states V.42bis/MNP 5 means that the modem can support either V.42bis or MNP Class 5.

Using MNP Class 5 data compression with already-compressed files (for example, with files that carry a .ZIP, .ARC or .GIF extension) can actually slow down the data transfer instead of speeding it up. The reason for this is that the overhead associated with trying to compress a file that has already been efficiently compressed is significant, while the file itself isn't decreased in size. Indeed, using a compression technique on an already compressed file can increase the size of the file rather than decrease it.

level and transmission speed, however, are only possible if the data is capable of being compressed (some types of files are more readily compressed than others) and the phone lines are very clean. (See Table 9-1.) Thus, manufacturers qualify their claims by saying their modems run at *up to* 38,000 bps. Modems capable of these high transmission speeds were once very expensive, but 9,600-bps modems with V.42bis and MNP5 now sell for less than $300.

Although V.42bis modems have the capability of transferring data at 14,400 bps, the quality of most phone lines may make it impossible to achieve those rates (again, high data rates require very clean phone lines). Also, there is no use buying a 14,400 bps modem if the modems you will be sharing information with are capable of only 9,600 bps (unless, of course, you expect that condition to change in the near future).

Some modems are capable of higher data through put than the serial ports commonly found on PCs. Most PC RS-232 serial ports have a maximum data transfer rate of only 19,200 bps, but the fastest modems now have data rates of as much as 34,400 bps. This means that there are modems faster than the serial port you may be intending to attach to them. The best solution is to use an internal high speed modem. Internal modems have their own built-in I/O ports that are capable of handling the higher data rates.

An alternative to using a modem with built-in data compression is one that requires considerably more user interaction—using a third-party compression

Modem data rates versus "effective" throughput

While the difference between baud and bps is mainly academic, the difference between a modem's data rate and its actual throughput can be very important. The throughput of a modem (the actual amount of data which it can send or receive over a period of time) can be either higher or lower than its data rate (the number of bits per second at which it transmits and receives data). Error detection and correction lowers the actual throughput of the modem while data compression increases it.

Simply stated, the throughput of the modem determines how long it takes to send or receive a file while the data rate is only a measure of the rate at which the modem is transmitting or receiving. The two can be compared to the rated miles per gallon of a car. While a car's MPG rating may be set by the department of transportation, the actual amount of gas you will use will be determined by the type of driving you do. Similarly, the data rate of your modem is set by the manufacturer, but the actual speed at which you can send and receive files is affected by the types of files, noise on the line, and the protocols that are used to transmit and receive files. With a modem, time is literally money, either because of connect charges or long distance charges or both. Thus we should be more interested in how long it actually takes to send and receive the files than the modem's data rate.

Baud and bps are not the same

While the earliest PC modems operated at both 300 baud and 300 bps, higher speed modems operate at different baud and bps rates. The baud rate is the number of times the signal that the modem uses fluctuates per second. The bps rate is the number of bits, or binary digits, that the modem can send in one second. Medium and high speed modems transmit and receive more than one bit with every signal change. Most 1,200 and 2,400 bps modems operate at 600 baud while most 9,600 bps modems operate at 2,400 baud.

Even though most people use the terms baud and bps interchangeably, they are not the same. From a user standpoint, it doesn't really matter too much unless you are interested in being technically correct.

utility such as PKARC, PKZIP, or LHARC to compress large files before sending them over a modem. Stand-alone data compression programs such as these are normally more efficient at data compression than the on-the-fly compression used by data compression modems. For one thing, they can make multiple passes over the data in order to optimize the compression. The penalty for this more efficient compression, however, is a requirement for user intervention to both compress and decompress a file.

If you want to transmit a compressed file to someone who doesn't have the decompress program (that is, you want to send a file that has been compressed with PKZIP, but you know the recipient won't have PKUNZIP or might not be able to figure out how to use it) use the ability of PKZIP to turn a .ZIP file into a self-extracting .EXE file. Then the recipient need only type the file name for the file to extract itself. The program ZIP2EXE, which turns a .ZIP file into a self-extracting .EXE file, adds only about 15 KB to the file size. While that translates into a minute of extra transmission time at 2,400 bps, the ability to send a compressed file to anyone, regardless of whether or not he or she has the decompression utility, may more than compensate for the additional time.

The amount of transmission time you save by compressing files depends on the kinds of files you're sending. Graphics files can typically be compressed by

30 to 40 percent; most, such as GIF and TGA, are already partially compressed and can't be reduced much more. Text and CAD files can be compressed by 50 to 70 percent. Some files, such as executables, don't lend themselves to compression at all. The following table shows the susceptibility of various file types to compression.

Table 9-1. Compression ratios of various file types

File Type	Typical Extension	Typical Compression Ratio
Text files	DOC, TXT	2:1 to 3:1
Database files	DBF	2:1 to 4:1
Spreadsheets	WK1, XLS	2:1 to 3:1
CAD drawings	DWG	2:1 to 4:1
Executable files	EXE, COM	2:1.5 to 1:1
Graphics	PCX, TIFF, BMP	2:1 to 10:1
Compressed graphics	GIF, TGA, FLC	1.5:1 to 1:1
Compressed files	ZIP, ARC, LHA	1:1 to .95:1.95*

* Attempting to compress files that have already been efficiently compressed may actually cause the files to expand in size rather than decrease.

Automated and background transmission

Even if you can compress a 1-MB file down to 300 KB and send it over a modem that's operating at 9,600 bps, you'll still waste about five minutes waiting for the file to be transmitted. This single transmission of a small file could bring your entire system to a temporary halt. Fortunately, you still have a few tricks at your disposal.

The easiest solution is to use the ability of many communications programs to send and receive files when you're not otherwise using your system—perhaps during your lunch hour or late at night. If you send late at night and the transmission is long distance, you'll also save on phone charges.

Modems that can send and receive in the background even from a machine running DOS are a more expensive solution. The good news is that transmitting in the background frees up your system's CPU and other resources; the bad news is that getting set up for this method requires the purchase of some sophisticated hardware and/or software. One such product is the Intel Connection Coprocessor (see Figure 9.3).

CompuServe speed

What kind of throughput can you expect to get with the new 14.4 modem? For example, if you're calling the CompuServe Information Service, will you be able to download files at the rate of 14.4 KB per second? That would mean you could download Version 6.0 of *PC Magazine*'s 473 KB benchmark in about half a minute, couldn't you? If your modem supports V.42bis or MNP5 compression, which can increase file transfer throughput by a factor of four, that download should take only about 8 seconds, right?

Wrong.

You'll find that downloading will actually take at least 10 minutes. CompuServe users logging onto the fastest modems CompuServe offers are lucky to achieve 700 characters per second on downloads.

What's going on? For one thing, the 14.4 speed of your modem is actually bits per second, while the 473 KB file is bytes, so you're immediately off by a factor of 8. For another, the fastest access supported by CompuServe is currently 9,600 bps, not 14.4 KB. Also, CompuServe does not offer any type of dynamic compression, such as V.42bis or MNP5. so the V.42bis capability on your modem is of no use. And you can only communicate at top speed when there's no noise on the phone line forcing retransmission of a bit of information that may have been changed by noise.

And it's even worse than it sounds. Some CompuServe users have reported speeds as slow as 205 characters per second (cps) when downloading during peak times, which would indicate that the bottleneck is partially at CompuServe's end. When lots of people are talking to CompuServe's mainframes at the same time, CompuServe apparently can't keep up.

Just keep this in mind when you plan your communications. Like so many other vendor claims and misleading benchmarks, modem speeds aren't all they're cracked up to be.

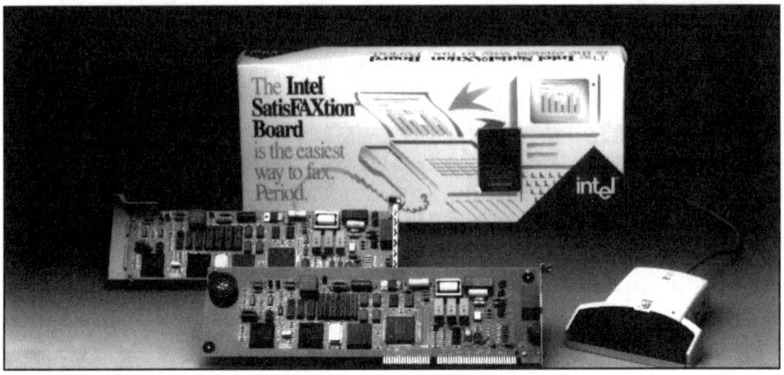

Figure 9-3. These modems have their own onboard processor so they can operate completely in the background.

With more advanced operating systems such as OS/2 2.0 and the forthcoming Windows NT from Microsoft, you can transmit and receive files in the background without significant impact on programs that continue to run

Sometimes slower is better than faster

Although it may seem contrary to the whole idea behind this book, sometimes it may actually be desirable to operate your computer at a slower rate than you normally would. There are two instances when slower is more desirable than faster. The case that applies to this chapter is the speed at which you operate your modem. While at first it might seem logical that you would always want your modem to operate at its maximum speed, or at least at the maximum speed your modem and the modem it is communicating with can operate successfully, there are times when you may actually want to operate your modem at its lowest speed.

Consider the case of an on-line service that varies connect time charges, depending on the speed at which you are operating. At the time of this writing, for example, CompuServe charges $12.50 an hour for 1,200 and 2,400 bps (bits per second) operation, $22.50 per hour for 9,600 bps operation, and only $6.00 per hour for 300 bps operation.

If you have a modem that supports 9,600 bps, clearly that seems to be the best speed for downloading files, and if your modem's highest speed is 2,400 bps you should use it at that speed when downloading files.

in the foreground. Even Microsoft Windows or DESQView can let a program transmit or receive as a background operation without overwhelming impact on foreground performance, unless you're transmitting with a protocol such as XModem.

Questions To Ask When Buying A Modem

Is the advertised bps rate the actual data rate or the "effective" throughput? While a high effective throughput might be nice, it's the actual data rate that matters most.

Can the modem drop down to speeds as low as 300 bps? If you plan to conference on a pay-per-minute line, you will probably want to use the inexpensive 300-bps mode. Some high speed modems can't run at such a low data rate (see Table 9-2 for a listing of modems and their data transfer rates).

But what if you were just using the service for interactive conferencing? Since the fastest possible speed at which you might be able to type and read messages during a conference session is less than 100 bps, you would be paying for more speed than you could possibly take advantage of if your modem was set to 1,200, 2,400 or 9,600 bps. In this case, it would make sense to operate at a speed with the lowest cost per unit of time.

So while the 9,600 bps or 2,400 bps rates make the most sense for file transfers, the 300 bps rate makes more sense for on-line conferencing. This is one of the few cases in computing when slower is better than faster. And you were probably wondering who in there right mind would still be operating a modem at 300 bps.

In fact, if that new superfast Belchfire 9,600 of yours doesn't go as low as 300 bps, it might make sense to buy and install an inexpensive 1,200 bps modem that does. With a difference in rates of $6.50 an hour, a $50 modem would pay for itself in less than eight hours of conferencing.

In what other circumstance is slower better than faster? When playing computer games that can't detect that you are operating the computer at a lower speed, of course. Most games can't be fooled this way but some, like early versions of Tetris, can.

Table 9-2. List of standard modem types

Modem Type	Data Transfer Rates (bps)
Bell 103	300
Bell 212A	1,200
V.22	600, 1,200
V.22bis	2,400
V.29	9,600
V.32	9,600
V.42bis	14,400

If you plan to buy a modem with built-in data compression, make sure the modems you will be communicating with support that compression. It won't do you much good having the latest and greatest in modem technology if all the modems you will communicate with are only capable of 1,200 bps.

If the modem is advertised as MNP, what level MNP should you get? MNP Classes 1 to 4 are for error detection and correction, while MNP Class 5 and up include data compression (see Table 9-3).

Table 9-3. Comparison of data compression standards and their efficiency

Data Compression Standards	Optimum* Efficiency
MNP Class 5	2:1
MNP Classes 7-9	3:1
V42.bis	4:1

*The actual amount of compression you achieve will depend on the file type.

What kind of service and support will the dealer you are going to buy the modem from offer? While modems are normally quite reliable, they can be tricky to configure. And the more features it has, the trickier it will be.

Data transmission costs

While the cost of a new high-speed modem may seem quite high, you might find it will actually pay for itself many times over. The following tables (Tables 9-4 through 9-7) show how quickly those phone charges can add up. It should be easy enough for you to create a similar table using your actual phone rates and expected data transmission requirements.

Table 9-4. Cost to send/receive 100,000 KB of files per month

BPS	Phone charges per minute			
	@ $0.10/min.	@ $0.25/min.	@$0.50/min.	@ $1.00/min
1,200	$1.11	$2.78	$5.56	$11.11
2,400	$0.56	$1.39	$2.78	$5.56
9,600	$0.14	$0.35	$0.69	$1.39
19,200	$0.07	$0.17	$0.35	$0.69
38,400	$0.03	$0.09	$0.17	$0.35

Table 9-5. Cost to send/receive 400,000 KB of files per month

BPS	Phone charges per minute			
	@ $0.10/min.	@ $0.25/min.	@$0.50/min.	@ $1.00/min
1,200	$4.44	$11.11	$22.22	$44.44
2,400	$2.22	$5.56	$11.11	$22.22
9,600	$0.56	$1.39	$2.78	$5.56
19,200	$0.28	$0.69	$1.39	$2.78
38,400	$0.14	$0.35	$0.69	$1.39

Table 9-6. Cost to send/receive 2 MB of files per month

BPS	Phone charges per minute			
	@ $0.10/min.	@ $0.25/min.	@$0.50/min.	@ $1.00/min
1,200	$22.22	$55.56	$111.11	$222.22
2,400	$11.11	$27.78	$55.56	$111.11
9,600	$2.78	$6.94	$13.89	$27.78
19,200	$1.39	$3.47	$6.94	$13.89
38,400	$0.69	$1.74	$3.47	$6.94

Table 9-7. Cost to send/receive 5 MB of files per month

BPS	Phone charges per minute			
	@ $0.10/min.	@ $0.25/min.	@$0.50/min.	@ $1.00/min
1,200	$55.56	$138.89	$277.78	$555.56
2,400	$27.78	$69.44	$138.89	$277.78
9,600	$6.94	$17.36	$34.72	$69.44
19,200	$3.47	$8.68	$17.36	$34.72
38,400	$1.74	$4.34	$8.68	$17.36

To determine how many months it will take for a faster modem to pay for itself, subtract the estimated cost per month of the faster modem from that of the slower modem, and then divide that number into the cost difference of the two modems.

For example, if you transmit 2 MB of files per month using a 2,400-bps modem at an average rate of $0.25 per minute, it will cost $27.78 per month. If you use a 9,600-bps modem, it would cost only $6.94 per month to send or receive the same files. If the 9,600-bps modem cost $375, it would take $375/($27.78 minus $6.94) or 18 months for the modem to pay for itself in phone bill savings.

CHAPTER TEN

The User, Keyboard, and Mouse

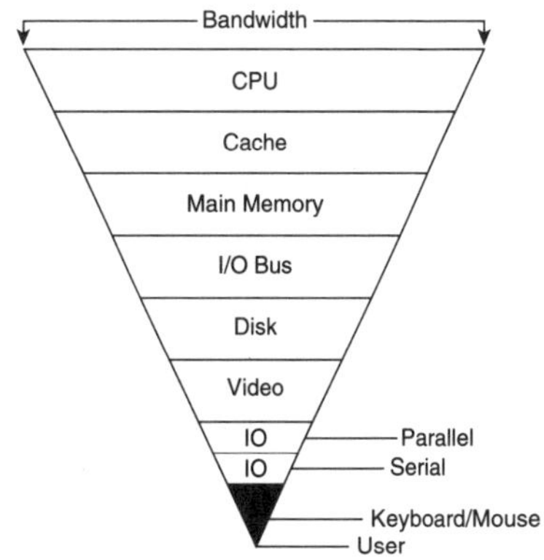

Data Funnel

You've probably noticed that the user is down at the smallest (meaning slowest) point of the data funnel. In fact, the user is often the biggest bottleneck in the computer system. Don't take this personally; the culprit is the way we interface with our computers, via our hands.

The keyboard, for example, is slower than any other system component in the data funnel. A high-speed typist can breeze along at something like 70 words per minute. That works out to about 350 bytes per minute, or a mere six bytes per second.

In this chapter, we'll look at some simple, practical ways to improve performance at the user, keyboard, and mouse levels.

Batch Files

A batch file is a text file containing commands that the computer executes. By creating some simple batch files with one- or two-character names, you can automate many of the tasks you perform frequently. (We won't go into great detail here about how to create a batch file; many books—almost every DOS book, in fact—cover this subject exhaustively.)

Let's say you want to load AutoCAD. Normally, this application is in the C:\ACAD directory. You type CD ACAD at the C:\ prompt to get into the AutoCAD directory, then type ACAD to load the program. If you want to invoke options with parameters at the same time, you also have to type those. Thus, your start-up sequence might look something like this:

```
CD ACAD <ENTER>
ACAD\Z:\FILENAME <ENTER>
```

It would probably take at least a few seconds to type in those two commands, assuming you typed it correctly. A short batch file containing these commands—which is really just a text file that has each command you enter at the DOS prompt on a separate line of a file with a .BAT suffix—would speed up the process considerably and eliminate the frustration of typos. If your batch file is called A.BAT, all you need to do is type A to send the commands at disk-drive speed.

As another example, perhaps you find that you change your CONFIG.SYS file frequently. You could create a batch file to call up your editor (edlin, EDIT, or your word processor), followed by your CONFIG.SYS file. For example, this batch file—call it ECS.BAT—would read

```
EDLIN C:\CONFIG.SYS
```

or

```
EDIT C:\CONFIG.SYS
```

or

```
CD WORD WORD C:\CONFIG.SYS
```

depending on which editor you use. A similar file—let's call it EA.BAT—could call up your editor, followed by your AUTOEXEC.BAT file.

You might also create batch files to perform the DOS clear screen and one that lists all files on drive C. For example, I replaced CLS with a batch file called C.BAT and created a batch file called ALL.BAT that issues the following commands:

```
CD /
DIR /S
```

If your fingers don't move at the same speed as your brain, you probably often find yourself typing DRI instead of DIR. If you create a batch file called DRI.BAT that executes the DOS command DIR, that typo will never again haunt you (although you have to make sure your batch files are put in a subdirectory that's in your DOS PATH so DOS can always find them).

You don't have to be a programming wizard to take advantage of the power of batch files; even a simple one can save you time. You've already spent thousands of dollars on a system that can execute millions of instructions per second, so why slow it down with a typing speed of a few characters per second?

Quick batch files without an editor

Sometimes you'll find yourself working on someone else's computer without a familiar editor, and all you want to do is create a quick batch file to save you from retyping some keystrokes in order to widen that slowest end of the data funnel. Well, you can, even without an editor.

Just enter a DOS command at the prompt that's a leftover from the days of CP/M: COPY CON, then type the name of the batch file you want to create.

```
COPY CON SPEEDUP.BAT
```

Now, you can simply type in as many lines of commands as you wish. When you're done with the last line, type the DOS character that signifies the end of a file by holding down the CTRL key and striking Z. The message on the screen should read:

```
1 FILE COPIED
```

Of course, the only editing you can do is of the line you're on by backspacing, so COPY CON isn't very flexible. But when you need to create a batch file in a pinch, it works just fine.

The %1 command

One of the most common batch file command, the %1, is so powerful in batch files that everyone should be using it. Yet until you see how it actually works, it seems awfully cryptic.

The %1 is used in a batch file to allow you to pass additional characters into the batch file at the time you start it. For example, if the name of your batch file is FLING.BAT and you type

```
FLING README.TXT
```

README.TXT gets passed into the batch file and replaces every occurrence of %1 inside the batch file. In other words, each time the batch file is actually run, the %1 symbol is replaced with the first set of characters that follows the batch file name.

As an example, let's look at the simple batch file you created to get around fumbling fingers. You created a one-line file called DRI.BAT that contained the following single line:

Macros

In the last two examples, you could have created a macro rather than a batch file. (Most power users have a combination of batch files and macros on their systems.) Macros let you assign a series of keystrokes to a simpler combination of keystrokes. There are two kinds of macros: those built with DOSKEY and those built with a third-party program such as RoseSoft Inc.'s Prokey. Both kinds are stored in main memory as part of a TSR, while application-based macros (such as those for Excel) are loaded from the disk drive.

Because a DOSKEY or Prokey macro is stored directly in main memory, the command is executed at memory speed. A batch file, on the other hand, is executed from the disk drive (at least the first time you run it; thereafter, it should be in your disk cache). The downside of macros is that they're a little more difficult to create than batch files. They also tend to be slightly harder to edit.

```
DIR
```

This file is supposed to help out when you accidentally type DRI instead of DIR. But there's a problem with this batch file: if you type DRI /p instead of DIR /p, the batch file will ignore the /p and issue a DIR command without the /p. By adding the %1 symbol to the batch file you can eliminate this problem. So now the one-line batch file DRI.BAT will read:

```
DIR %1
```

The next time you type DRI /p instead of DIR /p, the /p will replace the %1.

Once you have seen how simple yet powerful the %1 symbol can be when used in batch files you will probably look at batch files in a whole new light. You may be inspired to dig out an old DOS book and learn more about creating batch files. Once you've got %1 down, you'll want to try %2, %3, or %4. These are simply ways to pass a second, third, or fourth set of characters into your batch file. By the way, the technical term for this is *parameter passing*.

During the course of an average work session, you probably change from one subdirectory to another, type commands, get into and out of programs, change directories again, get into another program, and call up other files. You'll probably notice that you're performing certain actions over and over. How do you decide when to make one of these a batch file or macro? Whenever you find yourself typing the same series of more than three keystrokes more than twice a week, you've discovered a procedure that should be relegated to a batch file or macro.

A great deal has been written about macros, and most application programs have built-in macro facilities that are described in the documentation. Macros may be a bit more intimidating than batch files, but they can save you a lot of time once you know how to create them. And after all, now that you know about the data funnel, where would you rather have your programs executing—at the narrow tip of the funnel or up in high-speed memory?

DOSKEY

One of the new features of DOS, beginning with DOS 5.0, is a program called DOSKEY. Besides having an excellent facility for creating macros, it's also good at keeping track of which commands you're using over and over. If you have DOSKEY installed (to install it, just type DOSKEY), every so often during your work session you should type the following:

DOSKEY macros

The way you enter a macro into the DOSKEY utility is by typing the DOSKEY command followed by the name of the macro and then the commands that compose the macro. For example, to create a macro called C that edits your CONFIG.SYS file, you'd type

```
DOSKEY C=EDIT CONFIG.SYS <ENTER>
```

where <ENTER> means you press the ENTER key.

A more complicated macro called "FF" that finds files no matter where they are on your disk can be stored in RAM by typing

```
DOSKEY FF=CHKDSK/V $B FIND/I "$1" <ENTER>
```

What this macro does is execute the verbose version of CHKDSK, which lists every file on the disk. $b is replaced by the DOS pipe command, which means the verbose listing of all files on your disk is piped into the DOS FIND command with the /I "insensitive to case" switch and whatever parameter you enter after FF (in this case, the name of the file you're looking for).

Now, when you type FF AUTOEXEC.BAT <ENTER> the macro will display the pathname of each occurrence of a file named AUTOEXEC.BAT.

What do you do after you've entered a few of these macros into DOSKEY? Although they're sitting in memory, ready to execute at RAM speeds, the fact

```
DOSKEY /H <ENTER>
```

You'll then see a history (list) of all the commands you've entered since you began that DOS session (unless you've entered so many or such long commands that the DOSKEY buffer is full). If you see that some of the commands in your history are more than three characters long and appear more than twice, I'd consider making them macros or batch files.

that they're in RAM means they'll go away when you turn off your computer, and you don't want to have to rekey them.

So, once you've entered macros into DOSKEY, you can save them to a file called LOADMACS.BAT by typing

```
DOSKEY/M > LOADMACS.BAT
```

The following are a few more lines of a sample LOADMACS.BAT file, after an editor was used to add the DOSKEY command and comments explaining what each macro does. The $ sign is used in macros the same way the % sign is used in batch files.

```
rem *** Make new DIR and change to it ***
DOSKEY ND=MD $1 $T CD $1
rem
rem *** Type ASCII file with pauses ***
DOSKEY TYPE=TYPE $1 $B MORE
rem
rem *** Delete all files in a DIR and then delete that DIR ***
DOSKEY DD=DEL $1\*.* $T RD $1
```

Once you've captured all your macros into a LOADMACS.BAT file, you can use an editor to add the command DOSKEY at the beginning of each line. Then to automatically load those macros into memory each time you start your computer, add the command LOADMACS to your AUTOEXEC.BAT file.

Remember, this all depends on you having DOS 5.0 and installing the command DOSKEY in your AUTOEXEC.BAT file.

The Keyboard

Some keyboards lend themselves to faster data entry. One of these is the Dvorak keyboard. When the typewriter was invented, people could type faster than the speed at which the machines could function. A fast typist simply jammed the keys together. Typewriter designers and manufacturers had to figure out a way to prevent that. In the absence of keyboard buffers, they laid out the keyboard in such a way that it would actually slow down typing speed.

That's right, the keys are actually laid out on a typewriter in an intentionally suboptimal way. And because manufacturers of computer keyboards wanted (and rightfully so) to maintain compatibility with the typewriter, the keyboards most of us use today have that same suboptimal QWERTY keyboard layout (see Figure 10-1).

A man named Dvorak (no relation to computer guru John C. Dvorak) did research into the optimal keyboard configuration and designed a keyboard around that layout. If you want to go to the trouble of relearning the key positions, you can buy a Dvorak keyboard and probably improve your typing speed (and thereby enhance performance in that section of the data funnel). In the

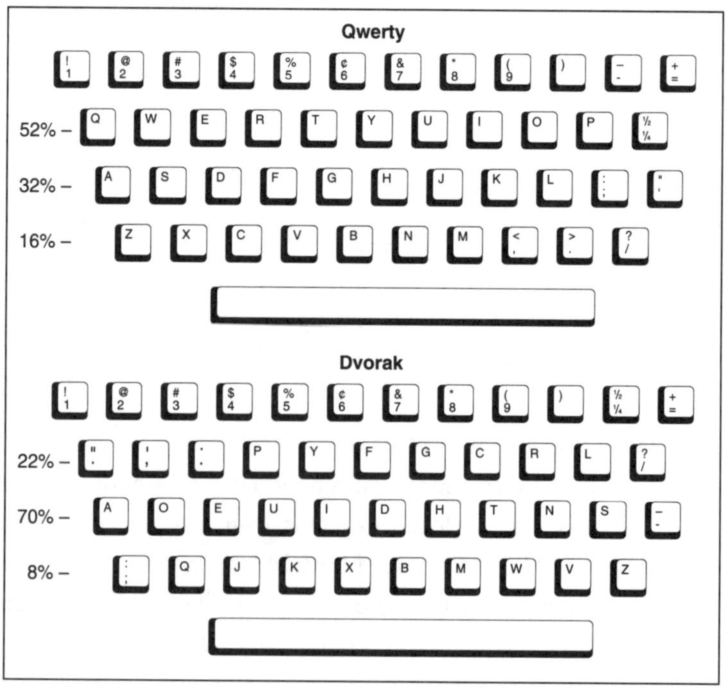

Figure 10-1. QWERTY and Dvorak keyboard layouts.

Dvorak keyboard, 70 percent of the keystrokes are made on the home row, compared to 32 percent with the QWERTY keyboard.

For most users, this isn't an easy way to improve performance. Buying a new keyboard (actually, some software will let you remap your keyboard to the Dvorak layout, but you won't be able to look down and see which key is which) and learning a different layout isn't a very practical solution. A more practical way to optimize your PC at the keyboard level is by skillfully implementing batch files and macros.

The Mouse

Although the mouse is easy to use, it's a very slow input device. Remember the calculations we did on the speed of input from the keyboard? They showed that we could only type a few characters per second. You would be lucky to get even that sluggish pace from a mouse (although a typical mouse command issued with a single click tends to replace three or so keystrokes). And while the mouse is a convenient way to interact with and input data, if you consider the time it takes to move, click, and wait through each command you'll realize how much time is wasted.

Nearly every program that accepts mouse commands also accepts keyboard commands. Take the time to learn some of these keyboard shortcuts (often called *hot-key combinations*). They're easy to learn; don't forget that the underlined letter in a mouse command is the hot key for that command. If you start using some of these hot-key combinations, you might see that you can get around much faster than with a mouse in some graphical user interfaces. For example, to exit a Windows application quickly, simply press Alt-F4 rather than going to the file bar, clicking on Close, and clicking on OK. To save a file in Microsoft Word, you could move the mouse to the file bar, pull it down, click on the Save command—or simply press Shift-F12.

I'm not advocating abandoning the mouse entirely—it's useful and easy to work with—but at least familiarize yourself with the software you're using. Many of the more common mouse actions can be replaced by keystrokes and hot-key combinations that will expedite the procedure and make you more productive. However, I wouldn't want to try to draw a circle with a keyboard, and a mouse beats a keyboard hands down when it comes to cutting and pasting.

Another alternative is the trackball, which some people think is easier to manipulate than a mouse. It's a matter of personal preference.

Also available are such exotic input devices as pen-based computers, natural-language input (from Natural Language Inc. and its licensees, which include Microsoft) and voice input (from Dragon Systems and Kurzweil). Just keep in mind that most of these devices result in performance degradation, at least at this point in their development. That is, it might take the computer longer to understand the spoken command "directory" than it would to simply type in DIR.

Voice input—improved performance?

It may seem logical to consider voice input devices—that is, devices that allow the user to speak to the computer instead of using a keyboard or a mouse—as performance-enhancement devices. In fact, as it now stands, voice input is actually more of a performance degrader than a performance enhancer. The reason is simple: It takes an enormous amount of computing power to change the sounds of a human voice into something the computer can understand. This computing power needs to come from somewhere, and to the extent that it draws on the computer's resources it will slow the computer's performance more then enhance it.

Whether or not voice input leads to more work being done by the user of the computer is a different question. If the method of data input leads to more work being done, then productivity is enhanced, which may be very desirable.

Although there has been a considerable amount of progress in voice recognition technology over the last few years, the use of voice input devices for the PC is still quite limited. The major barriers to more widespread use of voice input for the PC is the ability for the computer to recognize the voices of different people rather than the single person that it may have been trained for (called *speaker independence*) and the ability of the computer to separate individual words out of complete sentences (called *continuous speech recognition*).

Until these goals are met, voice input will remain limited to applications that can benefit from it, even with the above limitations.

CHAPTER ELEVEN

Optimizing for Major Applications

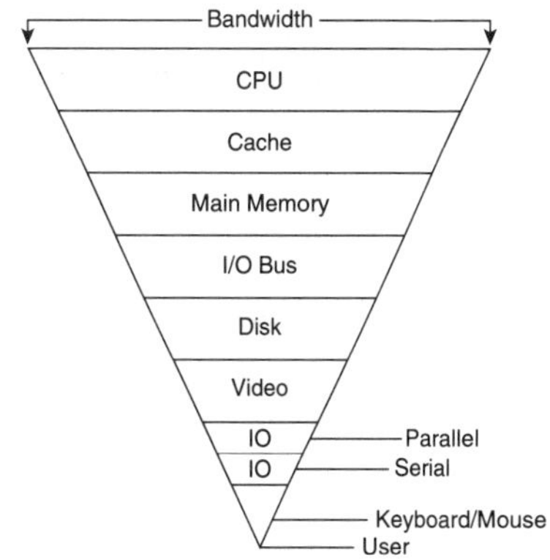

Data Funnel

In this chapter, we use the data funnel as a model for understanding which performance enhancement techniques are most appropriate for specific applications. Of course, no two PC configurations are identical and different applications make different demands on your computer; you should use the following information to provide some basic guidelines—rather than hard-and-fast rules—on where bottlenecks tend to form when using various applications.

For example, some applications rely almost entirely on the CPU and memory, and make only minor demands on the rest of the system. A large spreadsheet performing recalcs is one such CPU-intensive application, whereas a database performing a large indexing function is more of a disk-bound application. Applying this information to our model, we can easily see that moving to a faster CPU will do very little to improve a bottleneck in the disk drive: the two bottlenecks occur at different places in the data funnel.

Locating the Bottleneck

The easiest bottlenecks to identify are those in the lower sections of the data funnel. For instance, you can easily watch your computer's disk activity light and listen to the drive to see if your application is disk bound. I/O bottlenecks are also easy to spot since the computer waits for a slow peripheral device like a modem or printer. Obviously, determining whether your application is CPU intensive is much more difficult since there are no outward signs of CPU activity.

Sometimes memory problems can make the system look CPU bound. If your system seems much slower than it should after you have installed additional memory, the memory may not be configured properly or may be installed on a slow I/O bus (see Chapter 3).

Sophisticated Diagnostics

If you aren't satisfied with watching the disk drive light or with sensing the video speed, you can use a much more sophisticated method. Personal Measure from Spirit of Performance is a diagnostic program that graphs the application's use of various subsystems. The program gives you a very clear look at the amount of time your computer spends in various areas—CPU, disk, video, and even keyboard—in fact, it's a bit mortifying to see how much of the time the computer is waiting for us instead of the other way around. Such information is very useful in deciding which bottleneck to attack first.

Although Personal Measure produces a chart that looks intimidating at first, the figure is actually not too difficult to understand (see Figure 11-1). Personal Measure will also produce the same information in a tabular form that gives actual times and percentages (see Figure 11-2).

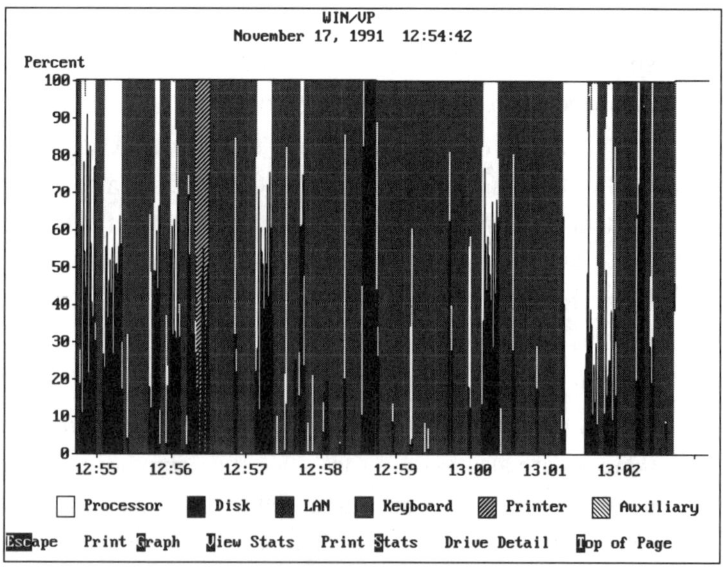

Figure 11-1. Personal Measure chart showing the relative amount of time spent by various subsystems.

```
                              WIN/VP
                    November 17, 1991  12:54:42

                       System Resources Used

        RESOURCE                TIME     PERCENTAGE      % OF TIME
                        hh:mm:ss.sss        OF TIME   W/O KEYBOARD

        Processor           1:32.447          18.18          54.31
        Disk                1:10.152          13.80          41.21
        LAN                    0.000           0.00           0.00
        Keyboard            5:38.209          66.52           ----
        Printer                7.628           1.50           4.48
        Auxiliary              0.004           0.00           0.00
        Total               8:28.440         100.00         100.00

                       Disk Activity Summary

    TYPE OF ACTIVITY        DOS     BIOS     DURATION
                          CALLS    CALLS  hh:mm:ss.sss
    File Reads             2157     3606       50.438  File fragmentation?
    File Writes             276      302       10.089
    Programs Loaded           6       19        0.553
    Directory Accesses      146      528        9.072
    Non-DOS Accesses          0        0        0.000
    Total                  2585     4455     1:10.152

    Average BIOS disk access time is    15.747 ms.

Escape   Print Graph   View Graph   Print Stats   Drive Detail   Top of Page
```

Figure 11-2. Same data as shown in Figure 11-1, but in tabular form.

Getting Software Specific

Next, we will look at some common applications to see where they typically have performance problems; we will then examine specific actions that can help.

AutoCAD

AutoCAD is a program that requires a great deal of computer power. It draws on nearly all of the PC's different resources. Why? Displaying a complex drawing requires a very high level of integer performance. Certain other operations, such as hidden line removal, require a lot of floating point performance. The large file sizes involved in most CAD drawings require substantial disk space and high disk throughput. The fact that .DWG files become even larger when they are loaded into memory places a heavy demand on system memory. And, of course, the graphical nature of CAD places a heavy demand on the PC's video system. Let's take a look at AutoCAD in relation to the relevant sections of the data funnel.

The CPU

It's well known that computer-aided design (CAD) is a very compute-intensive application. In other words, the faster the CPU, the better CAD programs perform. Considering the cost of the software and the likelihood that the AutoCAD users time is valuable, running AutoCAD on anything less than a fast 386 doesn't make sense. Using a 486 is even more desirable. However, as I've mentioned before in this book we are looking at ways to fully exploit the resources of the PC you have. So no matter what type and clock speed of CPU your PC is based on, the following should improve your computer's performance running AutoCAD. You may be surprised at the boost in performance some of our optimizing tricks can deliver.

Math coprocessors

Floating point is another aspect of performance in which CAD requires significant resources. Of course, the latest versions of AutoCAD and some of the other CAD packages will no longer even operate without a math coprocessor. Therefore, the addition of a math coprocessor is a moot point, at least, in relation to AutoCAD. If you don't have a math coprocessor, AutoCAD won't even run.

You should be aware that you are no longer limited to a single brand of math coprocessor. Currently, a variety of coprocessors are on the market: 387 compatibles, 387 compatible super-sets and non-387 compatibles. If you still haven't purchased your math coprocessor, you may want to look seriously at the Intel-compatible coprocessors. These products reportedly deliver some performance increases in floating point operations.

You're not going to see a very significant performance boost if you go with an Intel-compatible such as the Cyrix rather than the Intel 387. Since the compatibles cost about the same as or less than the Intel, and seem to provide more floating point performance, you may want to take a look at one of them.

One 387 compatible that deserves a close look is Intel's new RapidCAD processor. This chip actually replaces the 386 itself. And like the 486, this chip includes the CPU and coprocessor on a single chip. The RapidCAD chip offers significantly faster math coprocessor performance than a 387 running at the same speed, and, in addition, it offers slightly faster CPU performance than the 386 it replaces.

To benefit from the power of the more advanced coprocessors, the software has to be rewritten to take advantage of that particular coprocessor.

AutoCAD does not exploit the Weitek 3167 or 4167, although the three-dimensional surface rendering add-on for AutoCAD, AutoShade 2.0, does support them. Worse, if your 386 PC only has a Weitek 3167, AutoCAD won't run unless you have a software emulation of the Intel math coprocessor installed (several public domain versions of such software is available on the Autodesk forum on CompuServe, and Multix Inc. (214-239-4989) sells a $100 program called Soft87 that takes three to four times as long as an equivalent hardware alternative. In general, productive use of AutoCAD requires the presence of a 387 (or a 486DX with its built-in math coprocessor).

Some of the other CAD packages take advantage of the Weitek 3167 and 4167 math coprocessors. In such cases the addition of the Weitek chip should help performance. Although the marketing materials for the various packages will tell you if the program supports the Weitek chips, I'd check with the technical support department of the various CAD software companies to find out

Intel's RapidCAD upgrade

Intel has fought back against the cheaper math coprocessors being offered by its competitors with its RapidCAD upgrade, claiming performance improvements of as much as 70 percent. The RapidCAD upgrade actually consists of two chips: RapidCAD-1, which combines the functions of a 386DX CPU and the 387DX math coprocessor into a single device (much as the 486 chip does), and a RapidCAD-2 chip that fits into the math coprocessor slot.

As you might expect, users who have installed RapidCAD have noticed a much smaller improvement—say 20 to 25 percent—in most CAD operations. The exception is rendering, which delivers close to the 70 percent increase promised by Intel. And although Intel doesn't publicize it, the RapidCAD processor also increases your system's integer performance by about 10 percent.

The RapidCAD coprocessor works with 16-MHz, 20-MHz, 25-MHz, and 33-MHz versions of Intel's 386DX CPU.

how much of a difference the Weitek (or the Intel or the Cyrix for that matter) will make. The technical support people can also tell you in what specific areas you'll see the increased performance. The performance increase you'll experience won't match the claims of the coprocessors' marketing departments claims, and you'll probably find the support people are usually a little more realistic (since they don't want you to call back upset after you've bought a coprocessor and failed to see any improvement).

A final point while on the subject of math coprocessors and CAD. You may recall that the Intel 486DX microprocessor itself has a very fast 387-compatible math coprocessor built in. This is another reason to consider using a 486-based PC rather than a 386-based PC for CAD. Indeed, when *PC Magazine* compared 386-based PCs equipped with any of the coprocessors from Intel, Cyrix, or IIT, all were outperformed by a 486DX running at the same clock speed.

Memory

CAD programs, particularly AutoCAD, are memory hungry. But it's important to note how and where AutoCAD uses this memory. Autodesk deserves congratulations for their thorough documentation on how to optimize memory configuration for running AutoCAD. In the installation manual, there is a large section on how to optimize for AutoCAD and particularly on how to configure on the system's memory so that AutoCAD will run at its best.

Arriving at your optimal memory configuration for AutoCAD isn't necessarily straightforward. After all, AutoCAD is really a combination of two programs, AutoCAD and AutoLISP, and unfortunately these two programs require different memory resources. AutoCAD, in its most recent releases, takes advantage of extended memory. AutoLISP has been written to take advantage of expanded memory. As you can see, simply adding more memory is not the end of the performance upgrade for AutoCAD. (Actually adding memory is usually not the end of the story for any application.) Adding more memory will almost certainly benefit your AutoCAD performance up to a point, but you'll also need to properly configure it.

AutoCAD tries to keep as much of itself and your current files in memory as possible. Once it has exhausted all available memory, it starts to swap data out to the disk. When AutoCAD has run out of memory and is using the disk drive, the disk activity light starts blinking frequently. As soon as disk swapping begins, performance drops off dramatically. A glance at the data funnel shows why this happens: As long as the program and files can stay in the upper area of the funnel, data can move around rapidly. Crossing over the slow I/O bus and into the disk area narrows the funnel considerably. (By this time it should be obvious why this occurs: A hard disk being a mechanical device is far slower than memory.)

As much memory as you can afford is the right amount of memory for AutoCAD. You should be aware, however, that prior to release 11, AutoCAD couldn't take advantage of anything in excess of 16 MB, and prior to release 10 for 386, AutoCAD couldn't directly address any extended memory beyond 4 MB. Therefore, in configuring memory for use by AutoCAD, unless you are using release 10 or higher, adding more than 4 MB won't buy any direct performance improvement. But you can use the additional memory for disk caching and some other techniques we'll mention shortly. In any case, make sure that you have devoted at least 4 MB of extended memory to AutoCad itself and another 2 to 4 MB of expanded memory to AutoLISP. AutoCAD release 11 is significantly better than release 10 in terms of memory support.

AutoCAD release 11 doesn't have the 4 MB barrier, so you can take advantage of as much memory as your system can support, but keep in mind that AutoLISP needs some expanded memory. Refer to the AutoCAD *Installation and Performance Guide* that comes with the program for the optimum memory configuration.

Disk optimization

In addition to the demands that AutoCAD makes on your CPU, coprocessor, and memory, AutoCAD is very demanding of the PC's disk subsystem. AutoCAD's program files are very large, and the data files AutoCAD creates also can get large. These large files are what place heavy demands on the disk. Rather than buying a new, faster disk drive, you first should try the standard disk optimization techniques with your current disk.

As with most programs, AutoCAD will benefit from the use of a disk cache. Because of the large files that AutoCAD uses, the most effective disk cache size for AutoCAD is probably much larger than the cache size you would normally use for other programs. The best way to determine an appropriate cache size is to look at your drawing files (.DWG files) and make the cache a multiple of your typical .DWG file's size. This means that if a typical drawing file is 1 MB, you should have a 2- or 3-MB cache. If the typical file size is 2 MB (which is a very large CAD drawing), then you should create a cache of 4 or 6 MB.because normally you will be working with several files at once and you'll want to load the various files quickly as you need them.

If your file size is 1 MB and your disk cache is 1 MB you'll never be able to have more than one file in the cache at once. If you have individual files that are larger than the disk cache, the cache will be flushed constantly to replace it with different parts of the same file. This will be apparent when the computer seems to run faster without the disk cache than with it. If that is the case, then you may be better off with no disk cache than with a cache that is too small. But if you don't have megabytes of memory to spare, don't let this talk about multiple-megabyte disk caches scare you. Most CAD users don't have files of over 1 MB and can benefit from a smaller disk cache. (For a more thorough discussion of disk caching issues, see Chapter 6.)

With AutoCAD, a sophisticated disk-caching program is advisable. I would recommend one of the third-party disk caches like Super PC-Kwik or Power Cache Plus. Whether or not you use a large disk cache with AutoCAD, you should perform some of the standard disk optimization techniques: disk defragmenting, file organizing, and using the correct interleave.

Disk defragmentation

AutoCAD is especially prone to becoming bogged down once your disk has become fragmented. Ideally you should defragment your drive before installing AutoCAD (or any large program for that matter). If the AutoCAD program files are originally loaded onto a disk without a lot of fragmentation, they can't become fragmented over time.

Your data files, on the other hand, are subject to further fragmentation as long as they continue to be modified. Because AutoCAD's data files are often bigger than the data files of other applications, they are more prone to fragmentation. And because AutoCAD users often have relatively large disk drives, the files can become fragmented over a very large area. Therefore, AutoCAD users should defragment their disks on a regular basis. You probably will be surprised at how much faster your files load once AutoCAD has defragmented them.

File organizing

It would also be wise to use a file organizing program (most likely the same program you use for defragmenting) to try to keep your files close together on the drive. If AutoCAD is your main application, you'll want to put the program files at the beginning of the drive, close to the file allocation table (FAT), then follow the recommendation of the file organizing program on the placement of your data files.

Using a faster drive

Creating a large disk cache and implementing the above disk optimization techniques will go a long way toward reducing the disk bottleneck. But even using the optimization techniques, there's nothing like a fast drive to improve AutoCAD's disk performance.

Because most of the files that AutoCAD uses are large and accessed sequentially rather than randomly, a drive with a high transfer rate is paramount. You should choose a drive with one of the faster interfaces, ESDI, SCSI, or IDE. A drive with an ST-506 interface will definitely slow your disk performance. (Not all IDE drives are fast either so take a look at the specs before you buy.) And even though random access performance isn't as important in the CAD environment, the drives with fast transfer rates have fast access times as well. It probably goes without saying that when shopping for a new drive for CAD you'll want to get a drive with plenty of capacity. It doesn't have much to do with performance, but those big CAD files have a way of filling a drive up quickly.

Graphics

When it comes to video performance with AutoCAD there is good news and bad news. Some aspects of AutoCAD's video performance can be sped up dramatically, often times at relatively little cost. Other aspects can only be sped up by upgrading to a faster CPU.

REDRAWs, PANs, and ZOOMs

One of the most time-consuming activities in AutoCAD is waiting for REDRAWS, PANs, and ZOOMs. Fortunately, these processes can be sped up dramatically with software called Display List Drivers (DLDs). Starting with release 10, AutoCAD has the ability to support display lists. Display lists are a series of vectors that contain information about a drawing. Without display lists, AutoCAD stores information about a drawing in a complex hierarchical structure. Anytime you want to perform a REDRAW, PAN, or ZOOM, AutoCAD must decode this structure, which is a very time-consuming process. A display list stores this same information in a decoded format so that it is ready to be displayed much quicker. In fact, well-written DLDs can allow you to REDRAW, ZOOM, and PAN between two and ten times as fast as AutoCAD without the drivers could.

The best part about these DLDs is that they are very inexpensive. In fact, many graphics adapters include them as standard, so you may already own some. The only other cost is the memory they require. While the DLDs themselves typically take up less than 100 KB of memory, they do require additional memory to hold the display list. The amount of memory necessary to store the display list will vary depending on the drawing, but it usually will be between half and twice the size of the drawing itself. Ideally this is extended memory, but if memory is tight, the better drivers allow you to page out to disk. Considering the performance gains, it's well worth adding some additional memory to your system if it's necessary to support the drivers.

As I mentioned, many of the video card manufacturers now supply DLDs with their cards. But there are some excellent third-party drivers available as well. The leader in this field is Panacea, which provides most of the drivers that ship with video cards. The drivers they sell at retail include features not available with the drivers shipped with the cards. If you are using AutoCAD 386, release 10 or 11, you should definitely give DLDs a try.

DRAWs and REGENs

Display list drivers have their limitations since they don't affect the speed of REGENS or DRAWs. It takes additional hardware to speed up these operations. Although it may surprise you, some of the disk optimizing techniques that were just mentioned can help these operations. The reason for this is that the drawings have to be read from the disk before they can be displayed. So improving disk performance will help here as well. The real key to faster DRAWs and REGENs, though, is more processing power. One place that this can come from is a faster CPU. The faster CPU is not only going to increase performance on DRAWs and REGENS but nearly all other operations as well. This is the case in a VGA system in which the CPU does most of the work necessary to drive the display.

Another way to improve performance of DRAWs and REGENs is to use a graphics coprocessor. You would use a graphics card that has its own graphics coprocessor, although the performance improvement provided by these coprocessor-based graphics cards may not be as impressive as you might hope, there is some good pricing news, however. The price of the boards based on the 34010, which has long been the standard for AutoCAD graphics enhancement, have dropped considerably over the last year or so. It used to be that any card based on the 34010 cost well over $1,000 and often closer to $2,000. Now, because many these boards are being repositioned as Windows accelerators, a number of 34010-based cards are selling for less than $600, and. some are even being advertised for less than $300. These cards also work with display list drivers. In fact, there can be some additional performance gain from these cards because some of them can hold the display list in the memory of the card, which eliminates the need to send the information over the slow I/O bus.

In addition to the many 34010-based cards for AutoCAD, many of the GUI accelerator cards sold primarily as Windows accelerators also offer excellent AutoCAD performance. These cards include 8514-based cards, 8514-like cards, and special GUI accelerator cards. Because there are many variables in the evaluation of the relative performance of the various graphics adapters available for AutoCAD, you should consult one of the many reviews in the PC publications. While the general interest PC publications review CAD graphics adapters, the CAD publications like *Catalyst* and *Cadence* review these types of products regularly.

With Windows, CAD graphics performance appears to have as much to do with the quality of the drivers as it does with the specific hardware. This has two implications: First, drivers can improve over time, so if a certain board doesn't fair well in performance comparisons, the manufacturer can always improve the drivers. Second, the best drivers are often available from third parties such as Panacea. When tuning your system for an application such as AutoCAD, many of the performance issues involved in optimizing the video subsystem can have a dramatic effect on performance.

Plotters and printers

Plotting and printing AutoCAD files can be a major bottleneck on your PC's performance. The best way to avoid this bottleneck is to get the printing and plotting jobs off your computer and onto another. If you have the luxury of having an additional system available, it's worth considering turning that system into a dedicated, or at least semidedicated, plot station. Although this won't necessarily make the printing or plotting any faster (in fact it may slow it down if you dedicate a slow system to this task), it will free up your PC faster so that you can get back to work. And like the print buffer products mentioned in Chapter 9 plot buffer products also are available.

Summary

Although the emphasis in this book is on hardware optimization techniques rather than productivity techniques, many different utilities and productivity enhancers are available to use with AutoCAD. These programs include file viewers, file organizers, word processors, drawing converters, and all kinds of other utilities to make the life of a CAD user easier. The best way to locate these types of programs is to look for advertisements in *Catalyst*, *Cadence*, and the other CAD publications.

CAD needs as much CPU and floating point as you can get and as much memory as possible within the bounds mentioned in this chapter. All the disk optimization techniques, including, disk caching, defragmentation, and file organizing, are appropriate for CAD. Display list drivers will speed certain graphics functions, even when using a VGA card. Plotting is slow, so try to get it off your machine. Although there's no substitute for a fast CPU and a fast hard drive, the above-mentioned techniques will make up a lot of the difference.

Databases

Common wisdom is that database programs do not have particularly heavy CPU or memory requirements. People always think the biggest bottleneck in a database program is in the disk subsystem. In fact, while it's true that database programs are very disk intensive, going to more memory or a faster CPU definitely impacts the performance of database programs like dBASE IV and Paradox. The impact on SQL databases like SQL Server and Oracle can be even greater. For example, the SysMark92 database scores can increase 43 percent when a 486SLC2 upgrade processor is added to an IBM Model 56.

In the case of an SQL database, the CPU carries an even bigger burden because it has to "optimize" each SQL statement, which really means it has to figure out which is the fastest set of physical disk accesses that can satisfy a particular request for data specified in the logic of the SQL.

Memory is also extremely important to multiuser SQL databases. The chief reason Oracle for OS/2 runs out of gas at just over a dozen users, while Oracle for NetWare can easily support 50 users or more, is that OS/2 limits Oracle to 16 MB of memory while Netware 386 lets Oracle have 32 MB or more.

The main thing database programs like FoxPro, Paradox and dBASE IV do with more memory is cache. Actually, dBASE IV simply installs an external caching program called Hyperdisk. FoxPro and Paradox, in contrast, use as much memory as you have in your 386-based machine, and they use much of that for internal buffering of data. When a database program can take advantage of extended memory as these two can, it may be better to give it to the database program rather than to the external disk cache. The database's internal caching is custom tailored to speeding database performance. Also, if you use two caches, you're going to end up with two copies of everything in cache, one in the internal cache and one in the external, and the program is going to have to run through two lookup tables to find anything.

Before you shut down your external cache, however, it would pay to follow our most basic rule of thumb for optimizing performance: try it and see. It's not unusual for common wisdom to fail on at least a few particular hardware and software configurations.

The bottom line is that type and clock speed of your CPU will have an enormous influence on database performance. A faster CPU speeds up access of data that's in a program's internal cache as well as speeding up indexes, sorts, and searches.

On the other hand, a faster CPU will not help much if your program is completely bogged down by a slow disk subsystem. This is bound to be true for those PC databases that cannot take advantage of more than the 640 KB provided by DOS. In that case, disk caching becomes the top priority.

Disk optimization

There is more than a modicum of truth in the belief that databases are disk-intensive programs. That means disk optimization techniques can improve the performance of a database program without requiring you to buy a faster disk drive.

Defragmentation

Defragmentation can be somewhat effective at improving database program performance. Although normally a database performs lots of random accesses, many operations are sequential in nature. Indexing entails a certain amount of sequential activity and sorting has a large sequential component. Copying files is exclusively a sequential operation. Using a defragmentation program to assure that your database files are located contiguously on the disk gives you optimum performance for these sequential operations.

File organization

File organization also can be useful for improving database performance. Even though records are often accessed at random from multiple files, it is still desirable to have the related files located as close to each other as possible. This is assuming that the database files are only a few megabytes or less in size. If the files are tens or hundreds of megabytes, then it is probably not possible to keep them close together.

Some administrators of large databases do the opposite of keeping the files close together. They spread their database files over two or more disks so they can have multiple disks seeking records at the same time. While you might think this would be effective only in a multitasking environment, it can provide a surprisingly strong performance boost even in a single-tasking environment like Novell NetWare.

The most common technique is to put a database file (or table) on one disk and that file's index on the other. Since many operations require reading or writing the index and the data files one after another, you gain a great deal in performance by dedicating a disk read/write head to each operation. Without the two heads, each of which never leaves the tracks occupied by its respective file, a single disk head must thrash back and forth between the two files.

If you are using a database in a multitasking environment like UNIX or OS/2, there is even more to gain from the technique of splitting tables among multiple drives. One approach is to put files that are often "joined" on different drives, which yields precisely the same benefit as the approach of putting a table and its index on different disks. If one database is accessed exclusively at one time and another at another time, putting these two databases on different disks won't help since one disk will always be idle.

This technique is most effective when used with bus mastering SCSI host adapters, because the SCSI drives will leave the bus free while they are seeking data. And, if the SCSI bus is on a bus mastering card, the SCSI bus will leave the rest of the system free, except when it is requesting data or actually transmitting it.

Interleave

As always it is important to make sure that you are using the optimum interleave on your drive. If your PC is a 16-MHz 386 or faster, this should be 1-to-1.

Disk caching

Disk caching, when a database program is already caching internally, can be counterproductive, as mentioned earlier.

In Chapter 6 we talked about RAM disks and in Chapter 7 about solid-state disks. Both could greatly improve your database performance. A RAM disk, as you'll recall, is a section of memory set aside and configured to appear to be a real disk drive. A solid-state disk is a device that appears to be a disk drive but contains semiconductor memory chips instead of magnetic media on a spinning platter. The RAM disk makes use of the computer's memory, while the solid-state disk uses its own memory. To be effective, these devices should be large enough to store the entire database. This kind of storage is volatile, however. A power failure before the data is written out to nonvolatile storage would be a disaster.

Disk drives

Having a fast drive is critical for optimum database performance. Because the most time-consuming database operations are random record accesses, it's important to have a drive with fast access times. Certain operations involve continuous sequential accesses, so a fast data transfer rate is also desirable. Fortunately, the drives with the fastest access times generally have high transfer rates as well. Since drive latency can be a big factor in random accesses, drives to be used for databases should also have low rotational latency.

Video

Your PC's video subsystem should have very little impact on the speed of your database (the only exception being a database that runs in a graphical environment, such as Windows). The extent of the slowdown caused by a GUI is basically limited to the amount of time it takes to display a screen once a record is located. In this case, the video enhancement techniques recommended for Windows will help. But they help speed appearance of the display to appear faster. Faster video won't affect any of the other database operations.

Spreadsheets

Spreadsheet program performance is very difficult to improve. Unfortunately, most spreadsheet applications aren't going to benefit as much from the optimization techniques discussed in this book as other applications will. The notable exceptions are those spreadsheets that run under Windows, such as Excel or Lotus 1-2-3 for Windows These programs will benefit from the performance enhancement techniques I mentioned in Chapter 11.

If a character-based spreadsheet like Lotus 1-2-3 is running very slowly, it's probably compute-bound. As I mentioned earlier, the only way to break a bottleneck at the CPU level of the data funnel is with a faster CPU or one with a higher clock speed. And, unfortunately, getting a faster CPU means either a CPU upgrade board (if your system will support it, or a new motherboard or computer.

Of course, math coprocessor manufacturers herald their products as deliverers of big performance boosts for your compute-bound spreadsheet. But a coprocessor will provide a significant performance increase to a spreadsheet program only if you are using certain operations. Math coprocessors are best at speeding up exponential and logarithmic functions, trigonometric functions, and operations such as square roots. A math coprocessor will not speed up a typical recalculations if the spreadsheet is primarily composed of columns and rows with totals and subtotals. Before investing in a coprocessor to speed up your spreadsheet, call the technical support department of that spreadsheet vendor and ask them whether they think a math coprocessor will speed up your spreadsheets.

There is a chance that your spreadsheet is disk bound. If this is the case, you should see a lot of disk activity (the disk light will be blinking on and off) while working in your spreadsheet program. If your spreadsheet is slowed by a lot of disk activity, then disk optimization techniques will help. And number one on the list of disk enhancements is installing a software disk cache. The proper size will be the size necessary to keep the disk light from flashing when the spreadsheet program is being run.

If you're using a character-based spreadsheet and you are bothered by how slow your system is scrolling through your spreadsheet, you may benefit from a faster video card. If you've noticed that it takes a long time to draw charts and graphs, it's more likely that a faster CPU is the only solution. The impressive number that many graphics adapters achieve on the benchmark programs are unlikely to translate into equally impressive graphics performance with your spreadsheet programs.

Word Processing

Fortunately, you can optimize word processing applications, like most other PC applications, via a number of different optimization techniques. (But keep in mind that we cannot optimize the user's typing speed. That much is up to you.)

Disk Cache

Most of us would like to improve our word processor's speed in loading and saving files—particularly larger ones, spell and grammar checking, and scrolling through text. Loading and saving files are obviously disk intensive operations. Before you buy a new drive, I suggest installing a disk cache. I recommend a cache like the most recent version of SMARTDRV, which caches both reads and writes. You should also consider increasing the size of your disk cache if you already have one installed.

Make sure that your disk cache is large enough to hold your main word processing program, a few of your typical files and your spelling checker's dictionary. To check the file size, run a DIR of your word processor's directory and look for the largest files. DOS 5.0 makes this easy by allowing you to sort files by size (DIR /OS).

RAM disk

If you are using a large disk cache and your drive light is still frequently active, you may want to try using a RAM disk—particularly if you notice the activity when performing such tasks as spell check. Create a RAM disk (see Chapter 5) and then copy your spelling checker's dictionary into the RAM disk. Reconfigure the word processor so that it knows to use the dictionary in the RAM disk and not the one on the hard drive. Your spelling checker should fly through your document next time.

A word of caution though. If you use the RAM disk for an updateable dictionary—one that allows new words to be entered, you'll need to copy the updated dictionary back to the hard drive before turning off your computer.

Desktop publishing

As users of nearly all desktop publishing (DTP) programs have found, DTP is very demanding of the computer's resources. Most of what is covered in the next chapter on optimizing for Windows applies to DTP programs as well. This is the case for both Windows-based and DOS-based DTP programs, since both have graphic interfaces and page displays that slow your system down. The only difference is that Windows users running a word processor or spreadsheet program may not require the highest performance CPU, while DTP users should use the fastest CPU they can afford. Even a fairly modest DTP project bogs down a slower CPU.

While graphics acceleration can be very useful for DTP, the graphics accelerators that have been designed specifically for Windows may not support a DTP package like the non-Windows version of Ventura Publisher. So before investing in a graphics accelerator, make sure it has the drivers for your package. For those who can't afford faster hardware, you'll have to rely on the standard disk optimization techniques and the productivity tricks mentioned in the DTP user's manuals. Such tasks as keeping text greeked and hiding images whenever possible normally are mentioned. And, while it certainly isn't a low-cost solution, a full-page monitor will save you having to scroll up and down the page frequently, which can mean considerable time savings.

Video

Word processing often entails a considerable amount of scrolling. Most character-based word processing programs scroll fairly quickly. However, word processors with GUIs often look very slow when scrolling. Although updating your video card's drivers can help a bit, you will probably see more significant gains by replacing your video card with a faster one. VGA cards based on the Tseng Labs ET4000 chip, such as the Diamond Computer Systems SpeedSTAR or the Everex Systems Viewpoint, are generally faster at scrolling than VGA cards based on other chips. But if you really want top scrolling speed, think about replacing your VGA card with a graphics accelerator. Video cards based on the S3 graphics accelerator, such as the Diamond Computer Systems, Stealth, or the Orchid Fahrenheit 1280, effectively improve the scrolling speed of word processors under Windows.

Although a faster CPU will speed nearly any video performance, I wouldn't recommend that as a way to get better video performance.

Disk defragmenting

Although we might expect that only document files would become fragmented since they are frequently overwritten and updated, you should know that even program files can be fragmented. If, when you installed your word processor, your hard disk was fragmented, the program files are probably fragmented and will take much longer to load than they should. You can defragment these files using the methods covered in Chapter 6. Since program files are only read from (and not written to), once they have been defragmented they should stay that way.

In contrast, document files can become fragmented again. And large fragmented files can slow your word processor significantly. Fragmentation can be a problem even with small files since these files create gaps in the disk that DOS fills with other files, thereby slowing disk access to all applications. Defragmenting is always a good practice, especially for those who frequently use word processors.

Print spoolers and buffers

Printing is important to word processing, yet printing is one of the biggest bottlenecks to system performance. Short of replacing your printer with a faster one—a costly solution—you can avoid the printing bottleneck by using a print spooler or print buffer. A print spooler or print buffer will not speed up the printing itself, but they do free the rest of the system so you can continue with other operations while printing takes place in the background.

For a single computer attached to a printer, print spooler software—such as Print Cache from Laser Tools—is probably the most cost effective solution. If several computers are sharing a printer, it makes sense to set up a print buffer.

Don't install an expensive network if you will only use it as a printer sharing device. If all you need is to share a printer among multiple computers look at printer-sharing devices that include a print buffer. It might be wise for you to use the difference in cost to buy a faster printer or additional printers that will actually speed printing itself.

If you are printing documents formatted in Postscript, your documents will be considerably larger than if they were not formatted in Postscript. You should use considerably more memory for the spooler or buffer.

CPU

Word processing applications are generally not bottlenecked by a slow CPU. Before upgrading your CPU, make sure that you have looked at the other areas I've covered. Once you have optimized your drive and video subsystems, then a faster CPU may be the only alternative. But make that choice when it becomes necessary.

Networks

Whole books could be written on optimizing for networks. Fortunately, the documentation for Novell NetWare, the most popular LAN, does devote considerable time to optimizing.

Performance of NetWare, as with most networks, is very much drive dependent. This makes sense if you consider that NetWare is chiefly providing file services and print spooling services, both of which involve lots of reading and writing of disk files. In fact, you might think that file serving was so disk intensive that the speed of the file server's CPU doesn't matter.

As with databases, however, a high-performance CPU will help a great deal in improving network performance on a server machine, in part because manufacturers, realizing how important disk speed is to the file intensive operations of a network file server, include very sophisticated disk caching as part of the network operating system. In effect, many of the operations involving files are moved up automatically into the fastest part of the data funnel, which means that more memory and a faster CPU will have a tremendous effect on the performance of a network.

So if you have a file server with a large number of nodes, consider adding more memory to it, because NetWare will use it for very sophisticated disk caching.

There is good news and bad news associated with the sophistication of NetWare's caching. The good news is that it is very tunable. You can adjust for block size and number of files cached. You can optimize for write-back, for reads or writes, and a whole array of variables. The bad news is that it's going to take some fine-tuning on your part. But the time spent tuning the disk parameters can benefit you considerably.

Before you assume that adding memory and configuring it properly is the only solution to your NetWare performance problems, don't forget about the disk drives themselves. A fast disk subsystem is going to buy you a lot in the NetWare environment.

Because NetWare is a multitasking operating system, many of the techniques that aren't effective for DOS can work well with NetWare. NetWare can take advantage of bus mastering disk controllers and the SCSI drives capabilities to operate somewhat independently of the SCSI bus. A 32-bit bus with bus mastering, such as EISA or Micro-Channel, can provide more benefit on a file server than it would on a typical stand-alone machine. And the ability of NetWare to stripe files across multiple drives can be beneficial for large file transfers.

Before investing in a disk array as the solution to the file server disk bottleneck, investigate carefully. You'll recall that most arrays are intended more for system availability than for performance. (Of course, there's nothing wrong with improved system availability, but you shouldn't be paying for improved availability when what you are after is improved performance.)

One of the drive enhancement possibilities not mentioned in Chapter 7 is an intelligent disk server. An intelligent disk server is a special (and expensive) drive subsystem that includes its own micro-processors, high- speed RAM cache memory and multitasking operating system to off-load all disk input and output activities from the file server. The intelligent disk server controls write data to disk or tape drives, and its high-speed cache reduces or eliminates even the rotational latency associated with the majority of data seeks. An example of this type of product is the LAN server family from Sanyo Icon. An intelligent disk server can provide extremely fast data access in network environments that would bog down traditional file servers, even those configured with lots of memory and fast drives. If you have particularly heavy file server demands, these are an option that should be explored.

Another key way to improve server performance is by using multiple network interface cards in the server. This is particularly true if the interface cards are bus-mastering cards that can run independently of each other and of the main CPU.

Network nodes

Before we discuss improving the performance of a network node (individual workstation), we must point out that the network is a major bottleneck. Consider that any data the node requires from the server must pass over the relatively slow network. And before the data can be sent over the network, we must wait for other nodes on the network that are also requesting data to have their requests serviced.

Thus, the more we can keep off the network, the better off we are. So if you have a choice between having your programs and data stored locally on your own drive or remotely on the server, it is likely that local access will be quicker. (The exception would be if you have a floppy-only system or a very old and slow hard drive.)

On the other hand, there are good reasons to keep data stored on the server. Most file server administrators back up the server on a regular basis, so if your files are stored on the server, they will be backed up. If your files are all stored locally, you must be responsible for backing them up regularly. You will have to decide which is best for you.

That's not to say that there's nothing you can do to speed up a client PC's ability to read and write files across the network. In general, upgrading from an 8-bit network interface card to a 16-bit card is a good idea, for example. You probably won't see any benefit, however, from moving to a bus mastering card on a client PC.

Peer-to-peer networks

Peer-to-peer networks are those that do not require a special file server per se but instead allow all computers on the network to access files on the drives of all other computers. Peer-to-peer networks generally are installed in less demanding environments than are dedicated file servers. Peer-to-peer networks are often found to be less expensive and easier to administer than a dedicated file server system, particularly in cases where a limited number of users are on the network.

The most popular peer-to-peer network is LANtastic from Artisoft. LANtastic, like most of the other peer-to-peer network products, includes its own disk-caching software. As you might expect, my advise would be to use a disk cache with these peer-to-peer networks. (Third-party disk caches may work with the peer-to-peer networks, but they often do not work with the dedicated file server products because the disk cache software often operates at a higher level than the network operating system and thus don't recognize the disk calls as such.) The disk cache in a peer-to-peer network stores information in local memory, which saves having to go out onto the network as frequently to retrieve files.

CHAPTER TWELVE

Optimizing for Windows

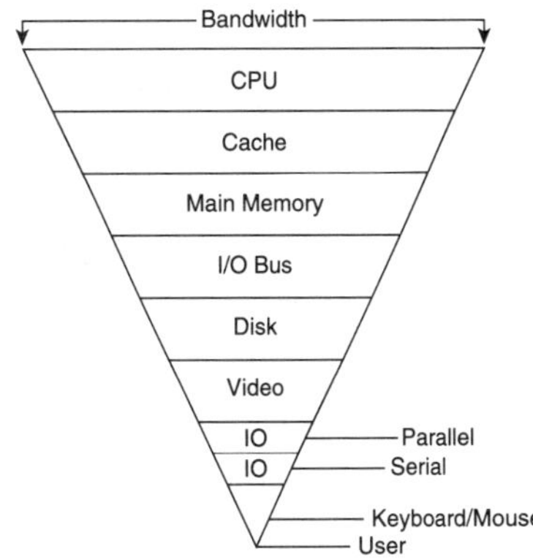

Data Funnel

In this chapter, we'll look at how you can tune your system to get the most out of Windows. Although Windows is known for giving DOS users an excellent graphical user interface that allows them to run more than one program at a time, it is also recognized as a shameless resource hog. It draws extensively on many elements of your system, bringing several parts of the data funnel into play. We'll cover each of these areas in turn, starting at the top of the funnel.

We'll also take a quick look at the performance implications of two 32-bit operating system environments that can run Windows programs, OS/2 2.0 and Windows NT.

Windows Modes

The Windows 3.0 environment has three operating modes: real, standard, and enhanced. Windows 3.1 has just the latter two. Version 3.0's real mode provides maximum compatibility with previous versions of Windows applications (those designed to run under Windows 2.0, 286, or 386). This is the most limiting of the Windows modes because it allows Windows to access only the first 640 KB of memory. In other words, it cannot access extended memory. Real mode is the only one available to computers with 1 MB of memory; it is essentially XT mode.

Standard mode is Windows' normal operating mode. It lets you switch between DOS applications and provides access to extended memory. Standard mode requires more than 1 MB of memory and is essentially 286 mode.

Enhanced mode has the capabilities of standard mode but provides some additional features. Besides supporting virtual memory, it allows multiple Windows programs to run simultaneously (this is known as *multitasking*). It is much better at supporting DOS applications. It lets you run DOS applications in a window, cut and paste text selections between DOS windows, and can even run DOS applications in the background. Of the three modes, enhanced is the most demanding of the PC's resources. It requires a 386 or better CPU and at least 2 MB of memory. Enhanced mode is also called 386 mode.

It's tempting for 386 and 486 users to run in enhanced mode, thinking they'll get the best performance. But that's not always true; the features are enhanced, not the performance. In fact, if you measure performance in terms of execution speed, standard mode is a better choice. Your programs will probably run a little faster in standard mode than in enhanced mode because Windows has less to worry about; for example, it's not multitasking or dealing with virtual memory.

However, if you find yourself working in more than one program most of the time, enhanced mode's multitasking ability might improve your productivity by eliminating the need to wait for one program to finish what it's doing before going to the next. If you don't really do two things at once but switch between programs often, enhanced mode is slightly faster at switching between programs than standard mode.

The speed penalty of running DOS programs in a Windows window

If you care about performance, and you run DOS applications in Windows 386 enhanced mode, run them full screen as much as possible. If you run them in a partial-screen window, which is easy and convenient under Windows 3.1 now that you can choose the size of the font with which the DOS window is drawn, you'll pay for the convenience with a huge performance hit. The problem is that Windows has to handle in software the screen updating that a DOS application normally handles by writing directly to your video card's buffers. You'll have to run DOS applications in a window rather than full screen to cut and paste from a DOS application to another window. But other than that, you'll probably find the extra performance strain (not to mention the eyestrain) will make you want to keep DOS applications full screen as much as possible.

Enhanced mode also lets you use more memory than is actually available to you. It does this with *virtual memory*. While there can be benefits from virtual memory, performance isn't one of them. Virtual memory is actually the reverse of disk caching. Instead of storing frequently accessed information in fast memory as a disk cache does, it stores program code and data on the disk drive. While virtual memory allows you to run more programs than you have DRAM for, you'll pay for it with vastly degraded performance.

So keep these trade-offs in mind: Windows runs a bit faster in standard mode than in enhanced mode. If you have only one program executing most of the time, you probably don't need multitasking. (Don't confuse multitasking with task switching: Windows' standard mode allows task switching, so you can load multiple applications at one time and switch between them; it doesn't allow multitasking—that is, multiple programs don't really execute at the same time.)

Unless you have some pressing need to have several programs open at the same time and don't have 4 MB of RAM or more, you probably don't need virtual memory—it's annoyingly slow. If you must have many programs loaded and you find them swapping to disk (you'll know this is happening when the disk light comes on), add more memory to your system. Remember, just because you're using a 386 or 486 CPU doesn't mean you want to run Windows in 386 mode.

Real mode is faster than enhanced and standard, but it doesn't provide enough memory to run most programs. Most Windows programs can't even be loaded in real mode (which is why Microsoft dropped support of it in Windows 3.1). If you have to run Windows on an XT, a notebook PC, or some other computer with only 1 MB of memory, you're going to be stuck with Windows 3.0, and only a handful of programs will be available to you. You should consider staying with DOS rather than running Windows in this kind of crippled environment.

CPU

In general, a faster CPU means better Windows performance. The problem is that, outside of replacing the CPU, you can do little to enhance Windows' performance at the CPU level. On the other hand, a 386/20 that has been optimized to eliminate system bottlenecks might well run Windows faster than a 486/25 that isn't tuned.

Does OS/2 offer reasonable performance for Windows programs?

OS/2 2.0 was initially touted by IBM as a better DOS than DOS, and a better Windows than Windows. Is it?

Well, no, particularly if you try to run OS/2 in a 4-MB machine. If you don't have at least 8 MB of RAM, I'd stay away from OS/2.

And even in an 8-MB machine, you'll find that Windows applications run much more slowly. For one, the version of Windows that OS/2 2.0 supports is Windows 3.0 rather than Windows 3.1, and Windows 3.0 is a slightly slower environment.

Bottom line to you is that Windows applications will load far more slowly and perform slightly more slowly than they do under Microsoft Windows. This is particularly true if you run Windows applications in a partial-screen window as part of the OS/2 desktop, rather than running them in OS/2's full-screen Windows environment.

On the other hand, when 32-bit OS/2 2.0 versions of Windows applications emerge, assuming they ever do, those applications should be faster and more powerful than their counterparts under the 16-bit Windows environment.

In other words, implementing the techniques presented in this chapter should provide a significant performance boost without upgrading to a faster CPU. If, after you implement these techniques, your system still doesn't run Windows fast enough, then you should consider a higher-performance CPU. Keep in mind that most of the performance techniques mentioned in this book will improve system performance regardless of which CPU your system is based on.

Memory Configuration

Memory is a critical area for PC optimization no matter what environment you're running, but it's particularly true for Windows. If you are running Windows, having plenty of memory and using it well can mean the difference between productivity and pain.

Although it's technically accurate to say that Windows 3.0 will run with 1 MB of memory, in practical terms anything less than 2 MB is ridiculous. And if you want to run Windows properly, you need at least 4 MB. Ideally, you should have at least 6 or 8 MB of main memory. (Because Windows uses DOS, a 16-bit operating system, the maximum amount of memory that Windows can recognize is 16 MB.)

Optimizing memory usage with Windows, as with most sophisticated programs, requires some thought; you can't just throw memory at an application and hope to solve the problem. Fortunately, because Microsoft realizes how important a role memory plays in Windows' performance, the Windows user's guide goes into considerable detail on how best to configure your system's memory. Microsoft recommends that you install as much extended memory as possible. In fact, if you don't need expanded memory for one of your older DOS applications, consider configuring all your available memory as extended. (In a 386 or 486 system, extended memory is usually the default for anything over the first 640 KB, so you don't ordinarily have to worry about this.)

The exception is a DOS program that uses expanded memory under Windows (such as Lotus 1-2-3 release 2). Windows has no problem supplying such programs with expanded memory if you have an expanded memory board on a 286 machine or you've loaded an expanded memory manager during boot on a 386 or 486 machine. You can do this with EMM386, the expanded memory manager that comes with DOS, with the expanded memory manager that came with your memory card, or with a third-party expanded memory manager, such as QEMM from Quarterdeck or 386-to-the-Max from Qualitas.

Disk Caching

Once you've increased your system's main memory to a minimum of 4 MB and configured it as extended, you'll want to convert a substantial chunk of it to a disk cache. As we've discussed, disk caching is an essential optimization technique; in fact, it's probably the most important thing you can do to speed up Windows. A properly implemented disk cache has a profound effect on Windows' performance.

Choosing a disk-caching program

Windows has its own disk-caching program called SMARTDRV. Although the name was a little ironic with version 3.0, considering that version of SMARTDRV.SYS was onc of the least intelligent disk caches available, SMARTDRV has one advantage over other disk caches in a very significant area: compatibility. Most of the third-party disk-caching programs on the market have exhibited compatibility problems when used with Windows 3.0, although they've worked hard at cleaning up their act in recent versions because of the tremendous success of Windows in the marketplace. You can be sure that SMARTDRV—since it's bundled with Windows—has no such problems.

If you're going to use SMARTDRV to implement a disk cache, you should probably try to find a copy of the version of SMARTDRV that comes with Windows 3.1, even if you're using Windows 3.0. In contrast to Super PC-Kwik, Power Cache Plus, other third-party products, and the version of SMARTDRV that ships with Windows 3.1, the original SMARTDRV was not a full disk-caching program; it was really more of a multitrack buffer. It stored entire tracks, or what it thought were entire tracks, of the disk. That's not an especially intelligent way to perform disk caching because programs often need only a few sectors of a track, so many of the kilobytes that compose the rest of the track are taking up cache memory needlessly. Besides, because many of the latest drives—especially IDE drives—use some sort of sector translation, there's no way for the original SMARTDRV to really know what constitutes a track.

Another drawback is that, according to the Windows 3.0 user's guide, the original SMARTDRV had an optimum size of about 2 MB. The early SMARTDRV appears to be very unsophisticated when it comes to managing its lookup tables; if the size of the cache goes too far beyond 2 MB, it could take the computer longer to find something in the SMARTDRV lookup table and load it than it would to load it directly from disk. (This is based on the assumption that you have a very fast disk drive and a slow CPU. If you have a typical disk drive and a 16-MHz or faster CPU, a large SMARTDRV disk cache should still be more effective than a small one.) For example, on a 16-MHz, 386-based PC with a 28-ms drive—a 4-MB SMARTDRV disk cache is faster overall than a 2-MB disk cache on the same system.

Of course, there's a dramatic performance difference between a 2-MB disk cache and no disk cache at all, even with the original SMARTDRV.SYS. And with a 4-MB cache, Windows itself—plus your data files and most of your applications—can operate entirely out of cache. You thereby avoid much of the need to perform repeated disk accesses or continuously traverse the slow I/O bus.

If you choose a third-party disk-caching program, go with a recent version and make sure it has been updated since the release of the Windows version you are using to prevent Windows compatibility problems.

Regardless of what disk cache you use, the best advice is to experiment with various disk cache sizes to see what works best for you.

The optimal disk cache size

The optimal size for a disk cache depends on your configuration and the applications you use most frequently. One way to determine the correct size is to start with a small cache—say 1 MB—and see how it affects Windows' performance. Does Windows feel any faster? At the same time, keep an eye on the hard-disk activity light on the front of your computer (or the drive itself). If you still see a lot of disk activity, try increasing the cache size by 512 KB. Once you've found the right cache size, you should only see drive activity when you load Windows or an application.

Don't get carried away; be sure to leave enough memory for Windows to operate in. (It's easy to see how much memory Windows has by going to the Help menu and choosing About Program Manager.) If you have a 4-MB system and devote more than 1.5 MB to disk caching, Windows might start acting up. Unfortunately, Windows doesn't always complain about a lack of memory with a "Not Enough Memory" message; it might either fail to load or start up in a different mode from the one you anticipated.

If your PC doesn't have multiple megabytes to spare, install at least a 256- or 512-KB disk cache. Even a small cache is better than no cache at all. One trap to be aware of when using SMARTDRV and Windows in enhanced mode is that Windows automatically reduces the SMARTDRV cache to the minimum specified size when it loads. For example, if you install SMARTDRV with a line like

```
DEVICE = SMARTDRV.SYS 512 2048
```

for Windows 3.0, or

```
SMARTDRV 512 2048
```

(in the AUTOEXEC.BAT for Windows 3.1) you might assume that Windows would leave the cache size at 2,048 KB until it needs additional memory, then gradually reduce the cache to 512 KB. Unfortunately, that isn't how Windows works. When loaded in enhanced mode, Windows immediately reduces the cache to the minimum. In this case, instead of having a healthy 2-MB cache, you only have a 512-KB cache. To make sure the cache is the size you want it to be, not the size Windows makes it, use a line like the following:

```
DEVICE = SMARTDRV.SYS 2048 2048
```

This forces Windows to leave the disk cache at 2 MB. Most users are running Windows in enhanced mode with a much smaller disk cache than they

Tips from the Windows Resource Guide

The following tips are offered in Microsoft's manual for the Windows Resource Kit.

- ❖ Upgrade to MS-DOS 5.0 and load DOS into the high memory area by setting DOS=HIGH or DOS=HIGH,UMB in CONFIG.SYS.
- ❖ Load HIMEM.SYS as part of your CONFIG.SYS and make sure this command comes before commands that load other applications or drivers into extended memory.
- ❖ Make sure the most recent versions of HIMEM.SYS, EMM386.EXE, RAMDRIVE.SYS, and SMARTDRV.EXE are stored in the directories specified in the command lines that load them in your CONFIG.SYS and AUTOEXEC.BAT files.
- ❖ Set FILES=30 in CONFIG.SYS unless one of your applications requires a higher setting.

realize. Windows usually installs itself with a line like DEVICE = SMARTDRV.SYS 256 512, minimizing the benefits of disk caching.

Disk Optimization

Whether or not you're using a disk-caching program, optimizing your disk drive is important if you want a performance boost in the Windows environment.

Defragmentation

Because Windows is a disk-intensive program, it helps to defragment the disk occasionally. In fact, you should do so on a regular basis. Chapter 6 explained how to defragment a disk; the disk and file organization techniques given in that chapter should also be useful.

- ❖ Set BUFFERS = 10 in CONFIG.SYS if you're using SMARTDRV.EXE. Higher settings will decrease overall throughput.
- ❖ Install RAMDrive to use the TEMP environment variable if you're using a diskless workstation or if you have limited hard disk space and have more than 6 Megabytes of extended memory. This will improve performance for the Print Manager and other applications that frequently create .TMP files.
- ❖ Load EMM386.EXE if you are running non-Windows programs that require expanded memory or if you want to allocate UMBs (upper memory blocks) for loading memory-resident TSRs and drivers.
- ❖ Load only the necessary TSRs and drivers before Windows. Whenever possible, load TSRs and device drivers into the UMBs.
- ❖ Use a color or a pattern for the desktop background instead of wallpaper: it will free up more memory for running applications.
- ❖ For 386 enhanced mode, create a permanent swap file on your fastest hard drive by using the 386 Enhanced option in the Control Panel.

File organization

The file organization techniques mentioned in Chapter 6 can also be useful when applied to Windows. If most of your time will be spent running Windows and Windows applications, it may be worthwhile to relocate those files on your disk. Use a disk optimization product, such as Norton Utilities or PC Tools to move your Windows files to the most efficient possible location.

The documentation for most disk optimization programs goes into great detail about the best locations for various types of files. And while this kind of tuned file organization probably won't give you the dramatic performance increases that adding more memory or installing a disk cache would, it should make your PC noticeably faster for a minimum of effort (and, if you already own a disk utility program that allows file organization, at no additional cost).

In general, the way to tune Windows by file organization is to move your Windows files to the outer tracks of the drive, which keeps them close to the file allocation table (FAT) entries. FAT entries are frequently accessed to determine the location to which to actually write new data to disk. Thus, you minimize the distance the read/write heads have to travel when they move from the tracks that contain the FAT to the tracks that hold the files. On drives that use Zone-Bit Recording, keeping frequently accessed files on the outer tracks allow the files to be read even faster because the transfer rate is higher there.

In contrast, large data files, such as large documents, spreadsheets, or graphics, should probably be placed on the inner tracks (where they won't become fragmented as quickly as files stored on the outer tracks). The actual programs—the .EXE and .COM files—aren't in danger of becoming fragmented because they're written only once (when they're installed) and only read from then on. Files can become fragmented only when they're written, not when they're read.

Swap files

One of the performance-boosting tricks often recommended in the Windows user manuals and in books about Windows is setting aside a certain amount of your hard drive as a Windows-only disk partition, known as a permanent swap file. This technique is only possible if you're running Windows in its enhanced mode. It presumably allows Windows to swap small pages of memory back and forth from memory to disk much faster than if it had to use DOS to swap the files.

However, if you have a properly defragmented disk and your files are relatively well organized, you probably won't gain much by implementing this technique.

The downside of this scheme is that it takes available disk space away from other programs and applications. It also takes disk storage space away from Windows itself when Windows is running in a mode other than enhanced. When part of a drive is being used as a permanent Windows swap file, that disk space isn't available or visible to other programs. Finally, a permanent Windows swap file may have compatibility problems with some IDE interface drives or drives that use sector translation. If you do decide to try this technique, refer to the Windows user's guide.

Temp files

Some applications create temporary files, called temp files, while they're working. The default location for these files is usually the root directory. If for some reason your root directory isn't located on your fastest drive, you should direct the application to put the files in a directory that's on the fastest drive. This situation could arise if you upgraded to a faster drive but left the root directory on the original drive. Even if you install Windows on the new drive (as you should), Windows will put the temp files in your root directory unless you tell it to do otherwise. The Windows user's guide explains how to direct temp files to alternate directories.

Faster disk drives

Because Windows is such a drive-dependent program, it can benefit from a faster drive. It's more desirable to improve your existing drive's performance than to buy a faster one, so try the drive optimization techniques presented in the preceding chapters first. If you decide you need still more performance improvement, you'll have to spend money on a faster drive. Of course, another more common reason to get a new drive is to increase storage capacity, particularly given that many Windows programs occupy 10 to 15 MB of disk space. Fortunately, larger disks tend to be faster disks in general.

Don't try to save money by buying an older, slower drive; look for one with an access time of less than 25 ms and a transfer rate of close to or better than 1 MB per second—in other words, an IDE, ESDI, or SCSI drive. An IDE drive would probably be the least expensive of the three. Try not to settle for a close-out MFM or RLL drive. Although they can be picked up at bargain prices, their performance and capacity will be disappointing.

RAM Drives

A RAM disk is a section of memory that's set aside to be used as if it were a very fast disk drive. (For an extensive discussion of the pros and cons of RAM drives, see Chapter 6.) Unless you have huge amounts of memory to spare, creating a RAM disk is probably not the best way to go. If you have a system with at least 8 MB of main memory, perhaps creating a RAM disk would be a practical step. If your system has 4 MB or less of main memory, however, you would be wise to set aside at least 1 or 2 MB as a disk cache rather than using it for a RAM disk.

The downside of a RAM disk is that it will be used only in specific instances. In the Windows environment, the usual recommendation is to create a RAM disk, then tell Windows to use the RAM disk for the temp files. Using a RAM disk in this way could be effective, but you would probably get the same result with a disk cache. One advantage of using a RAM disk rather than a disk cache is that a RAM disk can cache (that is, speed up) both reads and writes, while many disk caches can cache only disk reads. Because most programs perform about four times as many reads as writes, the fact that a disk cache doesn't cache the writes doesn't hurt performance as much as you might expect.

Even with lots of available memory and a fairly large disk cache, you may find yourself waiting for disk activity to finish. If you do, try installing a RAM disk and directing the temp files to it as recommended in the Windows user's guide and see if it speeds things up. For example, in an older version of CorelDraw, directing the temp files to a small RAM disk (only 256 KB) can cut the time it took to print a drawing almost in half. That was despite the fact that many megabytes of memory and several megabytes of disk cache were free. Obviously, it pays to experiment with different configurations.

I would advise against using a RAM disk with Windows except in certain cases. A RAM disk requires memory that is probably better used for disk caching or left as extended memory available to Windows and its applications. When you use a RAM disk, the memory allocated is really dedicated to a single task. When the memory is used for a disk cache or for Windows memory, it's available to many programs.

Graphics

The video subsystem is another critical bottleneck of your PC's resources. Consider the display of a typical character-based program. A maximum of 2,000 characters (80 columns x 25 rows) can be on the screen at one time. A typical Windows display, because it is graphical, has more than 300,000 individual pixels (640 columns x 480 rows) active at any given time. In addition, the characters of the character-mode display have a maximum of four attributes (on, off, bright, and blinking), while a pixel in a Windows screen can be one of 16 or even 256 colors. Manipulating all those pixels demands a great deal of CPU power.

Obviously, controlling a Windows display is much more work than controlling a traditional character display. Because standard PC display cards—including monochrome, EGA, and VGA—are really buffers where the CPU can store and manipulate the display information, the CPU must perform most of that work. Unfortunately, little can be done to reduce this drain on system resources that doesn't involve adding or replacing hardware.

If you're using an 8-bit EGA card, you could get better performance by upgrading to a 16-bit VGA. This is especially true on the 386 and 486, where the very fast CPU tends to be severely bottlenecked by the older 8-bit cards.

Keep in mind when comparing VGA cards that the driver used with the card can be as important to performance as the card itself. Because Windows requires special drivers to run in anything other than standard resolution (640 x 480 with 16 colors), manufacturers provide drivers with their VGA cards. These drivers affect the VGA card's performance considerably. The reason this is important is that one set of drivers for a card can be fast while another set is slow. A card might be relatively slow at a certain resolution, while at a different (possibly even higher) resolution the same card could be very fast.

Because drivers are software, they can be improved over time without hardware changes. If you've had your VGA card for a while, newer and faster Windows drivers are probably available. Many VGA card manufacturers provide bulletin boards from which you can download the latest drivers at no charge.

Windows accelerators

Even a fast VGA card with fast Windows drivers is a major bottleneck on most systems. (Look at where video is in the data funnel.) The only way to get fast Windows video performance is to assist the CPU with a special graphics processor. Fortunately, a number of very fast, relatively inexpensive graphics accelerators aimed at Windows users are on the market or soon to be released. These cards go a long way toward eliminating the video bottleneck. Some of these products have been around for some time and are being repositioned to take advantage of the widespread popularity of Windows, while others are new and designed specifically to improve Windows performance (Figure 11-1).

These cards can be much faster than VGA cards because they have dedicated processors designed specifically to run graphics functions. While such processors don't have the sheer horsepower of a fast 386 or 486, they can perform some graphics functions much faster than a 386 or 486. Many of the graphics processors also operate at higher clock speeds (40 to 60 MHz) than the CPU itself might. By assisting the CPU where it's slow—for example, in moving blocks of pixels or drawing lines very quickly—they let the CPU get back to its primary computing function that much sooner.

The graphics coprocessor that has been around the longest is the Texas Instruments 34010. Many of the cards based on this coprocessor have long been available with Windows drivers, but they cost more than $1,000. That was more than many of us were willing to pay just to speed up Windows. But the widespread popularity of Windows has helped move the price of a new breed of 34010-based graphics cards to between $300 and $600. If you're considering one of these cards, be aware that most of them don't have VGA support and thus require a separate VGA card when you're not in Windows.

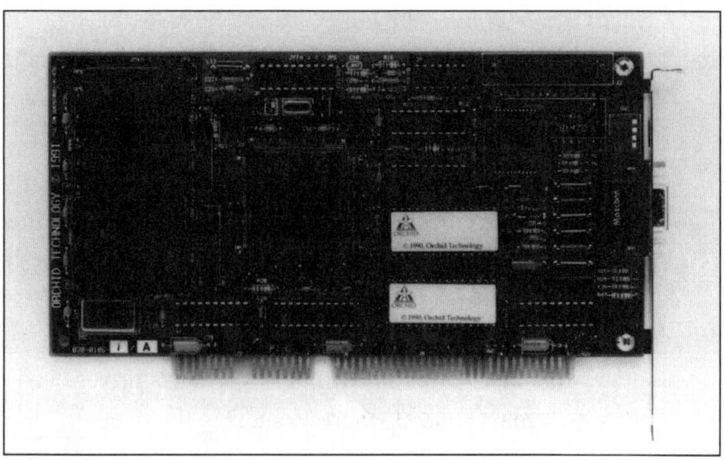

Figure 11-1. The Orchid 1280, one of the more popular Windows accelerator cards.

The 34010-based cards aren't the only way to accelerate Windows graphics; suddenly we're seeing a wealth of graphics adapters with accelerators specifically tailored to making Windows graphics run faster. For example, several cards that mimic IBM's 8514 are available, although they actually outperform the 8514 by running in noninterlaced modes and providing higher resolution. They generally list for less than $700, and some are priced under $500. The ATI Graphics Ultra card, for example, delivers an excellent performance boost to Windows graphics, and because it's 8514-compatible, it works with other programs that offer 8514 support.

The latest generation of Windows accelerator cards is based on chips like the Carrera 911 from a company called S3 (see Figure 11-1). This high-performance graphics chip also includes super VGA. Like many of the 34010-based cards and the ATI Graphics Ultra, the 911 takes advantage of dual-ported memory, called VRAM (for video RAM), for even better performance. Because the chip includes both accelerated graphics and VGA, cards based on it will be even less expensive than previous-generation products. A number of very fast Windows accelerator products based on this chip have emerged for less than $300. That's an incredible price considering a good VGA-only card cost that much not so long ago.

The S3 911 isn't the only new chip on the market; Western Digital (Paradise), Weitek, and Chips and Technologies also have chips and chip sets that allow for low-cost Windows accelerators.

What performance difference do these cards make? While they're from 2 to 20 times as fast as VGA cards on benchmarks, it's difficult to relate those numbers to a particular application. They won't make Windows run many times faster overall, since Windows still needs to contend with the disk and CPU bottlenecks. But they do make Windows graphics appear to "pop" onto the screen as opposed to the painfully slow screen updates you may be accustomed to.

Although there's really not much you can do to improve video performance without spending money, beyond checking with the manufacturer of your video adapter to see if a more recent (and faster) driver is available, the good news is that hardware is now available that improves performance at reasonable prices. And for those of you who have been struggling with Windows on a slower CPU, say a 16- or 20-MHz instead of a 33- or 50-MHz, the resulting performance gains should be impressive.

Is Windows NT faster?

Windows NT should be both slower and faster than Windows for DOS.

For regular Windows applications, you can expect that running them under regular Windows for DOS's standard mode will provide higher performance.

On the other hand, an NT version of applications that run under Windows for DOS should at least seem faster and definitely be more capable than their DOS Windows counterparts.

For one, Windows NT will let applications start a process in the background without seriously degrading foreground performance. That means you can start some process, such as formatting a floppy disk, that would force all activity to cease under the DOS version of Windows. Only when the activity ceases and the cursor changes back from an hourglass into a pointer can you continue. Under Windows NT, the formatting will happen in the background, and you can continue to work with other programs. In other words, you won't ever have to wait for the hourglass under Windows NT.

There should be some raw performance improvement as well. Windows NT is a 32-bit environment, which eliminates some of the overhead of the oddly segmented 16-bit architecture used by Intel chips to maintain compatibility with early versions of the x86 family. There are also performance benefits to be had from such advanced operating system features as threading and NT's ability to use higher-performance file system than DOS's standard FAT (file allocation table) system. Try setting up NT with HPFS (high-performance file system), and you'll see a measurable difference. You'll also discover that disk fragmentation is less of a problem when using HPFS.

On the other hand, be prepared to have somc heavy-duty hardware if you're going to run Windows NT. The minimum recommended memory is 8 MB, and 16 MB is a far better idea.

Finally, Windows NT provides a number of performance tracking features that will let you fine-tune performance in much the same way you can fine-tune NetWare or UNIX. A discussion of those tuning knobs is beyond the scope of this book; fortunately, the process isn't as obtuse as it is under UNIX or NetWare, because Windows NT provides a fine graphical user interface for the performance tuning parameters.

Summary

In this chapter we've looked at the three major areas in which PC optimization techniques prove the most effective: the system's main memory and its disk and video subsystems.

Windows needs as much memory as you can give it. Ideally, this additional memory should be configured as extended.

Certainly a fast hard disk with a low access time and high data-transfer rate will help you in terms of Windows performance, but it's more important to take full advantage of the drive you already have. Use a disk cache, defragment your drive, and organize your files.

If you don't want to invest several hundred dollars in a Windows accelerator card, at the very least you should have a fast 16-bit VGA card. If you bought an 8-bit VGA card a few years ago and have been putting off buying a 16-bit card, now may be the time.

Finally, don't let the Windows nomenclature lure you into running in 386 enhanced mode when you don't need to. Remember, enhanced refers to the features, not the performance.

By taking advantage of some of these suggestions, you can avoid having to buy a new computer just to make Windows run at an acceptable speed.

APPENDIX A

Hot-Key Combinations for Windows 3.1 and Applications

Generic (Applications and Windows Desktop)

Key Combination	Operation	Windows Program
CTRL + ESC	Display Task List	All
ALT + Space Bar	Display application's Control menu	All
ALT + Hyphen	Display document's Control menu	All
ALT + F4	Close active window	All
CTRL + F4	Close document window	All
ALT + TAB	Switch windows	All
CTRL + TAB	Switch document window	All
ALT + Backspace	Undo previous action	All
ALT + Letter	Display drop-down box denoted by letter	All
SHIFT + Up Arrow	Extend highlight upward	All
SHIFT + Down Arrow	Extend highlight downward	All
SHIFT + DEL	Cut selected data	Application
CTRL + INS	Copy selected data	Application
SHIFT + INS	Paste selected data	Application
+	Expand one level	File Manager*
*	Expand branch	File Manager*
CTRL + *	Expand all	File Manager*
Hyphen	Collapse all	File Manager*
SHIFT+Up Arrow or SHIFT+Down Arrow	File Manager**	Extended selection
CTRL+/	Select all	File Manager**
ALT + P	Pause processing queue	Print Manager
ALT + R	Resume processing queue	Print Manager
ALT + D	Delete print job	Print Manager

* Directory tree only

** Directory window only

Word for Windows

Key Combination	Operation
CTRL + F	Select font
CTRL + P	Select point size
CTRL + S	Select style
CTRL + B	Bold
CTRL + C	Center paragraph
CTRL + J	Justify paragraph
CTRL + L	Left-align paragraph
CTRL + R	Right-align paragraph
CTRL + INS	Copy to Clipboard
CTRL + Enter	Page break
SHIFT + DEL	Cut to Clipboard
CTRL + Backspace	Delete word left
SHIFT + INS	Paste from Clipboard
ALT + E	Open Edit menu
ALT + F	Open File menu
ALT + T	Open Format menu
ALT + I	Open Insert menu
ALT + M	Open Macro menu
ALT + W	Open Window menu
ALT + Enter	Repeat last operation
CTRL + W	Underline word
ALT + Backspace	Undo command
SHIFT + F3	Toggle case
F5	Go to...
SHIFT + F7	Thesaurus
F12	Save file as...
SHIFT + F12	Save file
CTRL + F12	Open file
CTRL + SHIFT + F12	Print file

Excel 3 and 4 for Windows

Key Combination	Operation
HOME	Select beginning of row
END	Select end of row
CTRL + HOME	Select cell A1
CTRL + END	Select cell last used
SHIFT + Space Bar	Select row
CTRL + Space Bar	Select column
SHIFT + CTRL + Space Bar	Select entire worksheet
F5	Go to cell or reference
CTRL + ?	Select notes
SHIFT + CTRL + Arrow	Select area to edge of data
CTRL + *	Select block of data
CTRL + /	Select current array
CTRL + \	Select row differences
CTRL + |	Select column differences
CTRL +]	Select immediately dependent formula
CTRL + }	Select all dependent formulas
CTRL + [	Select immediately preceding formulas
CTRL + {	Select all preceding formulas
ALT + =	Activate the Auto + SUM button
Backspace	Clear cell/activate formula bar
CTRL + ;	Display current date
CTRL + :	Display current time
CTRL + ‘	Copy formula from cell above
CTRL + “	Copy value from cell above
CTRL + Enter	Fill selected cells with entry
SHIFT + CTRL + Enter	Fill selected cells with array
F2	Activate formula bar
ALT + Enter	Repeat last action
ALT + Backspace	Undo last action
CTRL++	Insert cells
CTRL + -	Delete cells
DEL +	Clear dialog box
CTRL + DEL	Clear only formulas
SHIFT + DEL	Cut
CTRL + INS	Copy
SHIFT + INS	Paste
SHIFT + Arrow	Select in formula bar

Excel 3 and 4 for Windows, *continued*

Key Combination	Operation
CTRL + Arrow	Move by word in formula word
SHIFT + CTRL + Arrow	Select words in formula bar
SHIFT + END	Select to end of formula bar

Ventura for Windows

Key Combination	Operation
CTRL + U	Access frame tool
CTRL + I	Access paragraph tool
CTRL + O	Access text tool
CTRL + P	Access table tool
CTRL + S	Save
DEL	Cut
SHIFT + DEL	Copy
INS	Paste
CTRL + B	Renumber chapter
CTRL + R	Reduced view
CTRL + N	Normal view
CTRL + E	Enlarged view
CTRL + T	Show/hide tabs and returns
CTRL + W	Toolbox window
CTRL + V	Tag List window
CTRL + Y	File List window
CTRL + G	Go to page..
CTRL + 2	Add new tag
CTRL + K	Update tag list
CTRL + Enter	Line break
CTRL + D	Edit special item
CTRL + SHIFT + 2	Trademark
CTRL + SHIFT + R	Registered trademark
CTRL + Z	Send to back
CTRL + A	Bring to front
CTRL + Q	Select all
CTRL + L	Line attributes
CTRL + F	File attributes
CTRL + Q	Select all

Computer Caches

A cache is probably the single most important concept in computer performance. In simple terms, a cache is a place to hold data that will be accessed frequently. A cache uses memory that is faster than the memory normally used to hold data.

In terms of our data funnel, cache is an upper section in the data funnel used to temporarily store data that would normally be stored in a lower section of the funnel. A cache can be created to function at any level of the data funnel.

A computer cache is able to improve performance because computers use data from the same general area of memory for a relatively long period of time before moving on to a different area of memory. (A "relatively long period of time" means only a fraction of a second, but keep in mind that to a microprocessor, a second is a long period of time.) The fact that computers frequently use memory from the same area is called locality of reference.

There is seldom an opportunity to change the type of RAM cache your PC has, although sometimes you can increase its size. Because a lot of marketing mumbo jumbo relating to caches gets tossed around, however, a brief overview of some cache features would be helpful. Some of these principles also apply to disk caches.

Cache Organization

The first computer caches allowed only one possible location for data from any given memory address that might be stored in the cache. This architecture was called direct mapping. Direct mapping was a desirable feature since it required the cache controller (the circuitry that stored and retrieved cached data) to look in only one location to determine if the requested data was already in the cache. But fast cache memory is expensive and consists of only a limited number of storage locations, called blocks, so multiple slow memory locations were mapped to the same block of fast cache memory. Since only one memory location could be stored in a block at one time, different memory addresses would have to compete for the same block. Thus, even though there were lots of open blocks in the cache, the cache controller would have to replace one stored block with another that was mapped to the same location in cache. The cache was effectively overflowing even though it was still largely empty.

The use of a single set of blocks, called a way, did not make for the most efficient use of the available cache memory. The computer architects reasoned that if they could divide the cache up into more than one set of blocks—that is, into multiple ways—the likelihood of more than one memory address requiring a block at the same time would be reduced. A cache with two sets of blocks, or two ways, was called a two-way set associative cache. A cache with four sets was called a four-way set associative cache, and so on. The addition of multiple ways made for more efficient use of the cache memory because the more sets there are the less likely the cache will have to start replacing data before the cache is filled.

But the implementation of a cache with multiple sets of mappings is very complex. The cache controller in a multiple-way set associative cache must check multiple cache locations before it can determine whether the desired data is in the cache or not. And it must do this very quickly. If it takes longer to find something in the cache than it would to find it without a cache, the cache is actually a detriment rather than an enhancement. The many esoteric details of implementing one design over the other are far beyond the scope of this book.

In fact, you probably shouldn't even care what type of cache your system has. Because the type of set associativity a cache uses is only important when comparing caches of the same size—all the advantages of a multiple-way cache are more than overcome by a single way cache that's twice as large. A direct-mapped cache may not make as good a use of the available cache memory as a multiple-way set associative cache, but if it is big enough, it doesn't have to.

Replacement Policy

In a set associative cache, the cache's replacement policy is one of its most important features. The replacement policy determines what to remove from the cache when the all the necessary blocks are already in use and an additional memory location requires one of the blocks. The cache controller can chose a set to replace at random, it can chose the set that has used the block first, or it can chose the block that was least recently used. The least recently used block is probably the most desirable to replace, but it is also the most difficult to determine.

Hit Rate

Whenever the CPU finds the data it needs in the cache that is called a cache hit. When the CPU fails to find the data it needs in the cache that is called a cache miss. The ratio of cache hits to cache misses is called the cache hit ratio. The cache hit ratio is a measure of the relative effectiveness of a cache. The better the cache design or the larger the cache the higher the cache hit ratio. A well-designed RAM cache normally will have a hit ratio of greater than 90 percent.

If a relatively small amount of fast static random access memory (SRAM), say 32 KB to 64 KB, is enough for the CPU to find what it needs in this memory 90 percent of the time, the effect is almost as if the computer were equipped only with fast SRAM even though a vast majority of its memory is much slower RAM. By using a cache with a high hit rate, you can get the performance of a computer with a large amount of fast memory and no RAM cache for the much lower overall cost of a small amount of fast memory and a cache controller.

Write Through and Write Back

Factors besides the hit rate also affect the efficiency of the cache.

When the CPU writes new data to the cache, the cache controller must update main memory with the new data. By making sure that the information in the cache is the same as that in main memory the cache controller is said to maintain cache coherency. If the cache controller allows the data in the cache to differ from data in main memory, the data is said to be stale.

The simplest way to avoid having stale data is to make sure that every time the CPU updates the cache, the data is automatically written through to the main memory. This is called a write through cache. To prevent the CPU from accessing any data until the main memory has been updated, the cache controller must lock the CPU out of both the cache and the main memory until the write through has been completed. If the CPU needs to access the cache or main memory before the write through is completed, the CPU must wait. This will slow the overall performance of the CPU.

One way to prevent this problem is for the cache controller to update a small but fast buffer instead of directly updating the main memory. Because the buffer can be faster than the main memory, the cache controller can make the cache available to the CPU sooner. This method of updating the main memory is called a buffered or posted write through.

Another way to avoid the problem of making the CPU wait while the main memory is updated is for the cache controller to keep track of which data is stale and only update the memory when it must, not immediately after every memory write. This technique, which is called write back or copy back, is more difficult to implement but is faster than a posted write through. The concept of buffering, or posting, the writes can also be applied to the write back cache to further increase its performance as well. This is the most complicated of all techniques to implement, but it results in the fastest cache.

Cache size

Often the size of RAM cache your PC uses is set by the computer's designer and manufacturer and you can't change it (although some designs allow you to increase the cache size if you are willing to spend the extra money). So the size of the cache may be important to you before you make your purchase. This is a subject of endless debate in the computer literature. The debate is complicated because the decision rarely comes down to cache size only. There normally are many other factors involved, as we've discussed.

But all else being equal, a large cache is better than a small one. Because it can store more data before new data will overwrite the old data, and thus increase the likelihood that the data is in the cache. (Bigger is not necessarily better when you're talking about a buffer, because increasing the buffer size makes it take longer to locate any given piece of buffered data.)

If a large cache is always better, why aren't computers designed with multiple-megabyte caches? The reason is cost. The cost of memory fast enough to implement a RAM cache is very great relative to the cost of standard memory. So computer designers and manufacturers try to build the most effective cache they can with the least amount of memory possible.

Buffer Versus Cache

As we have seen, a computer cache can be very complex. Sometimes it is useful to try getting some of the benefits of a cache without its complexity. A buffer is similar to a cache, but it is much simpler. Typically a buffer is fast memory set aside to temporarily store data, much like a cache, but a buffer lacks the sophistication of a cache. In its simplest form, a buffer is a first-in-first-out (FIFO) device. It can be written to very quickly, and then it slowly writes out the data to some other device that can only accept the data more slowly. A buffer is used when the cost savings of a simple design outweighs the benefits of a more effective but also more complex and expensive design.

A key difference between a buffer and a cache arises when a buffer must be read from randomly. Because a buffer does not use sophisticated methods of storing the data, it cannot access its data as quickly as a cache. In fact, locating a particular piece of data in a buffer may require a sequential search from beginning to end. This means that the larger the buffer the longer it will take to locate the data (on average). Depending on the speed of the buffer relative to what it is buffering, a large buffer may be slower than a small buffer or no buffer at all. (This is why the original SMARTDRV.SYS, which is a track buffer, can actually be slower when it is configured with a very large amount of memory than when it has less memory.)

Summary

This discussion on caching applies mostly to the RAM caches—the cache that lies between the CPU and main memory. But as we have seen throughout the book, caches can be used in many places. In fact, nearly anywhere in the data funnel where there is slow throughput, you can reduce the bottleneck by implementing a cache or buffer. The further up in the data funnel you can place the cache the faster it will be and the more effectively it can eliminate the bottleneck. A RAM cache is very effective, even though it is only one level above the area it is caching. But a software disk cache is even more effective, because it is actually two levels above the area in the data funnel it is caching (that is, it moves the data up from the disk past the I/O bus to main memory).

The further up in the data funnel you place the cache, however, the higher the cost-of the cache per megabyte. So you must make a decision as to how much you are willing to spend to gain performance. Computer architects make those decisions for you when it comes to the on-chip cache of the 486 CPU, say, or the organization of our PC's RAM cache. But when it comes to the size and type of caches to use in all the other levels of the data funnel, you must make the decision yourself.

Interpreting Benchmarks

Many computer professionals have spent a tremendous amount of time over the years benchmarking computer systems and software. The results have been cause for great joy and great frustration. The real question is do you really gain a greater understanding of the computer and how well it performs?

According to Webster's Unabridged Dictionary, a benchmark is a point of reference. When used as a point of reference, a benchmark can be extremely useful. However, when used as the ultimate indicator of performance, or the *only* indicator of performance, it can be very misleading.

Nonetheless, benchmarks are important. We need some way to gauge the relative performance levels of computers, particularly a before-and-after gauge of the impact of a change intended to improve performance; benchmark testing provides such a way.

There is no doubt that the ideal way to measure and compare computer performance is to run the actual applications that the computer is to run in its normal work environment. Unfortunately, no easy or practical way to do this exists, although the BAPCo SysMark92 discussed later in this appendix may be the answer, particularly for organizations that don't mind spending $795.

In the case of comparing two different types of computers, the same program often will not run on both. For example, many of the programs that you would run on your PC will not run on a Sun workstation. So it is simply not possible to run your application programs on a Sun and see if it is faster or slower than your PC. Comparing application speed and features is often difficult and not necessarily an accurate assessment of performance.

The Holy Grail of benchmarks would be one that gives the desired results in a single number that accurately reflects all aspects of any computer's performance. While it can be argued that the BAPCo SysMark92 comes close to that goal for the most commonly used business applications, it is not universally applicable—it cannot be used to compare only Intel-based desktop computers that run DOS and Windows. And the applications tested may not match the application you wish to run on your computers. Since most application tuning is an attempt to increase the performance of a computer at a particular point in the data funnel, benchmarks that examine the performance of only that aspect of a computer can be very useful.

On the other hand, keep in mind that most applications draw on the various resources of your PC, so a single benchmark result can't be used as the only indicator of expected application performance. For example, a benchmark that measures CPU performance is not valid if the application you intend to run is very disk intensive. Another example of incorrect testing would be using a video benchmark test on applications that have a limited amount of video activity.

Ultimately, the only way to determine if the change you've made to your computer's configuration improves its performance is to run the application you care about before and after the modification, doing your best to ascertain the change in performance.

The Small Benchmarks

Unlike BAPCo's SysMark92, most benchmark tests are relatively small programs that try to test the performance of one particular component of a computer by generating artificial traffic to exercise that component. You can think of them as gauges of a computer's throughput in any part of the data funnel, although most benchmarks are not that clearly delineated and actually involve several parts of the data funnel. Thus, to accurately evaluate the results and performance of a benchmark test, you must understand what operations are being performed and what is being measured.

The best a simple, single-point-of-examination benchmark test can give you is a number that accurately reflects a single aspect of a computer's performance relative to other similar computers. When used as a point of reference, a benchmark test can be relevant and valid. If used for much more than that, it can be very misleading. Nevertheless the allure of benchmark testing remains. We are always searching for a simple, easy-to-understand number that can summarize a computer's performance. Four of the most common such numbers are the Whetstone, the Dhrystone, the Linpack, and the Livermore Loops benchmarks.

The Whetstone benchmark test measures math coprocessor performance. It records the time it takes to perform predefined floating point operations. The results of this test are expressed in terms of Whetstones per second, or millions of floating point instructions per second (MFLOPS). This benchmark test requires the installation of a math coprocessor.

The Dhrystone benchmark test measures integer processes per second and is an indicator of expected CPU performance for standard, non-floating point operations. This benchmark performs several classes of operations, including assignment, arithmetic, and control. It uses integer, character, pointer, string, array, and record operand types and is normally not affected by the installation of a math coprocessor. The results of this test are expressed in terms of Dhrystones per second. The results can be translated into VAX MIPS by dividing the result by 1,757, as we'll discuss later in this appendix. The name Dhrystone itself is a play on the name Whetstone.

The Linpack benchmark test has a high percentage of floating point operations. It is used to measure the performance of a computer in solving dense systems of linear equations. The algorithms concentrate on manipulating array elements with column-oriented results. Most of the work is done in a single subroutine, making this a measure of localized Fortran system performance. It should not be taken as a general measure of performance. The results of this benchmark test are expressed in terms of millions of floating point instructions per second (MFLOPS). This benchmark test requires the installation of a math coprocessor.

The Livermore Loops benchmark test is also a test of floating point performance. It contains a broad sample of generic Fortran computations. There are 24 kernels, each tuned to benchmark a different range of the Fortran development system being measured. The results of this benchmark are expressed as millions of floating point instructions per second (MFLOPS). This benchmark test requires the installation of a math coprocessor.

All of the above benchmarks have no I/O element so they are not influenced by the performance of the disk or video subsystem. You can obtain public-domain versions of each of these benchmarks from a number of sources, including M&T Online, which can be accessed through CompuServe or by dialing direct. Access via the direct number (415-358-8857) requires communication parameters of 8 data bits, no parity, and 1 stop bit.

The "Magic" Numbers

Some simple benchmarks have gotten unfounded reputations for accurately representing performance. Nevertheless, these tests can tell us something, particularly if they are run with the principles expounded in this book in mind. Examples include Norton's SI (which, incidentally, is a slightly different measurement since the release of the version included with Norton Desktop for DOS and Norton Desktop for Windows), Landmark, and PowerMeter.

Perhaps the best example of the problems with such numbers is the commonly used MIPS rating. An examination of MIPS shows just how convoluted computer benchmark numbers can be.

MIPS

Sometimes called the meaningless indication of processor speed, MIPS actually stands for millions of instructions per second. Interestingly, that is not what it actually measures, as you'll soon see.

MIPS is a commonly used measurement to show the potential performance of a computer. Actually, it measures the performance of a limited subset of the CPU's instruction set. Computer performance is much more than simply the level of CPU performance. There is no substitute for a fast CPU, but this alone can't deliver high performance unless the rest of the system is properly tuned.

Even using MIPS as the only indicator of relative CPU performance has its problems, because there isn't one widely accepted way to measure MIPS. However, some history is in order.

Back in the late '70s, Digital Equipment Corporation (DEC) was about to introduce a new minicomputer called the VAX 11/780. The DEC marketing department wanted to convey the power of this new machine by comparing it to the then-current IBM 370 mainframe. The IBM folks believed that their computer was capable of executing about 1 million instructions per second and marketed it as a 1-MIPS machine. The DEC marketers surmised that if their computer was roughly equal in performance to the IBM machine, it was also a 1-MIPS machine. The problem with this reasoning was that the IBM machine and the DEC machine executed different instruction sets; one million instructions on the DEC machine may not have done the same amount of work as one million instructions on the IBM. This fact was believed to be a minor technicality. One million instructions per second just sounded too good to be ignored, so the VAX 11/780 was rolled out as a 1-MIPS computer.

The popularity of the VAX minicomputer and the fact that it apparently had a MIPS rating of 1 made it a good comparison or benchmark machine. Subsequently, a computer that was twice as fast as a VAX was called a 2-MIPS computer, three times as fast a 3-MIPS computer, and so on. Some professionals questioned the claim by DEC and pointed out that the original VAX couldn't actually execute one million instructions per second. They were given an interesting and innovative reply—these were VAX MIPS, which had no relation to the numbers of instructions per second executed. That, of course, begs the question: if a VAX MIPS isn't really one million instructions per second, then how do we determine how many MIPS any computer is capable of?

The generally accepted way to determine the MIPS rating of a computer today is to run the previously discussed Dhrystone benchmark test and compare the results to the results of the VAX 11/780 running the same Dhrystone benchmark. This is somewhat like comparing the time it takes for a car to go one lap around a race track with the time it takes another car to go around a different race track, without knowing the difference in size between the two race tracks. Nonetheless, it does give us a number. And given the choice between a number of very dubious origin and no number at all, we consumers tend to go for a number. After all, would you rather hear that your computer is an 8-MIPS computer or that it's just a fast computer.

With all the above caveats about MIPS in mind, the way to determine the MIPS of your computer is to run the Dhrystone benchmark test and divide the results by the number earned by the VAX 11/780, which was 1,757. If your computer earns a Dhrystone of 3,514, it is twice as fast as a VAX 11/780 and thus a 2-MIPS machine, although that in no way means your computer actually executes two million instructions per second.

Don't be disappointed if the number you get is not quite as high as the MIPS numbers you've read in advertisements. There is no such thing as the one true MIPS number, due largely to continually improving compiler technology. The results of the Dhrystone benchmark test are influenced by compiler optimization, and compilers are continually changing.

Publication Benchmarks

Many of the popular computer publications use their own sets of benchmarks to compare the performance of various computers. *PC Magazine* and *PC Week*, for example, use the ZD Labs benchmark suite. These benchmark programs can be very useful if the publication provides the programs to the public so they can run them on their own machines. The benchmarks used by the Ziff-Davis publications can be obtained by mail from the respective publications or downloaded from ZiffNet, an on-line information service that is available on CompuServe or Prodigy. These benchmarks exercise a particular component found in the data funnel—video, bus, CPU, memory, disk I/O, and so on—and might be quite valuable for ascertaining the impact of changes you make based on specific suggestions or general principles described in this book.

Some publications, such as InfoWorld, try to make their benchmarks more directly relevant to actual performance by running popular applications and then reporting the results. While this can be of some benefit, these results can be just as misleading as those derived from the standard benchmarks. For obvious reasons, not everyone runs their applications in the same manner. A publication may report that one machine is faster at running a particular CAD program, but actually they are reporting that one machine is faster at running a given set of CAD operations. For those publications that use application-level benchmark tests, it is important that they explicitly define the exact operations that were being measured. Ideally, they should describe in great detail the tasks run against which files. In this way you can see if the results are relevant to your particular application.

Another issue to be aware of when looking at any benchmark results in publications is the frequency that the programs or test suites are updated. The results obtained by using the various versions of the benchmarks are usually not comparable to each other. It is important to compare results of each test that have been generated by using the same version of the program.

Do-it-Yourself

Of course, you can take this same application-based approach yourself, which will guarantee that you're testing the applications you really care about. Be aware that even when running the same program, you have a bewildering variety of different tasks you could be testing. Also be aware that to compare the performance of two computers running the same programs, you must duplicate the exact environment and set of tasks. Unfortunately, the only mechanism for capturing the use of a program and playing it back—a macro program—can have significant impact on performance, so you're still not going to be 100 percent sure that your results are accurate. Executing the activities by hand also introduces a number of variables.

Bottom line: This can be very expensive given the number of software packages that might have to be purchased and the very labor-intensive task of running tests and examining the results. The results are still open to question, and what you find today might not hold tomorrow if a new version of software is released.

A non-profit coalition called Business Applications Performance Corporation (BAPCo) has tackled the tough task of creating an application-based benchmark for comparing the performance of desktop PCs that run DOS and Windows. Later application suites from BAPCo will bring OS/2 and Windows NT into the picture.

BAPCo's SysMark92 automatically runs the best-selling business applications through a series of tasks designed to emulate the activities of real-world users of the software.

The suite is divided into five categories: word processing (using Word for Windows and WordPerfect), spreadsheet (enlisting Excel, Lotus 1-2-3, and Quattro Pro), database (dBASE IV 1.1 and Paradox 3.5), desktop publishing (PageMaker 4.0 and Ventura Publisher), software development (Borland C++ and Microsoft C), and graphics (Harvard Graphics and CorelDraw). A workload manager coordinates execution of each benchmark segment, verifies correct results, and reports the performance measurement. How fast is, say, 100 on the SysMark92? In early use of the SysMark92 at InfoWorld, the weekly news publication, some 50-MHz 80486 machines scored in the 160 to 170 range, while a Compaq 386/20e scored 40.42 and a Compaq 386/33 scored 62.42.

Running the SysMark92 is relatively simple because of all the work done by the BAPCo member organizations, many of which donated hundreds of hours to the task of creating the benchmark manager and scripts that ran the applications in question through typical real-world scenarios: for example, building a spreadsheet model, entering data, moving around the model to make changes and checking what-if results, creating graphs, rolling up one model with several others, and so on.

Even though it is completely automated, running the SysMark92 requires some effort. Loading the benchmark entails a 22-disk installation. So many disks are required because "crippled" versions of the executable files of the commercial programs used in the benchmark are included—you don't have to own the software used in the SysMark92 to run the test suite. And a full run of the suite will take most of a business day, the actual amount of time depending, of course, on the speed of thc computer tested.

While the $795 price of the SysMark92 suite may make it too expensive for individuals to justify the purchase, organizations with significant computer budgets will not find the price a barrier. For more information on SysMark92, you can call BAPCo at (408) 988-7654.

Myths, Placebos, and Suspected Placebos

Myths

Replacing your DRAM with faster DRAM

Several articles in PC publications have stated, in effect, "This system would have been faster if the manufacturer had used faster DRAM." Changing the speed of main memory in a PC can almost never result in faster performance. Most PCs are designed to operate with a certain speed of memory. Using memory slower than the designed speed will result in a "Parity Error" message followed by a system crash or will simply prevent the computer from operating at all.

Using faster memory than the memory the PC was designed for does not provide any performance benefit.

Replacing your CPU with a faster CPU

Replacing your CPU with a higher-clock-speed CPU may not increase your PCs performance unless you change other parts of the motherboard at the same time. For example, if you have a 386/25 and replace the 25-MHz CPU with a 33-MHz CPU without changing anything else on your motherboard, your system will run at the same speed as before. The reason is your computer has been designed to operate at a certain clock speed, which is set by an oscillator, not by the CPU. A CPU with a higher speed rating has merely been designed (or tested) to run at the higher speed, but it will only run at the speed of the oscillator, and it may be that the rest of the system cannot support a higher-speed clock.

This does not apply to the special clock-doubling CPUs that have been designed to deliver higher performance even when running at the same clock speed as the original CPU but are inserted into special "performance upgrade sockets" that manufacturers are starting to put onto their motherboards.

Placebos

Shadow ROM

I mentioned shadow ROM in regard to video ROM in Chapter 9, but some PCs have the ability to shadow the system ROM as well. In this case, the BIOS (basic input output system) is relocated from relatively slow ROM into faster RAM. While in theory it seems this would speed operations, in practice, shadowing the system BIOS does not improve performance. But shadow ROM has now become a standard feature for most high-performance PCs since customers have come to expect it. If your computer doesn't have it, don't worry, your performance isn't suffering. Even with PCs that do support system ROM shadowing, you may have to disable it for compatibility reasons, because some programs expect to find the BIOS in a certain location and may cause problems when it's not where it expected it to be.

The one operation that system ROM shadowing can definitely speed up is the initial POST (power on self test) when you first start your computer. It is debatable whether by making your computer boot faster you have actually improved performance.

FASTOPEN command

Later versions of MS and PC DOS include a command called FASTOPEN, which is supposed to store information about the location of your recently accessed files in memory. The FASTOPEN command is often mentioned in other books as a way to improve disk performance, we have not noticed increased disk performance by using it. The fact that I have never felt any increased disk performance together with the many compatibility warnings that disk optimization and file organization programs include about FASTOPEN leads me to believe that the command is more trouble than it is worth. If you are using a disk cache program, there is definitely no need to use the FASTOPEN command.

Suspected Placebos

Permanent swap file

The Windows user's manual mentions that setting up a permanent Windows swap file can improve disk performance when running Windows in enhanced mode. If it does, it certainly doesn't improve it by very much. The downside of a permanent Windows swap file is that it takes disk space away from non-Windows applications and can cause compatibility problems with certain IDE drives.

Bus master controllers

There are disk controller cards are available, called bus master controllers, that have their own processor. This gives them the ability to take control of the I/O bus and operate independently of the PC's CPU. The standard AT bus allows only a single bus mastering controller, while the EISA and Micro-Channel buses can support multiple bus masters. In theory, a bus master controller should be able to deliver higher performance than a standard disk controller because the bus master can free up the CPU to work on other tasks while the bus master controller performs its task.

While bus master controllers can improve performance with a multitasking operating system such as UNIX or Novell, it is doubtful whether they can deliver any additional performance in a DOS environment. Given the fact that they are normally quite expensive, bus master controllers are difficult to justify if you are running DOS or DOS and Windows.

Smaller drive partitions are faster than large drive partitions

You might think that if you partitioned your hard disk into multiple small partitions of about 20 MB each, your access time will be faster than if you partition the drive as one large partition. After all, the average access time for each of the smaller partitions should be less than the average access time for the single large partition, right? This is true from benchmark standpoints, since the smaller partitions have fewer cylinders and average access time is dependent on the number of cylinders (more cylinders increases the largest distance over which the head has to seek), however, it is not true from a practical standpoint because during normal computing, your files should not be spread out over very many cylinders. So your actual access times should be well under the average access time anyway. Occasionally running a disk optimizing program will do more than partitioning your drive into small partitions. The down side of partitioning your drive into many partitions it can become unmanageable. With a large drive you can end up wasting a lot of time as you search for files on drives C, D, E, F, G, and so on.

Average seek time is the most important factor in evaluating a drive's access time. Some drive manufacturers offer truncated drives simply to improve the average seek time. In practice, the truncated and untruncated drive are likely to deliver the same real-world performance because your accesses are likely to be in the same general area.

Unconventional Performance Techniques

Most of the techniques covered in this book are generally accepted techniques for enhancing computer performance. But additional techniques, best described as unconventional, may be frowned on by your PC manufacturer and may in fact violate your warranty.

Delaying the Refresh Cycle

This technique needs a little background explanation. The main memory of most PCs is composed of DRAM chips. DRAM memory must be refreshed on a regular basis, which means that a small charge must be sent to every memory cell on a DRAM chip every so often or the chip will lose the information it was storing. This charge is called a refresh, and it is sent to the DRAM many times per second. During the time that the DRAM is being refreshed, the CPU cannot access the PCs memory. The PCs performance is slowed by a few percentage points because of the CPU cannot access the memory during the refresh cycle.

Current DRAM chips don't need to be refreshed as often as the older DRAM chips did, but many PCs are still being designed with refresh cycles that reflect the specifications of the older memory. Some computer hackers have discovered that if they delay the frequency with which their CPU refreshes its DRAM, they can squeeze another one or two percentage points of performance out of their PCs. This technique is not recommended.

Pushing the Chip

Chip pushing refers to running a CPU at a higher speed than it is rated by the CPU manufacturer. Chip manufacturers test their chips and certify them to run properly at a certain clock speed. This rate of speed is normally marked on the chip. Chip pushing goes back to the days of the original IBM PC AT. The original PC AT was apparently designed to operate at 8 MHz, but IBM decided to ship it as a 6-MHz computer. The PC AT was designed to use a socketed crystal chip that determined the computer's clock speed, and that crystal chip could be removed relatively easily. Some users discovered that if they removed the original 6-MHz crystal and replaced it with an 8-MHz crystal, the computer still worked well. This was a quick and relatively easy way to get a 30 percent performance increase.

Needless to say, replacing a computer's crystal chip with a faster one may violate the computer's warranty and can lead to unpredictable results.

Over the years, determined hardware hackers experimented with replacing the oscillator (later PCs used oscillators instead of crystals) in an effort to get a performance boost. The process became much more difficult when manufacturers started soldering in the oscillator instead of placing it in a socket.

The process of chip pushing was generally confined to hardware hackers experimenting on their own machines. Occasionally a computer manufacturer would use these techniques when desperate to ship the next generation of computer but confronted by a shortage of the proper CPUs. After such practices were reported a few times in the computer trade press, they were largely stopped.

The Ice Cap

One of the more interesting methods of achieving higher PC performance uses a device called the Ice Cap.

The faster a semiconductor device runs, the hotter it becomes. Once they exceed a certain speed, they reach a temperature beyond the operating temperature recommended by the manufacturer. Indeed, the chip may actually fail before the temperature reaches the manufacturer's highest temperature rating. One company that recognized this fact is Velox Corp. They developed a solid-state cooling device capable of keeping a chip cool, even when it is run at much higher speeds than intended by the manufacturer. The device, called an Ice Cap, can cool a CPU down to as low as 0° centigrade.

Velox has been able to push a 33-MHz 486 chip to run at 50 MHz by cooling it in this manner, and will soon probably push a 50-MHz to an even higher rate. Of course, Intel does not condone this method of performance enhancement, but it is being used by a number of Velox customers. The problem with running a chip at a speed that has not been tested by the manufacturer is not knowing whether the chip is truly functioning properly. While it is possible to make certain that the computer will function at the higher speed, it is not possible to test the validity of all the CPUs operations without very sophisticated test equipment used by the CPU manufacturers. The computer may appear to run software correctly, but there is no simple way to make sure that it will always produce the correct results. For those willing to live with that caveat, the device is available from Velox in a number of configurations. Velox sells the Ice Cap alone for computer designers that want to experiment with higher clock speeds. They also sell motherboards complete with the Ice Cap and a CPU for those who want to build a system that runs at a higher speed than is currently available.

Simply cooling off the CPU and increasing the system's clock speed by replacing the motherboard's oscillator is not all that is necessary to make a PC run faster. The motherboard itself must be designed to run at the higher clock speed. Cranking up the speed, Ice Cap or not, will not make the entire system run faster. All of the circuitry must be designed to support the higher speed.

Versions of DOS

MS and PC DOS

The version of MS or PC DOS you use does not seem to have much impact on performance, except DOS 5.0. Version 5.0 does free up more of the first 640 KB of memory, which can be quite useful if you are short of memory below 1 MB. This is particularly true when you are running a computer on a network. Follow the directions included in the DOS 5.0 manual to create as much regular DOS memory as you can; performance will increase in many situations.

MS DOS 5.0 includes some very useful productivity features as well. The most important of these is the DOSKEY program. DOSKEY not only allows you to scroll through previous commands, but also allows you to edit these commands and reexecute them. These features can save a lot of time if you use DOS from the command line and not from within a shell program or Windows. Another excellent feature is a macro program that allows you to assign a number of keystrokes or instructions to a few keys.

DOS 5.0 also supports disk partitions larger than 32 MB. This means that you will no longer need a third-party driver to support large disk partitions. Support for large partitions was introduced in DOS 4.0, however, a number of compatibility problems made DOS 4.0 less than attractive for most users.

DOS 5.0 also includes the MEM command first introduced in DOS 4.0. The DOS 5.0 MEM command is more flexible than the previous one, allowing you to see exactly how your memory is configured and which programs are using it. This can be very useful when you are configuring or reconfiguring the memory in your PC.

So all in all, DOS 5.0 does have a considerable number of productivity features that can help you increase performance and productivity.

DR DOS 5.0 and 6.0

If you are about to upgrade from an older version of MS or PC DOS to DOS 5.0, you may want to try DR DOS 6.0. DR DOS 6.0 actually includes a disk-caching program and a data compression utility as well as many of the features mentioned for MS DOS 5.0. DR DOS 5.0 and 6.0 have both received a number of favorable reviews.

Company Listings

CPU Manufacturers

Advanced Micro Devices Inc.
P.O. Box 3453
Sunnyvale, CA 94088-3453
(408) 732-2400
(800) 222-9323

Chips and Technologies Inc.
3050 Zanker Rd.
San Jose, CA 95134
(408) 434-0600

Intel Corp.
P.O. Box 58119
Santa Clara, CA 95052-8119
(408) 765-8080
(800) 722-7772

Coprocessor Manufacturers

Advanced Micro Devices Inc.
P.O. Box 3453
Sunnyvale, CA 94088-3453
(408) 732-2400
(800) 222-9323

Chips and Technologies Inc.
3050 Zanker Rd.
San Jose, CA 95134
(408) 434-0600

Cyrix Corp.
2703 North Central Expressway
Richardson, TX 75080
(214) 234-8387

Integrated Information Technology Inc. (IIT)
2445 Mission College Blvd.
Santa Clara, CA 95054
(408) 727-1885

Intel Corp.
P.O. Box 58119
Santa Clara, CA 95052-8119
(408) 765-8080
(800) 722-7772

Weitek Corp.
1060 E. Arques Ave.
Sunnyvale, CA 94086
(408) 738-8400

Disk Controller Manufacturers

Adaptec Inc.
691 S. Milpitas Blvd.
Milpitas, CA 95035
(408) 945-8600

BusLogic, Inc.
4151 Burton Dr.
Santa Clara, CA 95054
(408) 492-9090

Disk Controller Manufacturers, *cont.*

Ciprico Inc.
2800 Campus Dr.
Minneapolis, MN 55441
(612) 559-2034

Core International Inc.
7171 N. Federal Hwy.
Boca Raton, FL 33487
(407) 997-6055

Distributed Processing Technology (DPT)
140 Candace Dr.
Maitland, FL 32751
(407) 830-5522

Future Domain Corp.
2801 McGaw Ave.
Irvine, CA 92714
(714) 253-0400

Interphase Corp.
13800 Senlac
Dallas, TX 75234
(214) 919-9000

Mylex Corp.
34551 Ardenwood Blvd.
P.O. Box 5035
Fremont, CA 94537-5035
(510) 796-6050
(800) 77-MYLEX

Pacific Magtron Inc.
5688 Weddell Dr.
Sunnyvale, CA 94089
(408) 744-1188

Perceptive Solutions Inc. (PSI)
2700 Flora St.
Dallas, TX 75201
(214) 954-1774

Promise Technology Inc.
1460 Koll Cir., Bldg. A
San Jose, CA 95112
(408) 452-0948

Qume Corp.and Data Technology Corp.
1515 Center Point Dr.
Milpitas, CA 95035
(408) 942-4000

QPI
260 S. Milpitas Blvd.
Milpitas, CA 95035
(408) 942-4242

UltraStor Corp.
15 Hammond St., Ste. 310
Irvine, CA 92718
(714) 581-4100

High-Performance Disk Drive Manufacturers

Core International Inc.
7171 N. Federal Hwy.
Boca Raton, FL 33487
(407) 997-6055

Hewlett-Packard Corp.
11311 Chinden Blvd.
Boise, ID 83714-1023
(800) 323-6000

Hitachi America, Ltd.
50 Prospect Ave.
Tarrytown, NY 10591
(914) 332-5800

Maxtor Corp.
211 River Oaks Pkwy.
San Jose, CA 95134
(408) 432-1700

Micropolis Corp.
21211 Nordhoff St.
Chatsworth, CA 91311
(818) 709-3300

Microscience International Corp.
1015 E. Brokaw Rd.
San Jose, CA 95131
(408) 441-1456

Prima International
3350 Scott Blvd., Bldg. 7
Santa Clara, CA 95054
(408) 727-2600

Seagate Technology, Inc.
920 Disc Dr.
Scotts Valley, CA 95067
(408) 438-6550

Western Digital Corp.
8105 Irvine Center Dr.
Irvine, CA 92718
(714) 932-5000

Disk Arrays

Compaq Computer Corp.
P.O. Box 692000
Houston, TX 77269
or: 20555 State Hwy. #249
Houston, TX 77070
(713) 370-0670

Core International Inc.
7171 N. Federal Hwy.
Boca Raton, FL 33487
(407) 997-6055

Legacy Storage Systems Inc.
25A South St.,
Hopkinton, MA 01748
(508) 881-6442

MicroNet Technology Inc.
20 Mason St.
Irvine, CA 92718
(714) 837-6033

Micropolis Corp.
21211 Nordhoff St.
Chatsworth, CA 91311
(818) 709-3300

Storage Concepts Inc.
1622 Deere Ave.
Irvine, CA 92714
(714) 852-8511

Solid-State Drives

ATTO Technology Inc.
1576 Sweet Home Rd.
Amherst, NY 14228
(716) 688-4259

Solid-State Drives, *continued*

Hitachi America, Ltd.
50 Prospect Ave.
Tarrytown, NY 10591-4698
(914) 332-5800

Imperial Technology Inc.
2305 Utah Ave.
El Segundo, California 90245
(310) 536-0018

Liberty Systems Inc.
160 Saratoga Ave., Ste. 38
Santa Clara, CA 95051
(408) 983-1127

Newer Technology Inc.
7803 E. Osie St.
Wichita, KS 67207
(316) 685-4904

Seagate Technology
920 Disc Dr.
Scotts Valley, CA 95066
(408) 438-6550

Accelerated Video Adapters

Actix Systems Inc.
3060 Tasman Dr.
Santa Clara, CA 95054
(800) 927-5557

ATI Technologies Inc.
3761 Victoria Park Ave.
Scarborough, Ont., MIW 3S2 Canada
(416) 756-0718

Beaver Computer Corp (BCC)
1610 Crane Ct.
San Jose, CA 95112
(408) 944-9000

Diamond Computer Systems Inc.
532 Mercury Dr.
Sunnyvale, CA 94086
(408) 736-2000

Hercules Computer Technology
921 Parker St.
Berkeley, CA 94710
(510) 540-6000

Liberty Systems Inc.
160 Saratoga Ave., Ste.38
Santa Clara, CA 95051
(408) 983-1127

Matrox Electronic Systems, Ltd.
1055 St. Regis Blvd.
Dorval, Quebec, H9P 2T4, Canada
(514) 685-2630

Nth Graphics
1906 Kramer Lane, Ste. A
Austin, TX 78758
(512) 832-1944
(800) 624-7552

Opta Corp.
2525 E. Bayshore Rd.
Palo Alto, CA 94303
(415) 354-1120

Orchid Technology
45365 Northport Loop W.
Fremont, CA 94538
(510) 683-0300

Spectragraphics Inc.
GSS Personal Graphics Div.
9590 S.W. Gemini Dr.
Beaverton, OR 97005

Manufacturers of Graphics Accelerator Chips

ATI Technologies Inc.
3761 Victoria Park Ave.
Scarborough, Ont., MIW 3S2, Canada
(416) 756-0718

S3 Inc.
2880 San Tomas Expy.
Santa Clara, CA 95051
(408) 986-8144

Texas Instruments
Computer Video Products
P.O. Box 1443
Houston, TX 77251-1443
(713) 274-2000

Weitek Corp.
1060 E. Arques Ave.
Sunnyvale, CA 94086
(408) 738-8400

Western Digital Corp.
8105 Irvine Center Dr.
Irvine, CA 92718
(714) 932-5000

Software Manufacturers

Novell, Inc.
70 Garden Ct.
Monterey, CA 93940
(408) 649-3896
DR DOS 5.0 and DR DOS 6.0

FastTrax International
8880 Ensenada Ave.
Berkeley, CA 94707
(510) 883-9561
Disk optimizing software

Geoworks Inc.
2150 Shattuck Ave.
Berkeley, CA 94704
(510) 644-0883
(800) 772-0001
Graphic Operating Environment

Gibson Research Corp.
35 Journey
Aliso Viejo, CA 92656
(714) 362-8800
Disk optimizing software

Lasertools Corp.
1250 45th St., Ste. 100
Emeryville, CA. 94608
(510) 420-8777
Print spooling software

Microsoft Corp.
1 Microsoft Way
Redmond, WA 98052
(206) 882-8080
MS DOS and Windows

Multisoft Corp.
15100 S. W. Koll Pkwy.
Beaverton, OR 97006
(503) 644-5644
Disk caching software

Panacea Inc.
Post Office Square
24 Orchard View Dr., Ste. 4
Londonderry, NH 03053-3376
Display list drivers

Software Manufacturers, *continued*

Quarterdeck Office Systems
150 Pico Blvd.
Santa Monica, CA 90405
(310) 392-9851
Memory managers

Rosesoft Inc.
P.O. Box 70337
Bellevue, WA 98007
(206) 562-0225
(800) 869-7676
Macro-creating software

Spirit of Performance Inc.
73 Westcott Rd.
Harvard, MA 01451
(508) 456-3889
Performance diagnostic software

Symantec Corp.
10201 Torre Ave.
Cupertino, CA 95014-2132
(408) 253-9600
Norton Utilities

Zenographics Corp.
4 Executive Circle, Ste. 200
Irvine, CA 92714
(714) 851-6352
Print spooling software

Memory Board Manufacturers

Acculogic Inc.
13715 Alton Pkwy.
Irvine, CA 92718
(714) 454-2441

AST Research Inc.
16215 Alton Pkwy.
Irvine, CA 92718
(714) 727-7902

Everex Systems Inc.
48431 Milmont, Dr.
Fremont, CA 94538
(510) 498-1111

Intel Corp.
P.O. Box 58119
Santa Clara, CA 95052-8119
(408) 765-8080
(800) 722-7772

STB Systems Inc.
1651 N. Glenville, Ste. 210
Richardson, TX 75085-0957
(214) 234-8750

Peripheral Manufacturers

Buffalo Products Inc.
2805 19th St. S.E.
Salem, OR 97302
(503) 585-6005
(800) 345-2356
Print buffers

Pen-Based Operating Environment

GO Corp.
919 East Hillsdale Blvd., Ste 400
Foster City, CA 94404
(415) 345-7400

Glossary

A

access time. The amount of time that transpires from the moment information is requested to the moment it starts to be delivered. Access time is usually measured in nanoseconds for memory chips. For hard disk drives, access time is measured in milliseconds. *See also* average access time.

acronym. A term that is composed of the initial letters of the key words in a name; e.g., BASIC stands for Beginner's All-Purpose Symbolic Instruction Code.

active hub. A networking device that can be used either to link additional workstations to an existing network or to extend the distance between the workstations and their file server. *See also* hub.

active partition. The hard disk partition that contains the boot information and operating system. Your hard disk may be partitioned into two or three logical drives, e.g. C, D, and E. But only one of these logical drives can contain the active partition.

actuator arm. The mechanical device that moves the read/write heads of the disk drive over the platter.

adapter board or card. Usually used as a synonym for expansion card, add-on card, or circuit board. A device that provides an interface between the system and the peripherals attached to it. For example, a video adapter board connects the monitor to the PC.

address. The method of identifying the location in which data is stored. May refer to the disk, as in disk address, or to memory, as in memory address.

address bus. One or more electrical conductors used to carry the binary-coded address from the microprocessor throughout the rest of the system.

address space. Refers to the amount of memory that programs can use as a working area. During the execution of a program, both the program and the data it is using reside in the available address space.

algorithm. A step-by-step procedure, scheme, formula, or method employed to solve a problem or accomplish a task, for example, a subroutine in a software program.

alphanumeric. The character set on a keyboard is alphanumeric, i.e., a character set that includes letters, numbers, symbols and punctuation marks.

ampere. One ampere (amp) is the basic unit for measuring electrical current.

ANSI. Acronym for American National Standards Institute. ANSI sets important standards for the computer industry.

application software. Refers to a broad range of programs from basic business applications, such as spreadsheets, word processors, and accounting packages, to sophisticated high-end applications, such as CAD/CAM or CASE. Applications are the tools that you use to do your specific kind of work. They differ from the operating systems that control the computing environment in which you work or the utilities that perform some of the janitorial functions. *See also* operating system.

ASCII. Acronym for American Standard Code for Information Interchange. ASCII is the standard code for the computer representation of letters, numbers, punctuation marks, and control characters. Adherence to ASCII enables files to be transferred between computers that use incompatible file formats.

ASIC. Acronym for application specific integrated circuit.

AUTOEXEC.BAT. A special MS-DOS batch file that is executed whenever the computer boots up. This file enables you to set up the DOS environment the way you want it. For example, including the PATH command with all vital directories listed as parameters in your AUTOEXEC.BAT makes it a lot easier for you to call up programs or seek out data. You can also use the AUTOEXEC.BAT to engage important devices, such as your mouse, by including the commands that activate them.

availability. The percent of time that the subsystem keeps data available. A drive subsystem with redundancy built in generally has a high availability.

average access time. Sum of seek time and rotational latency. The average amount of time it takes for the actuator arm to move the read/write heads of a hard disk drive from one random platter sector to another. Often used incorrectly to mean seek time.

average seek time. The average amount of time it takes for the read/write heads of a hard disk drive to move to the track that contains the data that is to be retrieved.

B

backplane. The main circuit board of a computer into which the other circuit boards are plugged. A PC is often designed with the CPU and most of its support circuitry on one or more of the boards that plug into the backplane. In this case, the backplane is primarily a circuit board with connectors to hold the other circuit boards, and is known as a passive backplane.

backup. A duplicate copy of files. Backup copies may exist on the hard disk, diskettes, or tape. BACKUP is also an MS-DOS command that can be helpful if you're transferring files that are larger than the diskette's storage capacity.

bad sector. A disk sector that cannot be relied on to hold data due to a media flaw or damage to the format markings.

bad track. A part of the disk that cannot be read from or written to because of some flaw in the disk. Most hard disks normally have a few bad tracks. These tracks are mapped out when the drive is formatted so that they won't be used to store data.

bank. A block of chips or SIMMS that compose a section of memory that the microprocessor accesses as a unit in a single clock cycle. The bank must be as large as the data bus of the CPU, for example, 8, 16, or 32 bits plus a parity bit for each 8 bits, resulting in a total of 9, 18, or 36 bits for each bank.

base I/O address. The beginning address for an I/O port. The microprocessor in your computer looks for the base I/O address to find the proper port through which to communicate with a particular device.

base memory. The first 640 KB of memory located on the processor board.

BASIC. Acronym for Beginner's All-Purpose Symbolic Instruction Code. BASIC is a programming language traditionally bundled with the MS-DOS operating system.

batch file. A file containing a series of MS-DOS commands that are run automatically in a sequence rather than individually. See also AUTOEXEC.BAT

baud. A measure of data-transmission speed. Originally used to measure transmission speed of telegraph equipment, the term now commonly refers to the data-transmission speed of a modem.

BIOS. Acronym for basic input/output system. A program that provides the interface between the microprocessor, hardware components and software. The BIOS manages the video display system, the serial and parallel input/output, and all other peripheral devices. The BIOS resides in ROM but can be copied to RAM for faster execution. *See also* shadow RAM.

binary. The binary number system uses two simple digits—1 and 0. Computers employ binary at their most basic operational level to denote the only two possible electrical conditions—1 for on and 0 for off.

bit. Binary digit (1 or 0). The smallest unit of data that can be individually identified. Eight bits are equal to one byte.

block. A contiguous set of bytes, words, or records that are grouped for a specific purpose such as reading from the disk or storing on a memory module.

block fetch size. The size of the minimum amount of data retrievable from RAM memory whenever the data is not in cache. Block fetch sizes may be 4, 8, or 16 bytes, depending on the configuration of memory.

board. Printed circuit board (PCB) on which the chips, resistors, and connectors are mounted. Circuit boards include both the expansion cards and the processor board.

boot. To start up the computer and load in the operating system software. *See also* cold boot and warm boot.

BPS. Acronym for bits per second. Also often incorrectly called baud rate.

buffer. A temporary storage area.

buffered write (also called posted write). In a normal cache design, if the CPU requires access to the cache memory before the cache controller has completed updating the main memory, the CPU must wait. In a posted or buffered write design, the cache controller updates a small but very fast buffer instead of directly updating the main memory. By updating the buffer, the cache controller can free up the cache quicker than if it had to wait for slow main memory to be updated. Although buffered writes are most often associated with write-through caches, they can also be used with write-back caches.

bus. A group of electronic paths used to send data between parts of the system. On the system board, a bus connects the expansion boards via the expansion slots with the microprocessor. The disk bus connects the disk controller board with the diskette or hard disks via a flat ribbon cable.

bus speed. The rate at which the expansion bus transfers data between the expansion boards and the microprocessor. Also referred to as the bus clock frequency.

byte. A contiguous set of eight bits.

C

cache. A sophisticated high-speed buffer between two forms of storage or memory, for example, between the disk and the RAM memory. This process greatly improves the speed of access to the slower memory form.

cache coherency. Refers to the degree in which the cache memory has the same data that is in the main memory. Cache coherency would be less than 100 percent if data were changed in the main memory but not in the cache. For example, if a disk transfer put data into the main memory but did not put it in the cache, the cache coherency would be compromised.

cache hit. If the data that the CPU requests from the cache is already in the cache, it is said to be a cache hit.

cache miss. If the data that the CPU requests is not in the cache, it is said to be a cache miss.

cache tag RAM. A part of the cache memory that keeps track of the memory bank from which the data is being cached. Five bits are used to identify the bank from which the data is being saved, depending on the SIMM configuration.

card. *See* board.

cascade. To arrange open windows so that they overlap each other yet allow each title bar to remain visible.

central processing unit. *See* CPU

CGA. Acronym for color/graphics adapter. An earlier standard for color PC monitor displays. CGA is older than EGA, VGA, or super VGA and produces the lowest resolution.

character. A letter, number, or symbol that can be entered from the keyboard and be displayed on the monitor. Eight bits (one byte) define a character. *See also* byte and alphanumeric.

chip. A single integrated circuit or a group of integrated circuits enclosed in a small package, usually plastic or ceramic, that provide the electronic components for the system.

clock cycle. One complete vibration of the crystal that regulates the timing of a CPU. Measured in MHz.

clock pulse. A clock pulse is a signal that is used to synchronize the operations of an electronic system. Clock pulses are continuous, precisely spaced changes in voltage.

clock speed. The clock speed is the internal heartbeat of a computer and governs the speed of the processor. The clock circuit uses the steady beat generated from a quartz crystal to deliver a regulated stream of pulses to the processor.

CMOS. Acronym for complementary metal oxide semiconductor.

CMOS RAM. The real-time clock RAM memory chip in which your computer system's configuration data is stored. The CMOS chip is powered by a small battery, so it can retain its contents even while the system is shut down.

CMOS SETUP. A program stored in ROM that allows you to load and change the configuration information in CMOS RAM. *See also* EEPROM SETUP.

cold boot. Starting the computer by turning on the power or pressing the RESET button. A cold boot makes the processor execute all of the diagnostics. *See also* boot and warm boot.

COM port. A serial port used to communicate to a peripheral, such as a mouse, modem, printer, or other computer device. Most computers have two COM ports, COM1 and COM2. *See also* serial port.

command. An instruction. A word or phrase that tells the computer software to perform a specific task. For example, in MS-DOS, the command DIR instructs the operating system to list all files and subdirectories within a directory to the screen.

COMMAND.COM. An MS-DOS file that interprets the commands you enter from the keyboard. COMMAND.COM is the DOS command processor for any commands that are not in the files provided on the DOS disk. COMMAND.COM is version specific, and the operating system will not function if you use the wrong version of COMMAND.COM.

compute-bound. A program that is limited or restricted by the speed of the CPU.

CONFIG.SYS. A file that contains specific configuration information from which DOS determines how to load the RAM and what peripherals are to be used. CONFIG.SYS is used before AUTOEXEC.BAT is executed. It contains the number of disk buffers to be allocated, the number of simultaneous files to be used, and the names of any device drivers.

configuration. A description of the hardware and software that make up the system. The hardware configuration information is stored in the CMOS RAM and EEPROM. The software configuration information is stored in CONFIG.SYS.

contiguous. Adjacent, or adjoining. Referring to memory, indicates any parts of memory in which the addresses are directly adjacent to each other.

controller card (hard disk and diskette drive). An expansion card that allows the microprocessor to communicate with the disk drives or other device.

conventional memory. The first 640 KB of RAM memory on a DOS-based PC. There is actually 1 MB of conventional memory, but the 384 KB above 640 KB is reserved for system use.

coprocessor. A chip or set of chips that speeds up certain processes in the system.

CPU. Acronym for central processing unit. The microprocessor. *See also* microprocessor.

CRT. Acronym for cathode ray tube. A vacuum tube through which electron beams strike to a screen to produce luminous spots that taken together form an image. Computer monitors and TV sets both employ CRTs.

cursor. A symbol on the monitor screen indicating the next character position.

cylinder. A set of tracks on the disk that have the same address but that are on different surfaces of the disk. Usually, these tracks are aligned vertically and therefore form a cylinder if viewed as a stack of circles. *See also* track.

D

data. Numbers, letters, or symbols that represent information that the computer can interpret, process, and communicate to other devices.

data communications equipment (DCE). Refers to a type of serial communications interface designed for use with specific equipment. For a serial interface to work, one piece of equipment must be a data terminal equipment (DTE) interface, and the other must be a data communications equipment (DCE) interface. Most personal computers should use a DTE interface and most peripherals use a DCE interface.

data path. The number of bits handled at one time by the processor.

data terminal equipment (DTE). Refers to a type of serial communications interface designed for use with specific equipment. For a serial interface to work, one piece of equipment must be a data terminal equipment (DTE) interface and the other must be a data communications equipment (DCE) interface. Most modems, printers, and pointing devices, such as a mouse, use a DTE interface.

data transfer rate. Rate at which data can travel through a component or subsystem.

daughterboard. A circuit board that plugs into the system's motherboard. Used in some CPU upgrade architectures.

DCE. See data communications equipment.

default. Defaults are preset hardware or software settings that the computer uses automatically, unless you specify other settings. There are default drives—in most cases, the C drive, if you have a hard disk. In DOS, the directory from which you issue a command is the default directory, unless you specify otherwise using a PATH command.Most word processors have default settings for fonts, margins, and so on, which remain in effect unless you specify other settings.

defragment. To make files contiguous.

device driver. A software program that communicates with a peripheral device (for example, a video graphics interface or a hard disk). It handles sending/receiving data to/from the device, the likely errors that the device generates, and the differences in manufacturer's models of the devices.

DIP switch. Acronym for dual in-line package switch seen on many expansion cards. When you change the settings of these switches, you alter the circuits on the card and, in this way, enable or disable different features.

direct mapping. A caching technique in which each block of main memory is assigned a specific location in the cache memory.

directory. A portion of the space on a disk used to organize files into related groups at the user's discretion. Directories are also created automatically during the installation of many software applications in order to set up the proper hierarchical structure for the execution of programs. In MS-DOS, typing the command DIR displays a list of files and subdirectories within a given directory or on a specific disk.

dirty bit. A part of each cache location that identifies if the cached data has been rendered obsolete by being updated from somewhere other than through the cache. For instance, whenever a disk transfer into memory changes a RAM address, the corresponding cache dirty bit is set to indicate that the cache is invalid. The next time data is requested from the cache, this dirty bit forces the cache controller to get the data from main memory. It is transparent to every program except diagnostic programs.

disk caching. The use of a cache memory to store data that is frequently accessed on the disk to eliminate multiple accesses of the disk for the data. Disk caching is transparent to almost all the programs.

disk drive. A hardware device that provides for the storage of data either on diskettes or hard metal disks that have a magnetic coating. In most cases, the A drive is a floppy disk or diskette drive, and the C drive is a hard disk drive. A disk drive functions by spinning at high speed while moving a device called the read/write head across the disk's surface in order to read or write data in magnetic code.

disk duplexing. A method for safeguarding data by copying the data simultaneously to two hard disks on separate channels. In this way, if one channel fails, the data on the other channel is protected. Disk duplexing can also increase a file server's efficiency because read requests are sent to whichever disk can respond faster. Also, if two read requests occur simultaneously, they can be split and processed immediately. *See also* disk mirroring.

disk mirroring. A method for safeguarding data in which the same data is copied to two hard disks on the same channel. If one hard disk fails, the data on the other is still preserved. However, disk mirroring provides only limited safeguards because if there is a failure along the channel, both disks could fail and the data would be lost. *See also* disk duplexing.

DMA. Acronym for direct memory access. A method of transporting data between memory and peripherals without having to access the CPU, thus lessening the CPU's administrative burden and speeding up processing.

DOS. Acronym for disk operating system. In common usage, people often refer to MS-DOS, Microsoft's operating system for the PC, as simply DOS. MS-DOS is a collection of programs, such as command-line processors and device drivers, that control the interface between the user and the hardware devices. *See also* operating system.

DOS extenders. A collection of drivers and code that can be incorporated into programs so they can take advantage of advanced memory-managing capabilities of 386 and 486 CPUs, while keeping real mode DOS compatibility.

dot matrix printer. A printer that implements the dot matrix technique of generating characters out of a group of dots. Although dot-matrix printers are faster than laser printers, they produce lower-quality print.

download. To receive files.

DRAM. Acronym for Dynamic Random Access Memory. A type of RAM that requires continual refreshing (electrical recharging) every few milliseconds to retain its contents.

drive bay. The space in the chassis used to mount internal hard disk, floppy disk and tape drives.

dynamic random access memory. *See* DRAM.

E

EEPROM. Acronym for erasable electronically programmable read-only memory. A type of ROM chip.

EEPROM SETUP. A ROM-resident program that enables the user to configure certain hardware options, such as the type of memory chip installed or the size of base memory, without having to set switches or jumpers on the system board. The details of system configuration recorded via EEPROM SETUP provide the computer with information needed to properly initialize the system during the boot process.

EGA. Acronym for enhanced graphics adapter. An early standard for color displays. EGA provides resolution up to 640 x 350 pixels.

EMS. Acronym for expanded memory specification. *See also* expanded memory.

ESDI. Acronym for enhanced small device interface. ESDI is a hard disk drive interface that delivers a faster data transfer rate between the hard disk and the computer's memory.

expanded memory. RAM memory that exists above 1 MB and is accessed via EMS or LIM (Lotus-Intel-Microsoft) memory specifications. Expanded memory requires special hardware to be utilized by programs.

expansion slot. Located at the rear of system board. They consist of connectors and panels that provide rear access. The slots are designed to hold adapter cards for add-on options such as video, memory expansions cards, and various other devices. There are 8-, 16-, and 32-bit expansion slots.

F

fault tolerance. *See* SFT.

FAT. Acronym for file allocation table. A table for disk management that is created automatically during the disk formatting process. There is a FAT for every disk. MS-DOS employs the FAT to monitor the space on the disk to store or locate files.

file. A collection of data that is stored together and accessed as a single entity.

filename. The name assigned to a file on a disk. Filenames can be from one to eight characters, and can be composed of most letters, numbers or other characters.

filename extension. A three-character suffix that sometimes follows a filename. A period (.) separates it from the filename. The filename extension tells the operating system or other software something about the type of data in the file to the operating system. The following file name extensions are important and have special meanings in the MS-DOS operating system:

.BAT......Batch file
.COM.....Program files less than 64 KB
.EXE......Program files greater than 64 KB
.SYS......System drivers and programs.

Other extension conventions are used by individual programs.

file server. A dedicated computer, large hard disk, or other device that holds data or programs accessible to users on a local area network.

firmware. Program instructions that are stored in ROM and control hardware function. The system BIOS stored in CMOS is an example of firmware.

fixed disk. *See* hard disk.

force-true. Providing a signal required for serial communications that the serial device is not capable of issuing without modification. The modification is usually accomplished through the manipulation of jumpers on the device.

format. Refers to writing a structure on the disk into which files may be placed. FORMAT is an MS-DOS command that initiates processes to prepare a disk for storing data. Formatting has different meanings depending on the type of format and the disk being formatted.

FORTRAN. An abbreviation of formula translator. A programming language used primarily for creating scientific and engineering programs.

fragmentation. Uneven distribution of data on a disk. As files become updated, they are less contiguous on the disk. When data is added, the operating system stores it in whatever space is available. Consequently, parts of the file wind up in disparate areas.

front access. Signifies that a disk drive or other device is accessible from the front panel of the system.

function key. On an AT-style keyboard, the keys marked F1 through F10 or F12. These keys perform specific, preset functions, both in MS-DOS and various applications programs. These functions may vary from program to program. In applications for instance, F1 is almost always Help, and F10 is usually Exit. In DOS, F3 repeats the last input of characters from the keyboard.

G

Gigabyte (GB). A disk storage capacity measurement. Commonly meant to signify a billion bytes, but more accurately, one gigabyte is equivalent to 1,073,741,824 bytes.

glitch. Any temporary or random malfunction in hardware.

global. Pertains to an entire file, database, volume, program, or system.

googool. 1 followed by 100 zeros.

GUI. Acronym for graphical user interface.

H

handshaking. An automatic process that occurs between two computers or a computer and a device and establishes the parameters to be used in the exchange of data.

hard disk. A data storage device that stores the data on metal disks that have a magnetic coating. Hard disk drives provide faster access and larger storage capacities than diskettes. Sometimes referred to as a fixed disk.

hardware. The physical components that make up the system including the system unit, the disk drives, the diskette disks, the monitor, and all other tangible devices.

head. A device that reads from and writes to disks. Diskette drives have two heads, hard disk drives have several.

hidden files. A hidden file is a disk file that has been given a special status that prevents it from being viewed, changed, or deleted. DOS has two hidden files in every directory.

high density. Referring to 5.25-inch diskettes that have 1.2 MB of storage or 3.5-inch floppy diskettes that have 1.44 MB of storage.

high-level languages. Programming languages that are relatively easy to learn or develop in, such as BASIC, Pascal, or C.

hit rate. A measure of cache efficiency. The hit rate is the ratio of cache hits to cache misses, normally expressed as a percentage. All else being equal, the higher the hit rate the more effective the cache. Under some circumstances, however, a cache with a lower hit rate is faster than the cache with the higher hit rate. If the amount of time (number of clock cycles) it takes the cache to recover from a cache miss is too great, a cache with a lower hit rate but faster recovery time could be the faster cache.

host. A networked computer that provides services other than simply storing or forwarding data to the other stations. The term is used loosely. The host might be a mainframe, minicomputer, or file server that delivers many services or even a simple PC that is taken over by a remote caller.

host bus adapter. A board used to provide an interface between the system's I/O bus and a peripheral device. Although host adapters are often referred to as controller cards, there is a distinction: Host adapters are employed to interface with devices that have their own controllers built in (e.g., IDE or SCSI disk drives).

hot-key combination. A combination of keystrokes that are performed simultaneously to command the computer to perform a certain function. For instance, the hot-key combination of CTR-ALT-DEL<L> causes the system to execute a warm boot.

hub. A device implemented in some network topologies. A hub modifies transmission signals to allow networks to be expanded in the number of workstations it includes or lengthened to cover a greater distance. *See also* active hub.

I

IC. Acronym for integrated circuit.

icon. A picture intended to represent an idea to enhance ease of use in graphical interfaces. For instance, in Windows 3.0, the Print Manager is represented on the screen with an icon—a printer on a printer stand.

initialize. The process through which a system or a device is prepared for use. Initialization establishes the parameters at their starting values so that the computer and its various devices can communicate properly. Initialization takes place during the system's automatic start-up procedures.

input/output (I/O). The transfer of data in and out of the system.

interface. A connection between two devices or programs. The connection can be either tangible, as in a connector between the system and the printer, or intangible, as in the connection between two programs.

interleave. Measurement of the number of revolutions a hard disk must make before the computer can read or write one track (also called "groove"). The lower that number of revolutions, the faster the speed at which data can be transferred. Thus, 1:1 interleave is optimal.

interrupt. The way in which a device signals that it requires the CPU's attention. When the CPU receives an interrupt, it suspends its current activity and addresses the device's call for attention. Once the demand of the interrupt request is met, the CPU returns to the activity which had been suspended.

I/O. *See* input/output

I/O-bound. A program that requires a large number of input/output operations, resulting in an increase of CPU idle time. An I/O-bound program or application is bottlenecked at the I/O subsystem level of the data funnel.

ISA. Acronym for industry standard architecture. A well-established bus standard that originated with the IBM AT.

J

jumper. A small plug that fits over pins on a circuit board. Jumpers allow the various functions of the board to be enabled or disabled.

K

KB. *See* kilobyte

kilobyte (KB). 1,024 bytes.

kludge. Makeshift. Pertaining to a collection of mismatched components that have been assembled into a system of some sort.

L

LAN. Acronym for local area network. A group of computers, peripherals, and other devices linked together to share resources.

latency. A delay

LCD. Acronym for liquid crystal display. A way to make letters and numbers appear by reflecting light on a special crystalline substance. Because of its flat profile, low weight, and low power needs, LCD technology is often used in portable, notebook, and palmtop computers.

LED. An abbreviation for light emitting diode. A semiconductor device that emits light when power is applied to it. LEDs display information about the operation of the system.

linear address. A logical, or theoretical, location of data in memory, as opposed to a physical address, which is a real location of data on the chip.

lithium battery. A small, long-lasting battery that provides a constant power source for the CMOS memory so it retains system configuration and can continue to track the time and date even when the system is shutdown.

logical drive. A portion of a disk which with the computer interacts as if it were an independent disk drive. An area to which DOS assigns a drive name.

logical format. The third phase of the formatting process in which the DOS file structure is written to the disk. Logical formatting follows physical formatting and partitioning.

low-level formatting. *See* physical formatting

LPT port. The DOS designation for the I/O ports used to communicate with printers and similar devices.

M

macro. A series of recorded keystrokes and/or mouse actions that can be played back at a later time. DOS 5.0 has a macro program called DOSKEY. There are third-party macro programs, such as ProKey. Windows 3.0 includes an accessory called the Recorder that allows you to create macros from inside Windows.

math coprocessor. An integrated circuit. A microprocessor designed specifically for performing mathematical calculations. A math coprocessor performs these calculations faster than the CPU, and by doing so, frees the CPU for other activities. See 80387 and 3167.

megabit. 1,048,576 bits or 1,024 kilobits.

megabyte (MB). 1,024 kilobytes (KB) or 1,048,576 bytes.

megahertz (MHz). A measure of frequency equal to 1,000,000 cycles per second. Used to indicate the speed of a CPU.

memory. An electronic data storage component. Refers to either the disk or the RAM components.

memory manager. A program, such as QEMM 386, that provides the user with control over how system memory is used. For example, a memory manager may allow extended memory to be used as expanded memory or can load device drivers or TSRs into high memory.

memory-resident. Denotes programs that stay active in memory while other programs are operating. Usually you can switch between programs using hot-key combinations. Also called TSRs (an acronym for terminate and stay resident), such programs can be terminated and yet stay resident in the system's memory.

MFLOPS. Acronym for a million floating-point operations per second. A measure of computing power. Also known as MEGAFLOP.

MFM. Acronym for modified frequency modulation. A magnetic recording technique used for some disk drives.

Micro Channel Architecture. IBM's bus standard interface used in PS/2 systems.

microprocessor. An integrated circuit. Usually used to refer to the CPU. A microprocessor performs arithmetic calculations, makes logical decisions, and in conjunction with the operating system, directs the operation of the computer.

microsecond. One millionth of a second.

millisecond (ms). One thousandth of a second.

MIPS. Acronym for millions of instructions per second. An important way of measuring the speed of a CPU.

modem. An abbreviation of modulator-demodulator. A device that enables computer equipment to communicate via telephone lines.

modes. *See* Windows modes

monitor. The video screen on which the system displays images and text.

monochrome. Using a single color (or shade) to display text and images.

motherboard. *See* system board.

MS-DOS. The trade name for Microsoft Corporation's disk-based operating system for the IBM PC and IBM AT compatible personal computer systems.

MTBF. Acronym for mean time between failures. The average amount of time that a component or subsystem can run before it fails. The higher the number the higher the reliability.

multitasking. The performance of at least two tasks at a time. For example, running a spreadsheet program and a word processor simultaneously. UNIX and OS/2 are multitasking operating systems. Windows 3.0 provides multitasking features for DOS users.

multiuser. A system in which two or more people, using different terminals, can access one computer simultaneously. UNIX is a multiuser operating system.

N

nanosecond (ns). One billionth of a second.

network. An interconnected group of computers that can share data and peripheral devices.

network adapter card. A circuit board that is installed in an expansion slot and enables the computer to communicate with other nodes on a network. Also called a network interface card (NIC).

node. A computer on a network.

O

on-line. When a peripheral, such as a printer or a modem, is on-line, it has an open and operative communication link to the communication. The term is also used in another sense; for example, on-line help means that Help text is available on computer rather than simply in printed form.

operating system (OS). The group of software programs that manages the computer, its components, and peripherals and handles communication between the user, the applications, and the computer. MS-DOS, OS/2, and UNIX are examples of operating systems.

optical disk. A disk that encodes data as a series of reflective pits that are read or written by a laser beam.

overlay. A part of a program that is loaded into memory only at the times it is required.

P

page. A 64-KB portion of main memory addresses.

parallel. A form of data transmission in which the data is sent one byte at a time over several wires that each carry one byte. In parallel transmission, all the bytes arrive simultaneously, as opposed to serial transmission in which bits arrive one by one.

parallel port. A connection for a printer or similar peripheral. LPT1 and LPT2 are parallel ports.

parameter. A variable in a command line that can be replaced by different values depending on the specific actions the user wants accomplished.

parity bit. An extra bit assigned to each eight bits to verify that the memory or communication hardware has correct data. *Odd parity* indicates that whenever the parity bit is set, there is an odd number of bits. *Even parity* indicates that whenever the parity bit is set, there is an even number of bits.

partition. The contiguous set of cylinders that you designate as a logical drive during the partitioning phase of the disk format.

peripheral. Any computer device used to input or output data to another device or person. Peripherals can include printers, tape drives, plotters, display units, scanners, modems, and other devices.

physical formatting. The first step in preparing a hard disk drive for use. The physical format determines the physical location of the data by writing the addresses of the cylinders and sectors on the drive.

pixel. Abbreviation of picture element. The smallest dot that can be delivered on a screen or a printer.

platter. The disk(s) in a hard disk drive. Most hard disk drives have three or more platters, each with data recorded on both sides.

plotter. A peripheral device that draws figures with a pen and paper.

POH. Acronym for power on hours. Normally used in conjunction with MTBF to indicate that the MTBF number applies to the number of hours that the component or subsystem is actually running before it fails.

port. A physical connection to the computer or the logical (software) path that leads to that physical connection.

posted write. In a normal cache design, if the CPU requires access to the cache memory before the cache controller has completed updating the main memory, the CPU must wait. In a posted write design, the cache controller updates a small but very fast buffer instead of directly updating the main memory. By updating (posting) the buffer the cache controller can free up the cache quicker than if it had to wait for slow main memory to be updated. Although posted writes are most often associated with write-through caches, they also can be used with write-back caches. (Also called buffered write.)

power-on self test (POST). A set of diagnostic programs that are automatically executed when the system is cold booted.

power supply. An internal electrical power unit in the system that changes the external AC voltage into DC.

print queue. A list of files that are waiting to be printed.

printed circuit board (PCB). A piece of fiberglass material which has circuits on it.

printer buffer. A memory device that accepts printer output from one or more computers and transmits it to the printer. It lets the system free itself for other tasks.

printer spooling. Printing in the background mode while other tasks are being performed.

processor. An integrated circuit that receives, interprets, and executes instructions. It can be the microprocessor or a math coprocessor.

processor board. *See* system board.

program. A set of instructions that directs the computer to perform a function.

prompt. Either an icon or a character sequence that appears on the monitor screen to indicate that the computer is waiting for input.

protected mode. An address mode in Intel 80x86 processors that enables them to address up to 16 MB of actual memory and 4 GB of virtual memory. Protected mode, as opposed to real mode, can be used by multi-tasking applications.

Q

QWERTY keyboard. Basis for standard English-language keyboard layout found on most typewriters and computer keyboards.

R

RAM. Acronym for random access memory. The system memory in which programs and data are held temporarily while the system is operating. RAM is electronic memory that requires constant electrical power to hold the data, as opposed to hard disks or diskettes, which use a magnetic process. There are two types of RAM, DRAM and SRAM.

RAM disk. A RAM disk is a simulation of a disk drive created in main memory.

read/write head. A device that reads and writes data on a magnetic disk or tape.

real mode. An address mode of Intel 80x86 CPUs which addresses up to 1MB of memory and can be used only by single-tasking applications.

refresh. To recharge a device that cannot hold its contents. For example, DRAM chips require constant refreshing to maintain their charged bit patterns.

resistor SIP. *See* single in-line package.

resolution. The degree of sharpness of a displayed or printed character or image. For example, a resolution of 680x400 delivers 680 dots across each of 400 lines.

RLL. Acronym for run length limited. A magnetic encoding scheme that increases the density of storage 50 percent more than MFM. *See also* MFM.

ROM. Acronym for read-only memory. Memory that is permanently or semipermanently set with the same data or program. ROM memory is preserved even when the computer is turned off.

root directory. The main or top-level list of files and subdirectories on a logical disk drive.

S

scroll. To move through a list or block of text that is larger than the current window or screen.

SCSI. Acronym for small computer system interface. An interface standard used to interface hard disk drives, diskette drives, tape drives, and CD-ROMs to the computer system. SCSI allows multiple, high-performance peripheral devices to be connected in a chain. Each has its own address. Data and control signals are sent along the chain, and only the specifically addressed device responds.

sector. A division of a track on a disk. A typical DOS sector contains 512 bytes.

seek time. The amount of time for the read/write head to position itself over a track.

serial. A type of data transmission in which the data is sent one bit at a time over a single wire. *See also* parallel.

serial port. A communications port used to connect peripherals such as modems and mice. COM1 and COM2 are serial ports.

settling time. The time required for the read/write heads to stop vibrating once they have been moved to a new track.

SETUP. CMOS and EEPROM programs that allow you to configure system hardware. *See also* CMOS SETUP and EEPROM SETUP.

SFT. Acronym for system fault tolerance. Methods for duplicating data on multiple storage devices to protect against severe data loss. *See also* disk duplexing and disk mirroring.

shadow RAM. A technique used to load a duplicate copy of BIOS ROM into RAM. This duplicate BIOS enhances system performance because it provides zero-wait-state access to the BIOS.

SIMM. Acronym for single in-line memory module. A small printed circuit board that has chips.

single in-line package (SIP). A small plastic or ceramic box that contains an integrated circuit and connectors. It is connected to a socket on a printed circuit board.

small computer system interface. *See* SCSI.

SRAM. Acronym for static RAM. Memory that holds data without requiring continual refreshing (electrical recharging) to maintain the data, as opposed to DRAM. *See also* DRAM and RAM.

startup. *See* boot, warm boot, and cold boot.

subdirectory. A directory that is contained within a directory. *See also* directory and root directory.

super VGA. Acronym for super video graphics array. A standard for monitor displays. Super VGA delivers the highest level of resolution (fineness of detail, sharpness of image) in the range of standards from CGA through EGA and VGA to super VGA.

SWAP file. A special file created only for use when Windows is running in 386 enhanced mode. It allows Windows to turn disk space into virtual memory.

system. Refers to the computer, monitor, and all connected peripherals.

system board. The central circuit board inside the computer. It holds the CPU and the bus. All other components connect to it in some way. Also known as motherboard or processor board.

T

terabyte. A measurement for very large disk capacity. One terabyte is the equivalent of 1,099,511,627,766 bytes.

third party. Company other than original manufacturer.

tile. To display windows in such a way that each window occupies roughly the same amount of screen area without overlapping.

time slicing. A function of multiprocessing that divides a CPU's time among several applications.

track. One of many concentric circles that hold data on a disk surface. A track consists of a single line of magnetic flux changes. Each track of the disk is divided into sectors.

trackball. An input device similar to a mouse except it remains stationary while the user spins a ball to position the pointer on the video screen.

track-to-track seek time. The amount of time it takes for the read/write heads to move between adjacent tracks.

TSR. Acronym for terminate and stay resident. *See also* memory-resident.

U

uninterruptable power supply (UPS). A device that supplies battery power to the computer so that you are not subject to data loss or interruption from power outages.

V

VGA. Acronym for video graphics array. A standard for monitor displays. VGA delivers the next to the best level of resolution (fineness of detail, sharpness of image) in the range from CGA through EGA and VGA to Super VGA.

virtual memory. A technique used to simulate the existence of additional memory by a kind of sleight of hand in which the apparent location of memory is shuffled around. 386- and 486-based computers can use up to 4 gigabytes of actual memory but up to 64 terabytes of virtual memory.

virtual mode. An operating mode in which CPUs can emulate 386- and 486-based CPUs. Virtual mode makes both downward compatibility and multitasking possible. DESQview/386 and Windows 3.0 use this feature to run multiple DOS-based programs at once.

volt. The basic unit of measurement for electrical pressure.

W

wait state. A cycle of the system in which the processor has to wait for the memory to complete its cycle. The ideal system has zero wait states.

warm boot. Restarting the system by simultaneously pressing CTRL, ALT, and Delete.

watt. The basic unit of measurement for electrical power.

window. A rectangular area of the screen that is used to contain a program or document.

Windows modes. Windows 3.0 has three distinct operating modes: real, standard and 386 enhanced. See also real mode and standard mode.

workstation. Formerly meant a class of computer that had a UNIX operating system, high-resolution display and networking capability built in. Currently ambiguous term since many PCs can be configured to conform to such a definition. Some have referred to a new classification of *personal workstations.*

WORM. An acronym for write-once read-many. Optical storage device.

write-back. Type of cache in which the cache controller updates the cache and then sets a bit to indicate that the cache contains data that is different from the memory itself. The controller then frees up the CPU to proceed without having to wait while the controller updates the main memory. The data in the cache is written to the memory at a later time. Because a write-back cache frees the CPU immediately, it is faster than a write-through cache. However a write-back cache is more difficult to implement. Also called copy-back.

write protection. A condition that allows data to be read from a disk but prevents data from being written to the disk.

write through. A type of cache in which the cache controller updates the main memory (writes through) at the same time that it updates the cache. Because the main memory is slower than the cache memory, there is a delay while the main memory is updated. Should the CPU need access to either the cache or the main memory before the cache controller has finished updating the main memory, it will have to wait until the update is completed. Because the cache controller causes delays to the CPU, a write-through cache is slower than a write back cache. A write-through cache is easier to implement than a write-back cache.

Index

T

Tell us what you think and we'll send you a free M&T Books catalog

It is our goal at M&T Books to produce the best technical books available. But you can help us make our books even better by letting us know what you think about this particular title.Please take a moment to fill out this card and mail it to us. Your opinion is appreciated.

Tell us about yourself

Name____________________

Company____________________

Address____________________

City____________________

State/Zip____________________

Title of this book?

____

Where did you purchase this book?

- ☐ Bookstore
- ☐ Catalog
- ☐ Direct Mail
- ☐ Magazine Ad
- ☐ Postcard Pack
- ☐ Other

Why did you choose this book?

- ☐ Recommended
- ☐ Read book review
- ☐ Read ad/catalog copy
- ☐ Responded to a special offer
- ☐ M&T Books' reputation
- ☐ Price
- ☐ Nice Cover

How would you rate the overall content of this book?

- ☐ Excellent
- ☐ Good
- ☐ Fair
- ☐ Poor

Why?

____

____

What chapters did you find valuable?

____

____

____

What did you find least useful?

____

____

____

What topic(s) would you add to future editions of this book?

____

____

____

What other titles would you like to see M&T Books publish?

____

____

____

Which format do you prefer for the optional disk?

☐ 5.25"   ☐ 3.5"

Any other comments?

____

____

____

☐ Check here for M&T Books Catalog

M&T BOOKS

2500

NO POSTAGE
NECESSARY
IF MAILED
IN THE
UNITED STATES

BUSINESS REPLY MAIL
FIRST CLASS MAIL PERMIT 2660 SAN MATEO, CA

POSTAGE WILL BE PAID BY ADDRESSEE

M&T BOOKS
411 Borel Avenue, Suite 100
San Mateo, CA 94402-9885

PLEASE FOLD ALONG LINE AND STAPLE OR TAPE CLOSED